MEDIA TECHNOLOGY

Critical Perspectives

ISSUES in CULTURAL and MEDIA STUDIES

Series editor: Stuart Allan

Published titles:

MEDIA TECHNOLOGY
Critical Perspectives

Joost van Loon

 Open University Press

Open University Press
McGraw-Hill Education
McGraw-Hill House
Shoppenhangers Road
Maidenhead
Berkshire
England
SL6 2QL

email: enquiries@openup.co.uk
world wide web: www.openup.co.uk

and

Two Penn Plaza, New York, NY 10121–2289, USA

First published 2008

A catalogue record of this book is available from the British Library

ISBN10: 0 335 21446 0 (pb)   0 335 21447 9 (pb)
ISBN13: 978 0 335 21446 4 (pb)   978 0 335 21447 1 (pb)

Library of Congress Cataloging-in-Publication Data
CIP data has been applied for

Typeset by RefineCatch Limited, Bungay, Suffolk
Printed in the UK by Bell & Bain Ltd, Glasgow

The *McGraw·Hill* Companies

CONTENTS

ACKNOWLEDGEMENTS

This book could not have been written without the generous and selfless support of many people. The ideas that are contained here are the result of countless interactions and conversations with people I have met over the last 20 years, at various places, and to whom I am greatly indebted (my sincere apologies to anyone omitted from this list who should be on it): Barbara Adam, Lou Armour, Ulrich Beck, Marc Berg, David Berry, Roger Bromley, Michel Callon, Claudia Castaneda, Simon Charlesworth, Matt Connell, Nick Couldry, Kingsley Dennis, Marc Deveney, Bella Dicks, Greg Elmer, Caroline Farey, Willem Fase, Sarah Franklin, Anne Galloway, Paul Gilfillan, Mels Hoogenboom, Alan Hunt, Penelope Ironstone, Richard Johnson, Willem Koot, Scott Lash, Bruno Latour, Celia Lury, Siobhan Lynch, Annemarie Mol, Ray Nzereogu, Hannah Rockwell, Ian Roderick, Ida Sabelis, Michael Schillmeier, Rob Shields, John Tomlinson, Neil Turnbull, Jeremy Valentine, Alex van Spijk, Emma van Spijk, James Walker, Harry Wels, Ian Welsh, Petroc Willy, Carsten Winter, Andreas Wittel, Dave Woods, Stephen Yates, Sierk Ybema, Tao Zhang, many students who I have worked with over the years and the many anonymous players on RuneScape who were kind enough to share their experiences.

However, I want to give special thanks to Stuart Allan, who has been extremely patient and most helpful, as a series editor, and made numerous valuable comments on the earlier version of the manuscript; Chris Cudmore from Open University Press, for his patience and generosity; Neal Curtis, who has kindly read parts of the manuscript, and provided me with some very useful criticisms and comments; and Emma Hemmingway, with whom I have done part of the research that informs this book, and whose sense of humour and wit have allowed me to continue with a smile. I also want to thank Nottingham Trent University for enabling me to write this book.

Finally, I wish to thank my wife and soulmate Esther Bolier, whose loving support and patience exceeds everything a person could possibly ask for, and my children Amy,

Mark, Anna and Claire, for continuing to bring joy to our lives and making the long evening hours spent writing and editing this work endurable.

Parts of Chapter 2 have been published as 'McLuhan and his Influences' in D. Berry and J. Theobald (eds) (2006) *Radical Mass Media Criticism. A Cultural Genealogy.* Montreal: Black Rose Books, 161–76.

Biography

Joost van Loon is professor of Media Analysis at the Institute for Cultural Analysis of Nottingham Trent University. He is the author of *Risk and Technological Culture* (2002) and coedited *The Risk Society and Beyond* (2000). He has also written numerous articles on technology, risk, and social and cultural change and is editor-in-chief of the journal *Space and Culture*.

SERIES EDITOR'S FOREWORD

'So far, relatively few people have witnessed the modern television under domestic conditions,' observed G.V. Dowding, an Associate of the Institution of Electrical Engineers, in 1935. 'No doubt the generally accepted idea is that it is pretty crude and is little more than a tiny, dim flickering picture which is tiring to the eyes and doesn't show much more than shimmering spots and splotches. Probably many will decide to wait for "improvements," believing that everything must at its very beginning be only a ghostly precursor of better things to come.' While this view proved to be the case – television would not become a familiar feature in middle-class homes until the 1950s – there is little doubt that the extraordinary potential of this new technology was readily apparent to engineers, such as Dowding, at the time. Television had effectively arrived in Britain on 22 August 1932, the night the BBC launched its first experimental television broadcast service (even though the transmission standards to be adopted remained a matter of fierce contention between the rival technological systems of the Baird, Cossor, Marconi-EMI and Scophony companies). 'For ten years or so it hovered on the doorstep leading from the laboratory to the public spaces of practical politics and then, with a single leap, it was over,' Dowding remarked. 'The pessimistic prophets were shown to be false prophets.'

Evident in this brief account are several issues worthy of exploration for any enquiry into media technologies, ranging from public perceptions of technical quality and entertainment value, the commercial imperatives guiding innovation and invention, the connections between the 'laboratory' and the 'public spaces of practical politics' or even the evolutionary 'leap' of progress anticipated (or not) by prophets. More difficult to discern, however, is how the particular uses of a technology are *mediated* by the prevailing economic, political and cultural forces, structures and institutions in the wider society. Joost van Loon's *Media Technology: Critical Perspectives* represents a welcome effort to investigate an exciting array of pertinent issues in theoretical terms.

The central question posed by this book is: how does this process of mediation shape our lived experiences of technological change? In appraising a range of divergent responses to this question, van Loon argues that two aims must be kept in mind: first, the importance of analysing media technologies with a view to better understanding the contingent factors influencing their emergence, development and application; and, second, the need to show how media technologies play a crucial role in the (re-)configuration of social and cultural practices and formations. Accordingly, it is his contention that we must rethink familiar sorts of assumptions about media technologies, and in so doing alert ourselves to a range of different futures than those which seem to be prefigured by theories relying upon a certain sense of inevitability in their prognoses.

The *Issues in Cultural and Media Studies* series aims to facilitate a diverse range of critical investigations into pressing questions considered to be central to current thinking and research. In light of the remarkable speed at which the conceptual agendas of cultural and media studies are changing, the series is committed to contributing to what is an ongoing process of re-evaluation and critique. Each of the books is intended to provide a lively, innovative and comprehensive introduction to a specific topical issue from a fresh perspective. The reader is offered a thorough grounding in the most salient debates indicative of the book's subject, as well as important insights into how new modes of enquiry may be established for future explorations. Taken as a whole, then, the series is designed to cover the core components of cultural and media studies courses in an imaginatively distinctive and engaging manner.

Stuart Allan

1 | AN INTRODUCTION

Then there is the methodological problem posed by the conundrum of whether the now so self-evident term 'communication' can properly be used in connection with times and locations which manifestly were characterised by other terminology (drawn from mythology or religion). At any rate its enthronement in philosophy was based in John Locke's 'Essay on Human Understanding' on the scarcely generalisable assumption that communication means the rendering into speech of perceived ideas and consequently the linking of isolated individuals through 'bonds of language'. The only trouble is that philosophy omits to enquire how, without language, people are supposed to have arrived at their ideas and conceptions in the first place. Liberation from this unfathomable confusion came only with a technical concept of information which, since Shannon's 'Mathematical Theory of Communication', avoids any reference to ideas or meanings and thus to people. (Kittler 1996: 1)

Media are ubiquitous. This is not only because of the sheer increase in volume and diversity of equipment specifically designed to facilitate information and communication processes, but also because more and more objects are being turned into (communication and information) media. It is generally accepted that we 'communicate' not simply 'via' mobile phones or email, but also *by means of* hairstyle, make-up, clothing, wristbands, t-shirts, plastic carrier bags (i.e., displaying brands and logos, indicating 'where we shop' or 'what we buy'), etc. Indeed, our world can be characterized by an increase in *mediatization*.

With the advent of modern industrial societies in the nineteenth century, media have really become an all pervasive social force. First, in the form of transport (in particular, the steam engine) and soon followed by communication media, such as the telegraph and telephone, the industrial society in Western Europe and North America took shape as a world of high mobility of goods and (some) people, as well as increasingly wide-ranging and accelerating forms of communication (e.g., Harvey 1989; Giddens 1990). With the advent of radio and television alongside newspapers, one could argue, mass media emerged as a set of technologies capable not only of facilitating the communication between people across wider distances in shorter time, but also the *broadcasting* of information from very few to very many people. In particular, since the Second World War, modern societies across the globe have been caught up in this process of mediatization (Thompson 1995).

Yet, despite the rather obvious fact that we are becoming more and more reliant on an expanding range of communication media, it is perhaps remarkable that we do not give more thought to this process beyond such superficial observations. Mediated communication is something we *do*, rather than *think about*. This is not simply the case in everyday life, but also in the academy. For years, universities have expanded their research and teaching programmes in communication and media studies, and they continue to be popular subjects among students. At the same time, there is a relative lack of concern for media *as media*. Instead, we simply talk about 'the' media.

Rather than analysing media as phenomena, media and communication studies have continued to borrow their main analytical frameworks from other disciplines and theoretical cadres. This usually comes in the form of understanding media *in service of* something else, e.g., power, capital accumulation, ideology, social interaction and popular culture. Furthermore, this servicing has generally been approached as either 'context' or 'consequence', with mediation in-between as 'process'. Media were too often simply treated as the black box between corporations and consumers.

There are, of course, exceptions. These are studies of media processes that focused on mediation in terms of:

- organizational practices (e.g., Hall *et al.* 1978; Tuchman 1978; Schlesinger 1987; Cottle 1993; Harrison 2000);
- media products (primarily in the field of semiotics and screen theory and mainly concerned with media content);
- some sustained interest media-technologies, mainly from scholars associated with McLuhanism (although these rapidly faded away in the 1970s).

It was in the early 1990s, with the rise of 'studies of media use' (Silverstone and Hirsch 1992), that technology made a somewhat 'surprise' return. When we refer to media-use, we are actually looking at how people interconnect with technological agents in structuring their everyday lives (Moores 2005). The concept of technological agency will be further explored in Chapter 2. In essence, it refers to the idea that technology contains a capacity 'to act' (Latour 1988a). The question whether technologies are exclusively 'reactive' is not relevant here; what matters is that in everyday life, people interact with technologies *as if* they are capable of acting on their own accord and, thus, have agency.

It is here where media-technologies become *realized* in specific forms and no longer operate as 'pure potentiality' (of possibilities of things that could be done with them). It is *the use* that makes a hammer a tool for joinery or smithing, a means of destroying toys or a weapon of mass destruction. Use does not foreclose potentiality (a hammer could still be all of these things), but actualizes it, in temporary form, to become 'one' with the practice of handling it.

Indeed, the media-use paradigm has already given strong hints of how mediation is always contextualized by the cultural repertoires by which new technologies are introduced in domestic settings and how their use stabilizes over time. We now need to argue the same thing when linking content and technology as both aspects of the mediation process. This contextualization relates to the political economy of media as it involves questions of how mediation takes place as socially organized practices. The strength of a phenomenological approach to media is that it problematizes exactly that which most communication studies approaches take for granted: the medium. What this book will try to show is that an adequate media analysis should start with its reversal, expressed in McLuhan's (1964) famous aphorism: 'the medium is the message'.

Mediation as a black box

Most advocates of media studies would emphasize the need to bridge effect-, content- and context-orientated approaches; that is, they recognize that understanding media involves mapping and tracing the connectedness of specific contexts (conditions), contents and effects. This book offers a distinctive conceptual framework with which mediation processes can be theoretically, as well as empirically, explored and critically analysed. In doing so, it is concerned with the 'lynchpin' between context, content and effect: media. That is, what context-, content- and effect-orientated approaches have in common is that they are assuming media themselves to be a 'black box'; either as a transmitter of messages or an engine of meaning-production (also see Fiske 1990 for a similar critique).

The aim of a phenomenological approach to mediation should be to prise open some of the secrecies of this 'black box' and demystify them, so to speak. It is because, thus far, the three aforementioned domains of media studies have such vastly different conceptualizations of media (as organizations, texts or transmitters) that media studies have struggled to adequately conceptualize this lynchpin.

The context in which this will be done is predominantly, but not exclusively, modern Western society and culture. More specifically, it focuses on the role of media-as-technology. This is not because we need to assume that media analysis can be exhausted by a focus on technology, i.e., that there is nothing more to media than technology, but instead that a consistent focus on media-as-technology (hereafter 'media-technologies') can help us clarify the process of mediatization and contribute to an explanation of why especially communication media have become ubiquitous in modern society.

Media as phenomena

An underlying theme in this book is the desire to think more clearly and deeply about media by resorting to a more philosophically grounded theoretical engagement with media-technologies as phenomena. However, it should not be read as a radical departure from the existing domains of the growing field of media theory, but merely a conceptual recalibration. Whereas it will undoubtedly be somewhat at odds with most of the dominant strands in the wider domain of media studies, most notably the Marxist and functionalist approaches [e.g., political economy (Murdock and Golding 1977), hegemony theory (Hall 1980), public sphere theory (Dahlgren 1995)], as well as those inspired by liberal pluralism (uses and gratifications theory; Blumler and Katz 1974), audience studies (Ang 1985; Moores 1993), cultivation theory (Gerbner and Gross 1976), it is not necessarily incompatible with any of these. The aim is not to falsify other approaches, but merely to refocus our theoretical orientation to that which is at the heart of media studies, namely the process of mediation. It is hoped that a result of this reorientation, some of the aforementioned theoretical approaches may actually also attain greater clarity.

The approach of this book has a lot in common with what is growing into a distinctive field of its own, namely 'new media theory' (Elmer 2002; Gauntlett and Horsley 2004). New media theory includes both theoretical and empirically grounded analyses of digital media, telecommunications and the Internet, and is, by and large, well attuned to exploring media phenomena beyond issues of domination and resistance. New media theory has emerged out of a range of disciplines, which have converged around issues of technological innovation, and their social and cultural embedding or 'domestication' (Bakardjieva 2005; Berker *et al.* 2006). Although there are clearly close links with media studies, new media theory has not been subject to the institutional straightjacket, simply because it has not sought to obtain its own (inter-) disciplinary status.

Thinking about media is something we cannot do often enough. This is first of all because not only do we think 'through' media; media also structure our thinking (Curtis 1977). How we think is so closely bound to the media through which this thought is processed and by which this thought is generated, that we generally do not perceive thought as itself mediated. Hence, we normally take media for granted. It is in our very nature to take media for granted because as Marshall McLuhan (1964) provocatively said: media are 'the extensions of man [sic]'. It is usually only when new media are introduced that we are actively encouraged to dwell on their ontology as media, but such dwellings are often lacking in critical appreciation, as exemplified by the ubiquity of naïve knee-jerk reactions of celebratory optimism, as well as derogatory pessimism. When this happens, it seems as if all there is to media critique is mere opinion.

An example of this is the way in which the arrival of the Internet, in the late 1980s, sparked quite a few publications, which (unfortunately too often) were being reduced to the issue of whether the Internet is a 'good' or a 'bad' thing (Dovey 1996). The 'goodness' or 'badness' of this 'thing' called the Internet, of course, strongly relies on the moral, ethical or political principles that are implicitly or explicitly invoked by such evaluative comments. Hence, whereas for socialists the issue of commodification played a central role, for liberals it was the role of state intervention and, for conservatives, it was the extent to which the Internet would support or undermine the moral fabric of our culture. In each of these cases, the Internet itself remains of minor importance, it is simply reduced to being a vehicle of (undesirable) social and political consequences.

Mediation and politics

The example shows that much 'thought' about media has been cluttered by a preoccupation with evaluative political critique taking the place of a more phenomenon-orientated analysis. This is directly reflected in a key text book on media theory, which although over 15-years-old, is still a highly adequate summary of where we are: 'media theory is a branch of political theory' (Inglis 1990: 3). Media theory and media studies have insufficiently scrutinized the ontological nature of their object of study. That is to say, the analysis of media is, by and large, derived from an assumption that media are merely empty vessels that deliver content.

This explains why most media analyses have focused on either the political economy of media production, the semiosis of media texts or the sociopsychological effects of media consumption. This triad is a mere adaptation of the systems model which is still the predominant paradigm of communication studies (Fiske 1990). In all three, the medium is largely irrelevant because it is a mere instrument of either the accumulation of power and/or wealth, the organization and transmission of meaning, or the means by which people can experience (electronically generated) stimuli that may or may not be meaningful within their everyday life settings, and could have social and/or psychological consequences.

The purpose of this book is to drag the medium back into the spotlight. That is to say, it wants to offer another way of theorizing media that does not reduce the medium to a mere instrument. It will do so by providing an introduction to theoretical writings on media that either explicitly or implicitly enable us to question them. The work of media theory does not have to be invented from scratch; as much of it has already been done extensively. However, what has been lacking, thus far, is a sustained theoretical integration of the different approaches that have sought to explore and interpret media as phenomena in and of themselves.

As a result of an often overtly political agenda, students of media studies are presented with a view of media as merely a political instrument or site of struggle. In the UK, this has been interpreted mainly in terms of issues over power and domination; in the USA it is predominantly discussed in pluralistic frameworks related to issues of access, balance and fairness; in continental Europe (as well all as in some non-western nations, such as China) the agenda has been more one of cultural regulation, in which media are seen as an instrument and venue of cultural policy. The consequence of this is that media studies presents itself to students as an appendix of political science, but it also creates the impression that media are merely instruments of political power, and sites of struggle and domination. This leaves the concept of media rather empty.

Mediation as social interaction

Other attempts to theorize the media have reduced mediation to forms of social inter-action. For example, John B. Thompson (1995) developed an approach to theorizing media based on social theory. The implicit assumption in this attempt is that media technology is merely a means of extending processes of *sociation* or social interaction. For example, Thompson's concept of '*mediated-quasi-interaction*' implies that the 'quasi' nature of interaction is the consequence of a technological intervention. In breaking up the face-to-face dialogical nature of speech, mediation performs a reduc-tion of social interaction to enable its instantaneous replication for broadcasting. Mediation is thus valued purely for its social features.

It could be argued that, in his own way, the late German sociologist Niklas Luhmann (arguably the most influential communication theorist in continental Europe) also attempted to develop an understanding of media as an extended form of sociation in his system-orientated version of social theory. For Luhmann (1982, 1990), the focus was on communication as a means by which systems operate and provide means to affect each other. This becomes increasingly necessary in a society marked by increasingly specialized institutions (media). Mediated communication becomes itself a specialized function, that is separated from other institutions. As a result of these increasingly specialized mediation processes, communication itself has become an object of con-cern, an object of study and a matter of regulation. However, what remains difficult to understand is what 'pure communication' entails (that is, communication without content).

Both Thompson and Luhmann reduce mediation to social functions. As a result, their models do not inspire inquiries into that which enables mediation in the first place, that is, technology. Mediation is technological exactly because (at the same time) it both reveals and conceals the process by which social interactions are 'enabled'. The problem with the separation of 'media' as a specialized institution is that it suggests that it is somehow removed from what social theory assumes to be 'the social' (Latour 2005). This, in turn, begs the question of what 'unmediated' social interaction might be. Too often, this is assumed to be interaction outside the so-called mass media of print, broadcasting and computing; i.e., the already separated and recognized media institutions. This, as we shall see next, is erroneous.

Mediation as cultural reproduction

Media can also be reduced to 'cultural tools'. For example, the work of Stuart Hall (1980) on encoding/decoding is a good example of how media are black boxes providing the 'encoding' of messages so that they can be transmitted. Decoding then becomes the work of human beings. The consequence of this thinking is that culture remains the work of humans only; and the role of media themselves remains relatively obscure; they are merely facilitators of 'text'. The fact that Hall's own interest in encoding and decoding was primarily geared towards understanding how dominant ideologies are (re)produced, further testifies to the dominance of a particular (narrowly defined) notion of 'the political' in the history of media analysis.

Finally, there are approaches to understanding media that primarily understand it as a means of (mass) communication. John Fiske's work (1994), which includes a well-developed technological analysis, is still primarily geared towards an instrumentalist approach of media as a means of (once again) political communication within everyday life settings of popular culture. For Fiske, the role of media technology is only interesting in so far as it further reinforces the skewed political consequences of the messages thus constructed. While placing a lot of emphasis on non-dominant interpretations (as forms of resistance), Fiske only partially engages in an analysis of how 'effects', such as dominant or resistant interpretations, are themselves technologically facilitated. To a large extent, his approach to critical media analysis remains a matter of positioning, the origins of which lie outside the realm of mediation itself, but are the consequence of a distinctive 'will' or 'ideological disposition'.

Technology as ordering

What unites many approaches to understanding media is thus a strong reductionist assumption that technology has to be understood as a facilitator, a device or tool, in service of something else. This 'something else' is deemed more fundamental and, as a result, the process of mediation is reduced to an epiphenomenon. Furthermore, it is quite remarkable that even if this 'something else' takes the form of a social, cultural or communicative process, ultimately it is always the political that surfaces as the supreme 'force' of motivation.

By focusing more closely on the specific features of technologies of mediation, however, media theory is able to reveal that the concept of the political is not exhausted by a focus on the public sphere, and the way in which 'the public' are organized by the state, as well as more civic deliberations (Dahlgren 1995). Instead the concept of 'the political' should be stretched a bit more to include the most banal events of everyday life, on the one hand, but also to the more psychological and existential attunements between human beings and more abstract technical systems, on the other hand. That is, a phenomenological approach to mediation enables us to question that which mainstream approaches to theorizing media have too often taken for granted, such as perception, cognition, mood and attunement. This is a rather more radical understanding of 'the political', which goes well beyond ideologies, institutions and regulations.

While the political is by no means irrelevant, a case needs to be made for understanding media '*as such*', that is to say, not as instruments or tools, but as 'agents' of political, social and cultural processes. This is why we need to start a refocusing of media analysis with a phenomenology of mediation in terms of technology.

This is not to suggest that media are only technologies; indeed, media could be equally seen as social systems, organizations, businesses, cultural phenomena and political actors, to name but a few. However, whereas such approaches are abundant in the literature, there is a comparative lack of integration of perspectives on media technology into the field of media studies. Too often, media-technological analyses are being dismissed as 'technological determinism' without due consideration of what understanding media-as-technology might contribute on its own. What is particularly missing are attempts to connect media-analyses with more generic philosophical approaches to technology, although more recently, this is changing. Particularly noteworthy in this respect is the work of Friedrich Kittler (1997) which is now finding resonance in exiting recent publications, such as Fuller (2005) and Mackenzie (2002).

We cannot ignore that media are contested sites, and can provide means and instruments for—as well as agency to—the development and organization of collective action, tactical intervention and forms of 'resistance'. However, these terms should be reconsidered as part of the technological assemblage, rather than outside of it. This means that forces, such as 'stakes', 'interests' and 'motives', should be understood as part of what constitutes technologies.

Technologies 'enframe' the world; that is they *order* them in the double sense of providing a structure and commanding specific actions (Heidegger 1977; Adams 1993; Fry 1993; Van Loon 2000). This ordering constitutes the essence of mediation. This focus will also help us to reconsider the critique of 'technological determinism', which nowadays is used too often rather carelessly, to dismiss any form of criticism that seeks to attribute some active and creative power to the technological itself.

A good example of how media-as-technology enables us to understand the particular way in which the world we inhabit is being ordered is Walter Ong's (1982) historico-anthropological discussion of orality and literacy. Strongly influenced by the work of Marshall McLuhan, he argues that, in cultures where orality is the primary or only communications medium, human perceptions are structured on the basis of aural paradigms. In oral cultures, listening is the primary mode of perception and is materialized in an acoustic conception of spatiality. Acoustic space generates a specific modality of 'presencing' that is dominated by a timeless, but ephemeral referentiality that can only come into presence through repetition.

In contrast, literacy is both linear and geared towards the visual. Literary cultures 'preserve' referentiality in symbolic forms that can be passed on as objects and thus separated from the enactment of representation. It entails a 'splitting of the medium' into the enunciating actor (the author) and the enunciated act (the text). Whereas, in oral cultures, the medium remains a unified actor/act and thus always requires the presence of the enunciator, literary media enable the isolation of the enunciated act from the actor. The act can then be passed on as a separate item as it becomes the main performative part of the media product. Repetition is thus no longer the province of enunciation, but becomes technological (e.g., copying or printing a text). It is for this reason that Ong associates literary cultures with forms of alienation, which – at the same time – were also essential components for the development of civilizations.

Ong uses the contrast between orality and literacy to show that our very human being, that is what it means to be human, is intertwined with how we communicate, think and perceive. Indeed, his work shows that we need to focus more closely on the technological dimension of media and mediation as a way to sculpture an approach to understanding media that does not embrace an empty instrumentalism [which takes media as simply the means by which something 'more fundamental' is accomplished, such as collective (inter)action, socialization, propaganda or mass communication]. Following on from Ong's seminal intervention, it is possible to suggest that an adequate analysis of media technology should involve four key aspects: form, historicity, cultural embedding and embodiment.

Form

Ong's contrasting of orality and literacy provide a necessary deepening of (for example) McLuhan's more aphoristic reading of media history (see Chapter 2). It highlights, first of all, that the *form* of mediation has a significant bearing on the way in which communication works. Given the ubiquity of media today, it is a focus on technology-as-form that enables us to understand mediation as incorporating a vast range of different practices. Attention to form enables one to remain critical of any type of instrumentalism.

This first premise of this book is therefore that we have to analyse media in terms of their different *forms*, because it is through these forms that we can see how they facilitate the formation of particular logics in terms of modes of sensing, interpreting and reasoning. Whereas media studies have tended to favour analyses of content, and thereby primarily concerned themselves with questions of 'ideology' or 'discourse', an adequate media analysis should also contain a sensitivity towards the phenomena of media themselves and not just what they seem to 'contain'.

Only an inclusion of media-form enables us to study media *as such*. That is to say, a phenomenological approach to media begins with an appreciation of mediation as form. In this book I will therefore largely follow the phenomenological line that seeks to identify and explore the nature of media, that is, their ontology. In doing so, questions of politics (media as political instruments or engines of manipulation) and effects (media as transmitting stimuli or offering services) are secondary, and will only be invoked through a more primary ontological analysis of what mediation entails.

However, form on its own can only inform a very basic phenomenology. Part of a phenomenological approach is to focus on media as embedded in specific environments. Indeed, even if one takes a completely instrumental view of media (that is, media as vehicles for politics, social interaction or cultural reproduction), their phenomenological nature has to be understood in relation to the functions they fulfil and operations they entail as instruments. Indeed, as we have already stressed, when exploring the consequences of media-technological innovations, we always have to pay particular attention to the entire social, economic, political and cultural formation within which such media-technology systems operate.

Central to a phenomenology of media is therefore the way in which a focus on mediation enables us to connect to distinct conceptual domains:

- communication, as the '(inter)action' through which meaning comes into being (which is often truncated into debates over 'effects');
- culture as the 'context' as well as 'content' of that action (which is often further differentiated into issues of power, wealth and knowledge; e.g., Innis 1982).

James Carey (1992: 15) distinguishes between two different approaches to understanding the relationship between culture and communication as 'a transmission view of communication' and 'a ritual view of communication'. The transmission view focuses on communication as a process of sending and receiving messages over distances. The ritual view is much older and portrays communication as the key means of association (very similar to interaction), which is expressed in the etymological links with communion, community and commonness (Carey 1992: 18). Carey asserts that both have distinct religious origins. Transmission relates to preaching and evangelization; ritual communication to practices of worship, prayer and liturgical and sacramental ministry within congregations. It is perhaps because the culture of the United States has been traditionally dominated by Protestantism (Parsons 1973) that the transmission model has been far more dominant there than the ritual model, which has its roots in the Catholic and Eastern Orthodox traditions of the early Christian Churches and (premedieval) monasticism (Winter 1996).

As Communication Studies has been dominated by North American scholarship from the outset, it is perhaps no surprise that it has been, by and large, framed by the transmission model. Indeed, in North America the very infrastructure of telegraphy developed alongside that of the East-West railway (Carey 1992). The link between transportation and communication was a key component of the colonization of the 'Wild West' through settlements that displaced the more nomadic modes of inhabitation of native Americans. Its close relationship with transportation made it an almost self-evident part of the experience of colonization and the ethos of pioneering. Its primary orientation [Innis (1982) called it 'bias'] is towards overcoming the obstacles of space and geography. The idea of cultivating 'nature' that was conceptualized as barbaric and pagan, could indeed be seen as a redemptive act in itself. The role of communication in the coming into being of the United States is, thus, more than merely instrumental; its very substance of spreading 'the Word', indeed its civilization-labour (a term coined by de Regt 1984) is of fundamental significance to understanding how the dominant culture of North America was initially formed and still persists to this very day (Carey 1992: 16). Indeed, from this point of view, communication is inherently a 'moral enterprise'.

By contrast, the ritual view of communication has much closer ties with traditional scholarship, first in the realm of theology, but later spreading to philosophy and the social sciences. Since the birth of the modern academy in the nineteenth century, its links with the emergent social sciences (such as psychology and sociology) were so close that it was generally not considered necessary to study communications as a separate field, let alone discipline. For Carey, the lack of scholarship based on the ritual model in the US, reflects the latter's underlying 'weak and evanescent concept of culture in American social thought' (Carey 1992: 19). Hence, it is with this in mind that a phenomenological approach to mediation could also be invoked to sharpen a more cultural analysis of communication processes.

Historicity

As we have seen, media-technologies have pervaded almost all activities of human beings. This has two rather paradoxical manifestations in commonsensical perceptions of the role of media-technologies in human history. On the one hand, there is a generic and usually unquestioned acceptance of the assumption that media-technologies have *caused* many social, cultural, political and economic changes. Current examples of this can be found in aforementioned lamentations over the rise of the Internet and the death of face-to-face communication as determinants of an increasingly individualistic and *blasé* society. On the other hand, (media-) technologies are often 'taken for granted' to the extent that we don't even seem to notice their workings (that is, until they 'break down'). We do not think about our use of and dependency on media as having any effect on ourselves because they are merely things we use.

However, the paradox of media as autonomous causes versus invisible instruments is easily resolved if we take a more historical perspective. When we look at the history of distinct media-technological innovations, we discover a distinct pattern. When a new medium 'arrives', that is, when its 'usage' moves from experimentation in laboratories to taking on functions (i.e., 'settles') in everyday life, we notice their 'effects'. That is, we notice the difference that these media-innovations make to how we function as human beings. The more radical the innovation, the more its effect is noticed.

Hence, the arrival of the telegraph was a far more historically marked event than the arrival of the fax machine or the VCR. The radical nature of the telegraph was its ability to facilitate communications over great distances with the immediacy of face-to-face speech. It was the first electronic communication medium. The fax machine, however, arrived a century after the telephone. Its usage was more closely associated with moveable typesetting (print), which was – at least in terms of its appropriation of the alphabet – over 500-years-old by the time it linked up with telephony. The social embedding of the fax was merely a speeding up of mail, not a new way of getting in touch, for which the telephone was still far more appropriate and effective.

Hence, one cannot understand the nature of any medium without taking into account the *historical context* in which it came into being. This is the second premise that underscores this book. It is a fairly obvious point, but nonetheless needs to be made if only as an antidote to modes of thinking that attempt to read the 'essence' of a medium purely from its internal, technological properties. It is also an antidote against both poles of the false paradox: media are neither singular causes of social effects nor inconsequential instruments of social, political or economic action.

A return to Ong's work makes it clear that even within the most elementary media that we can already trace the complex, interconnected nature of mediation. Indeed, while speech and non-verbal communication have by no means been diminished during the course of human history, it is noticeable how many more media have been introduced since the beginning of time (e.g., itself a mediated event, mythologized by 'recorded history'). The introduction of inscription and writing, for example, in ancient Egyptian civilization, combined the use of language (a rule-bound, arbitrary system of symbols) in speech with the visual means of representation of cave painting.

Hieroglyphs are an interesting form of writing because they are 'little pictures' of 'things' they represent; this also entails a reduction of often complex visual realities to rather simplistic icons. This reduction, in turn, has to be compensated for by the invocation of connotations, which themselves have to be socially acquired through learning. That is to say, the first systems of writing also entailed a more formalized pedagogy of reading. This meant that a separation was made between understanding in terms of 'thought' as opposed to 'experience' and this, in turn, can be seen as the inauguration of formal abstraction (Ong 1982).

The arrival of the alphabet entailed the completion of the total abstraction of writing as a medium of representation. The simplicity of the alphabet, in which a relatively short number of characters can be put together to produce an infinite amount of 'words', became the major strategic advantage for the development of print in Europe. This is not the case in, for example, China, where the sheer amount of characters or ideograms inhibited the rapid spread of moveable typesetting and facilitated (not caused!) the consolidation of centralized control (Innis 1982).

However, the first consequence of the use of alphabetical writing was a radical extension of 'abstraction' in forms of communication and thus an increased emphasis on the development of 'reading' as a learned practice. The acquisition of know-how to use (read and write) the alphabet thus brought with it an incorporation of the logic of this abstract system. This logic was linear (letters making words, words making sentences, etc.). Whereas the alphabet was a lot easier to learn than hieroglyphs, because one acquires it through the linear logic that underscores it, it required a more radical transformation of perspective because of its shift of meaning from the primacy of icons to the absolute supremacy of symbols. Following Innis, McLuhan (1964: 86) argues that the shift to the phonetic alphabet led to a demystification of writing. This, in turn, entailed a loss of monopolistic power of the priestly caste over the realm of representation in favour of the military and political castes. As everybody could now learn to read and write, and it was no longer a lifelong enterprise; the printed word could be instrumentalized in the service of the pursuit of strategic power and the accumulation of wealth (see Chapter 2).

Cultural embedding

The articulation of the form of the medium within a specific historical trajectory opens up a whole new domain of analysis, namely how relationships between media have affected communication processes, i.e., the possibilities for *shared meaning*. The content of mediation is not independent from the form of mediation because, as McLuhan (1964) stated, '*the medium is the message*'. Even if we accept that this may be a bit hyperbolical, we can still appreciate the merits of emphasizing mediation in terms of evolution as it enables a historical sensitivity towards the way in which sense-making is organized. In simpler terms, the organization of sense-making is what we normally call 'culture'.

The third premise of this book is that media analysis requires a sensitivity towards the cultural embedding of mediation. This also means that we are always geared towards analysing inter-media relationships, because it is in the articulations between media that specific forms of sense-making become embedded in social forms and are able to 'endure' over time. Moreover, an awareness of cultural embedding enables us to look for transformations in the way in which sense-making relates to the sensibilities, experiences and anticipations of those involved in it (which can be human, as well as non-human actors). Culture highlights that meaning and significance emerge from *practices* and do not exist in themselves. In short, sense-making is an *enactment*, it is performative. This enactment will be primarily understood as 'technology-use'.

If we accept that the role of media- technology is ordering both in terms of structuring and commanding, how we perceive, think and communicate, it follows that there is no meaning outside mediation. The way in which the world is revealed and enframed, and thus becomes significant, following specific historical trajectories, which can also be mapped as media evolutions (as long as we include human actors in there as well).

In Chapter 2, we will see that these evolutions are very specific mediated nestings and sequences that can only be explained when taking into account their cultural embedding. That is, media evolutions are not haphazard or autonomous, but involve specific *selections*. These selections emerge from specific forms of engagement with the technology, i.e., their *use*. Technological use becomes binding over time as particular selections, in turn, affect how we perceive, think and communicate, that is, how we make sense. The emphasis on the enactment of sense-making enables us to identify specific modes of agency, subjectivity, intentionality, as well as necessity, determination and impact; in short, enactment highlights the process of motivation. All forms of mediation are *motivated*.

It is this understanding of mediation as motivated that enables us to return to the question concerning the political nature of mediation. This is the radical extension of the political that was referred to earlier. The political is not limited to collectively articulated opinions or interests, but to very particular instances of sense-making. These may impact on the way in which use becomes binding and thus affects the specific trajectories through which media-technologies are enabled to facilitate ('order') how we perceive, think and communicate.

Embodiment (and disembodiment)

It is difficult to envisage a human history without media and without technology. From archaeological digs of the earliest forms of human life, there is already abundant evidence of the use of technological devices such as tools and weapons. The Magdalenian paintings of the Altamira Cave in Cantabria Spain and, most famously, in Lascaux, as well as the paintings of the Chauvet-Pont-d'Arc Cave (both in France), are brilliant records of media used in visual representations of life events (Heyd and Clegg 2005). These paintings were embedded in oral cultures and often depicted animals. Human representations were extremely rare.

Whereas no consensus exists among archaeologists about the exact function of the paintings, it is not difficult to explain how they could have functioned within oral cultures. They ordered specific sensibilities towards the world, by illustrating experiences, thoughts and reflections. That is, the images did not represent how people thought, but ordered their sensibilities of being-in-the-world. In such cultures, the main modality of communication was not visual but oral.

Logically speaking, speech is in effect the first communication medium (Ong 1982). Although, in essence, not an application of any 'artefact' as tool, speech is a medium because it uses 'language', which is an abstract system of symbols based on arbitrary (but socially reinforced, reproduced and regulated) connections between sounds (words) and things. If we take speech as the 'arche typical' communication medium, it is perhaps easier to understand why McLuhan (1964) referred to media as 'extensions of man' [sic]. It is also easy to see that this medium has a direct connectivity with the human body, which is further underlined with the notion of nonverbal communication, in which the human body itself becomes an instrument, a medium, for the articulation and dissemination of meaning. This is, therefore, the fourth premise underscoring this book: the adequate analysis of media requires an orientation towards their *embodied* nature, which has a *logical* starting point in the human body itself.

Mediation extends the human body; its ability to perceive, to express itself, to 'reach out and touch' others across space and time. This is captured by the aphorism 'media are extensions of man'. The challenge of feminist theory, however, is that the human body is not a self-evident singularity, but itself differentiated (gendered) and politicized. This can be revealed by linking the previous concerns over form, historicity and cultural motivation with the concept of gender. Not only is gender heavily propped up by forms of mediation, it also affects the nature of mediation itself. This becomes particularly clear when reflecting on issues of subjectivity and identity.

Subjectivity and identity operate at the level of 'manifestations'; they are specific, modern, expressions of sensibilities. These should not be confused with the sensibilities themselves. To come to terms with how sensibilities are ordered, we should consider the nature of mediated embodiment in terms of what is perhaps more primordial: namely, power (force) and desire. That is to say, the embodiment of mediation has an 'affective' drive that, if we use the human body as an archetype, reveals itself, for example, in terms of 'sexual desire' (Eros). Hence, mediation can be understood through the prism of sexual desire as a movement towards unification, a physiological expression of drive to 'become one' (again).

The embodied nature of media, however, should by no means be exclusively understood in terms of the *human* body. 'Media as extensions of "man" ' is perhaps one of the less fortunate expressions used by McLuhan. Not only does it immediately pose the question of gender difference; it also brings up a rather problematic (and literal) anthropocentric view of the process of mediation as extending from a unique mythical origin (in terms of what Nietzsche called *Ursprung*, cited in Foucault 1977a) i.e., 'man'. This 'man' is too easily confused with modern 'man', the double agent of modernity: its arche and telos, its cause and effect, its condition and destiny, the measure and purpose of all things (Foucault 1970).

Instead of this mythical 'man', Matthew Fuller (2005: 63) proposes a more Nietzschean concept of the body as the 'starting point' for knowledge. For Fuller, this has two distinct advantages:

- it provides a materialist and action-based grounding of perception, ordering, indeed mediation;
- it bypasses the need to impose an *a priori* hierarchy of the organization of this mediation.

In simpler terms it seeks to avoid having to take-for-granted human intentions, motivations, concerns and interests as the sole origin of intelligible action (anthropocentrism). As a result, it does not have to assume that media evolution happens on the basis of some intrinsic human reason. The 'subject' of communication is thus no longer a privileged entity (i.e., the human being) whose status is derived from metaphysics, but instead is itself an *effect* of a sustained interaction between forces. Following Latour (1988b) we could further specify that these forces themselves are irreducible (to interests, beliefs, moral values, etc.). This, in turn, leads us back to Nietzsche's

(1992) concept of 'the will to power' as a means to describe this force of sheer being or 'vitality'. This will be discussed in greater detail in Chapter 5, where we will problematize the man-machine divide to develop a concept of mediation that does not rely on an anthropocentric concept of human-machine interfaciality.

Outline

Form, historicity, cultural embedding and embodiment/disembodiment are all intricately connected in a phenomenology of mediation. Yet, different approaches to understanding media-as-technology will have different emphases. For example, whereas the works of thinkers, such as McLuhan, Benjamin and Barthes, emphasize form, Innis, Williams and Baudrillard are much more focused on historicity. All of them were concerned with cultural embedding and, in particular, McLuhan and Benjamin were also concerned with embodiment.

The way to organize a discussion of their writings will always entail some form or arbitrariness, and it is for this reason that I have decided to use the split between medium theory and cultural theory, or between a transmission view of communication (as the North American tradition) in Chapter 2 and a ritual view (the European tradition) in Chapter 3. In order to move out of the artificial intercontinental stalemate that one may thereby end up with, Chapter 4 will discuss a different 'cutting across' form, historicity, cultural embedding and embodiment, by discussing feminist approaches, whereas Chapter 5 aims to radicalize a phenomenological approach to mediation by discussing in greater detail new developments in media theory, particularly those concerning networks and disembodiment.

The main method of analysis for this book will be to provide an in-depth discussion of a few key thinkers whose works highlight how we could theorize media-technology. This, however, is not to merely summarize their main points of view, but to help us think *with* them about the essential characteristics of media-technologies, and how they affect social and cultural processes. The purpose is thus not to give a summary of the field, but to explore how we could better understand the technological dimension of media-processes, which has been too often ignored in favour of analyses of media-content.

The best known approach to theorizing media-technologies is undoubtedly to be found in the work of Marshall McLuhan. It is not for nothing that McLuhan has given the seminal inspiration behind this book. However, it is simply wrong to assume that McLuhan's work is self-standing and entirely original. In fact, McLuhan was strongly inspired by a wide range of thinkers (including Heidegger, Bergson and Nietzsche) and his aversion to write in a traditional, scholarly manner should not lead one to believe that he was not himself an excellent scholar. Nor should we assume that McLuhan's approach has died with the thinker. It lives on remarkably well in the work of a number of influential contemporary scholars. Therefore, Chapter 2 introduces McLuhan in relation to a number of other thinkers, such as Innis, Postman, Carey, Levinson and Meyrowitz.

McLuhanism represents a North American media theoretical approach whose originality and depth continues to provide a strong focal point for analyses of media-technology (Babe 2000). However, there are also distinctive European traditions that could be invoked to develop a sophisticated understanding of the importance of the cultural embedding of the technological dimension of media analysis. The European traditions all share what Carey (1992) referred to as 'the ritual model' of media analysis (as opposed to the 'transmission model' that dominates North American communication studies).

Yet, Carey's useful distinction obfuscates the subtle differences between various trajectories of European thought. Chapter 3, therefore, introduces four different thinkers: Walter Benjamin, Raymond Williams, Roland Barthes and Jean Baudrillard alongside each other. In addition, the Chapter attempts to bring these traditions together into a more radical thesis on the future of society as a mediascape. Placing Benjamin's seminal article 'the Work of Art in an Age of Mechanical Reproduction' alongside Raymond Williams' writings on television, which have almost equal status as key texts on media technology within cultural studies, Roland Barthes' essay 'From Work to Text' (among others) and Baudrillard's work on symbolic exchange the simulacrum and hyperreality, enables us to see how a focus on media-technology has also helped to develop a more critical notion of culture that does not slide into sociological or political reductionism. Although by no means identical, all four theorists have placed 'culture' to the foreground of analysing media technology, using – often implicitly – an analytical framework inspired by a rather loose association with Marxism (although, they have refrained from reducing media technology to simply a means of production).

The Benjamin–Williams–Barthes–Baudrillard conjunction is not an immediately recognizable one, as they were working within quite different traditions. Yet, in quite distinct ways, all four situate media-technology at the heart of understanding cultural changes, similar to McLuhan. However, unlike McLuhanism, the Marxist influence has ensured a strong connection with more politically orientated media-analyses, such as those of the Frankfurt School, the Birmingham School and French Post-structuralism. They enable us to conceptualize media, culture and politics as interconnected fields, without subduing any one of them to the others.

Studies of technology, and especially media-technologies, have been dominated by men. On top of this, other traditions central to media-analyses, such as phenomenology and Marxism, have also been dominated by men. As a result, it is fair to say that there is an inherent masculinist bias in media-technological analyses. Whereas analyses of media content have become profoundly sensitized to the gendered nature of representation, this has not filtered strongly into considerations over the gendered nature of media-technology. This is the more remarkable since from its inception a phenomenology of media-forms also reveals their embodied being (media as extensions of 'man').

It is on the basis of this association between technology and the body, that Chapter 4 embraces the feminist challenge. However, this is not done in the form of an indictment, but as a means of deepening our understanding of the primacy of 'difference' that constitutes the essence of the 'historical' human body (rather than the metaphysical or theological notion of 'humanity' or 'mankind' in a non-gendered sense).

A clear angle in feminist writings on media technology is its focus on gendered embodiment alongside concerns over notions of domesticity, marginalization and social exclusion (Wajcman 1991, 2004; Cockburn 1992; Cockburn and Fürst-Dilic 1994; Spigel 2001; Haddon 2003). These analyses are invoked to displace rather abstract and grand ideas of many male media theorists, and bring in a more astute sociological and culturally-specific angle.

Feminist notions of media also enable us to situate media-technologies in relation to the cultural and political, as well as social fields, which is essential to understanding their impact on the specific gendered orderings, which characterize the modern western world. The chapter concludes with a critical appraisal of feminist reflections on media-technology, and points at some shortcomings and limitations, which also include the dangers of deploying an undifferentiated notion of gender itself.

However, as we have already seen, there remains a fundamental issue with treating embodiment on the basis of the primacy of the human body as it privileges 'man' as the subject of history and assumes a metaphysical hierarchy of social organization with the human as both origin and destiny.

Therefore, Chapter 5 extends the analysis of media-technology through modes of embodiment by means of an analysis of the emergence of what might be called a 'vitalist' paradigm. This vitalist paradigm is mainly derived from Nietzsche, but finds echoes in the more contemporary works of Deleuze and Guattari, Virilio and, most importantly for this chapter, Actor Network Theory (ANT), especially the work of Bruno Latour. As a theoretical perspective, ANT has thus far not been applied to the study of media-technologies. In so doing, the chapter also seeks to make more explicit the possibilities for linking a phenomenological media analysis with the emergent field of 'new media theory' with a particular focus on processes of disembodiment, which has given rise to the concept of 'networked being'.

There is no point in concerning ourselves with media-technology if we refrain from applying some of the generated insights to our own media-saturated, cultural environments. In the last 20 years, we have witnessed an explosion of digital and wireless communication technologies that have again radically reconfigured our everyday worlds in modern western society (although we are by no means equally affected by it or equally benefiting from it). The digital poses new questions regarding a phenomenological understanding of media-technologies. Specific attention needs to be given to digital media because they have forced us to radically rethink the matter of 'matter' and the nature of presence and the present (the virtual). The main aim of this chapter is to show how media-technologies connect to more general technological constellations and thereby have come to play a central role in the reconfiguration of the world we inhabit.

It should by now be clear that this book contains a dual purpose. On the one hand, it introduces the reader to a range of ideas regarding (media-) technologies that have – in many cases – occupied relatively marginal positions within the general fields of media and communication studies. In this sense, it is an attempt to alert the reader to some hidden treasures within existing works that can be unearthed to help illuminate our present condition, which is heavily mediated and mediatized.

On the other hand, it is an attempt to go beyond mere synthesis to make a more original contribution to media analysis. It aims to offer an alternative to the stalemate between technological determinism and instrumentalism without resorting to a simplistic notion of 'dialectics' (i.e., that it is a combination of both forces affecting each other). Instead, it wants to show how the stalemate is simply a product of 'bad thought' or – more charitably – a conceptual confusion. In doing so, it proposes to make a 'Nietzschean turn' in media analysis to steer away from 'reductions' of media processes to economic, political or social ones in favour of a more biophysiological and phenomenological understanding of media in which history, embodiment and form are recombined to provide an original framework for doing media analysis.

Suggested further reading

Carey, J.W. (1992) *Communication as Culture. Essays on Media and Society*. London: Routledge.
   This is an excellent account of how Medium Theory (Media Ecology) can be used to develop a far better and more critical appreciation of the distinctive role of media in communication processes. It has a strong North American and historically-orientated focus.
Moores, S. (2005) *Media/Theory. Thinking about Media and Communications*. London: Routledge.
   A very good and much more recent theoretical engagement with different ways of conceptualizing mediation processes. It has a strong sociological orientation on media technology.
Morley, D. (2007) *Media, Modernity and Technology. The Geography of the New*. London: Routledge.
   British media studies have been strongly influenced by David Morley and his most recent work provides a wide-ranging set of explorations of the field of media and cultural studies, and a discussion of disciplinary and methodological issues and concerns.
Ong, W.J. (1982) *Orality and Literacy. The Technologizing of the World*. London: Routledge.
   This book is a true landmark in media analysis. A highly original and thorough engagement with the shifts and transformations of human culture as it moved from a sole dependency on orality to a new reliance on literacy.
Williams, K. (2003) *Understanding Media Theory*. London: Hodder Arnold.
   An accessible introduction to different theories of mass mediation. Indispensable to those who are completely new to the subject.

2 | A CRITICAL HISTORY OF MEDIA TECHNOLOGY

As modern developments in communication made for greater realism they have made for greater possibilities of delusion. (Innis 1982: 82)

Our culture wants both to multiply its media and to erase all traces of mediation: ideally, it wants to erase its media in the very act of multiplying them. (Bolter and Grusin 2000: 5)

When people talk about 'media' they can refer to a wide range of different things. For example, '*the* media' is an institution operating within the structures of modern society alongside other institutions, such as 'education', 'health care', 'the police', etc. The 'the' indicates that the phenomenon is both singular and 'integral' in terms of its functions; that is, it contains all phenomena and operations involved in 'mediated communications'. In a similar vein, media are referred to as organizations, products, and, crucial for this book, as technologies. This book seeks to argue that approaching media as technology enables one to explain *what media are* more adequately than a focus on institutions, organizations or products. Moreover, through the course of this book, it shall also become clear that what media are, has a direct impact on *what media do*.

In this chapter we will explore one of the most influential trajectories of theorizing media-technology. It emerged from North America in the middle of the twentieth century and provided a radically different perspective on (mass) media from the then dominant schools of communication studies, i.e., functionalist systems theory and effects research (Babe 2000).

This innovative approach has been called both 'Medium Theory' and 'Media Ecology'. Both terms are complementary. Whereas the former highlights the central role of the medium as more than a tool or instrument, the latter term reflects the insistence on the relationship between the development of media and the influence of the impact on their environment as a dynamic system (hence ecology). It is this *combination* that is essential, and we must always remind ourselves to insist on both medium and environment as concomitant, not just or even primarily in terms of effect.

The first axis of innovation of Medium Theory lies in its focus on *media as a form of technology*. It paved the way for the emergence of a form of media analysis whose potential is still to be fulfilled, if only because it has all too often been misunderstood, but whose relevance for the present and the future is difficult to ignore. The second axis (Media-Ecology) is a shift of attention to the *interaction between media-technologies and their wider environment*. To a large extent, these interactions are facilitated by human actions and motivations, but as we have seen in the previous chapter, technological processes entail their own sense of agency as well; they, too, are capable of performing actions. These actions can be referred to as 'enframing' and 'revealing' (which are part of the same process) and are in essence ways of 'ordering' particular spheres of action.

The central figure in Medium Theory (Media Ecology) is Marshall McLuhan. McLuhan was a highly controversial figure both inside and outside the academic world. During his heyday in the 1960s, he was considered a guru, a prophet, the founder of a new calling for sociocultural theory and, in particular, 'media studies' (Miller 1971). In the 1970s he would lose that acclaim, as more and more of his imaginative and visionary ideas were discredited (Genosko 1998; Levinson 1998; Babe 2000). However, as it has become more and more clear that McLuhan's prophetic thoughts on the role of information and its global impact are perhaps now more adequate than ever before, it may not be such a bad idea to return to some of his works and reinstate some of its theoretical force. This chapter aims to present a brief analysis of the logic of McLuhan's theoretical work and highlight its usefulness for understanding the technohistorical dimension of mediation.

Starting with Harold Innis, who was McLuhan's mentor, this chapter will give an account of how human-cultural evolution can be understood as being co-dependent on technological innovation. Moving on to McLuhan, more specific items, such as print, radio and television will be discussed in terms of their alleged social and cultural implications. Specific attention will be paid to McLuhan's key phrases: media as extensions of man, narcissus narcosis and the medium is the message. Following this, the chapter addresses some of the more contemporary works that have been inspired by McLuhan's immense legacy. By asking to what extent their rather bold predictions have come true, we can ascertain what we can learn from this type of analysis. Finally, a more critical assessment shall be given of the limitations and pitfalls of perspectives associated with McLuhanism (Levinson 1997, 1998).

Technological and social change: bias in the work of Harold Innis

> We must appraise civilization in relation to its territory and in relation to its duration. The character of the medium of communication tends to create a bias in civilization favourable to an overemphasis on the time concept or on the space concept and only at rare intervals are the biases offset by the influence of another medium and stability achieved. (Innis 1982: 64)

Harold Innis is widely seen as a central figure within communication and media theory, although he is also rather controversial because his primary background was political economy and history, and his research was in particular concerned with the Canadian frontier economy (Heyer 2003).

Within communication studies, the concept for which he is most famous is that of bias. As a term bias was already quite well-known in communication studies. Alongside 'noise' it functioned as a signifier of dysfunctional elements within the media process. Whereas noise was used to describe external disturbances, bias referred to internally motivated distortions in the translation from original ideas and intentions into the message-as-received (Shannon and Weaver 1949). Hence, for mainstream communication theorists, bias was related to the agency of those involved in communication processes. As it was also undesired, practical implications (driven by the ideal of 'perfect' or 'effective' communication) often focused on the elimination of bias either by means of technological or administrative interventions and regulations. However, because the pragmatics of communication were generally framed within a wider concern for strategic (political, military) deployment, the elimination of bias was never as important as its manipulation (propaganda).

Innis, however, appropriated his background in law, political economy and history to develop a rather different and far more critical understanding of bias. According to McLuhan (1982), bias in Innis' work is primarily a research tool and a heuristic device (Comor 2003). Innis' usage of the term reflects a desire to return to a more fundamental notion of communication, one that is not cast in the highly instrumentalist and strategic mould of Shannon and Weaver's systems theory.

For Innis, communication is closely associated with transportation (it is only with the arrival of the telegraph that the two have become separated; Carey 1992). Therefore, the physical nature of the 'matter' of communication matters. This is not an unusual collocation. As Carey (1992) has argued, the association with transportation has dominated conceptions of communication within North American culture since the nineteenth century, which he referred to as 'the transmission view of communication', as opposed to the ritual view, which emphasized communication as a form of meaningful association. The problem, however, is that Carey fails to distinguish between two radically different types of transmission. On the one hand, transmission could focus on the act of 'passing'; on the other hand, it could focus on the matter being passed. The dominant paradigms within Communication Studies have only concerned themselves with the process of passing; that is to say, *what* is being passed is of secondary importance.

It is important to remember that Communication Studies emerged as a distinctive discipline in an age where electronic communication was already dominant. That is, it follows the logic of a complete separation of medium and content. This neglect of the medium, as medium, assumed an equivalence between orality and literacy. By not acknowledging this, Carey perhaps overemphasizes 'outcomes' and underanalyses process. In contrasting transmission and ritual, Carey may have consequently glossed over what is itself a fundamental break between a culture based on print and literacy, and one based on electronic communications. When pointing out the distinctive revolutionary implications of the telegraph, we should also acknowledge that its impact is more than historical and cultural, but deeply ontological, as well. Indeed, Innis reminds us that the matter-in-transmission matters and is the central part of the communication process. As a result, his model provides a radical alternative within transmission views of communication when compared with the dominant paradigms.

Shannon and Weaver's systems theory suffers from the particular 'bias' of having been conceived within an age of electronic mediation (radio and television). In electronic communications, the 'matter' of communication is ephemeral, both in terms of form and of content (see below). Their entanglement with politics, governance, economics and the military has been orientated towards the maximization of centralized control over information flows from the outset. Hence, within that thinking, the strategic-pragmatic focus of communication is a natural extension of the idea that the accumulation of knowledge, wealth and power requires forms of information processing that eliminate contingencies, such as unintended 'side effects', technological glitches, ambiguity and ambivalence (Kittler 1996).

Communication effects research (the other dominant paradigm in communciation studies according to Fiske 1990) suffers from a similar negligence of matter. In transforming communications media into generic providers of stimuli, the effects paradigm has separated 'effects' from the nature of the medium itself and thereby rendered a very simplistic notion of mediation in which substance is secondary to form. Media-effects research has very little to say about differences between media apart from the issue of which media are more 'effective'. In contrast, Innis offers us a way to understand media as '*affective*'. That is to say, for Innis the central question is how media 'involve' particular responses, both in terms of social forms as well as cultural-psychological predispositions (e.g., towards authority, critical thinking, etc.).

Innis' use of bias helps us to break out of the particular blind spot towards the nature of the medium, i.e., matter-of-transmission and matter-in-transmission. Bias enables us to put the contingency of medium-matters back at the centre of our thinking about communication. Because he returns to the earliest forms of communication (such as writings in clay tablets), he is able to reconnect transmission with the basics of transportation and makes the 'matter' of communication visible again (Innis 1972). In doing so, he reveals the particular limitations and conditions of each of the media that were being used, i.e., their bias.

Bias relates to matter (i.e., the matter through which mediation takes place, such as paper, the press, electronic wires, microprocessor, keyboard, etc.). Matter anchors mediation in a material world and grants mediation its molecular properties. Even in completely digitalized communications, matter still matters (as hardware); electricity still has to be generated and wireless still requires wires (Mackenzie 2005), all electronic flows still rely on material infrastructures.

Bias also relates to form. The form of mediation relates to the way in which matter is ordered and organized and put into place. The multiplicity of media-forms is still limited and conditioned by matter, and thus 'biased'; even if this may not be in a unidirectional, linear way.

Use provides a third dimension of bias. It is here where media applications become anchored in social practices; where media become 'bound' to specific performances. Again, multiplicity is inevitable, but bias emerges as that which attunes specific orientations; the calling for specific attention and thus also the overlooking of alternative modes of 'use'.

Finally, bias relates to know-how (which is orientated towards outcomes). It relates to the purposefulness of mediation, and the ways on which it calls upon particular skills and functions. Mediation is motivated and it is from this motivation that meaningful action emerges.

Together, these four axes of bias – matter, form, use and know-how – engender the contingency of mediation. The constitute what we call technology. Technology is constituted on the basis of the interplay between these four aspects and each technological form consists of its own unique articulation between them. These unique articulations emerge historically as a particular medium takes shape. This taking shape might also be called 'media-evolution'. Innis' insight stresses that far from an unwanted remainder of not-yet-perfect communication, contingency (random variation) becomes the force of history, the engine of change. Hence, bias is not a 'mere' heuristic device, but a radical intervention in thought.

Innis helpfully translates the term bias into a particular philosophical question: 'why do we attend to the things to which we attend?' and uses this question to show how bias can be understood as 'the nodal points through which what we know and how we know are produced and reproduced' (Comor 2003: 89). In other words, whereas it empirically operates as a reminder of the importance of contingency stemming from the 'matter' of communication, bias relates to the fundamental phenomenological question of the relationship between matter and thought: what motivates thought? Rather than the free will of the unbound philosophical mind, bias reminds us of Nietzsche's (1966) assertion that all philosophy is inherently a mere justification of particular cultural prejudices of the time.

Wealth, power and knowledge

Unlike Nietzsche, however, Innis looks for the structural reproduction of bias, rather than deriving his insights from a particular biophilosophy (i.e., vitalism). As a political economist, Innis himself was perhaps strongly biased towards the economic infrastructure of historical processes. More specifically, Innis was interested in how civilizations evolved in relation to three drives towards maximizing control: as a monopoly over wealth, a monopoly over power and a monopoly over knowledge (Comor 2003).

Comor's reading of Innis stresses that alongside his focus on economics, there is a significant political dimension to his communication theory as well. He points towards the centrality of control. Communication media can enhance the capacity of control of space or time. Sometimes this can take place simultaneously but, on other occasions, they can be mutually exclusive. For example, Innis argues that:

> [t]he monopoly of knowledge centring around the printing press brought to an end an obsession with space and the neglect of problems of continuity and time. The newspaper with a monopoly over time was limited in its power over space because of its regional character. Its monopoly was characterised by instability and crises. The radio introduced a new phase in the history of Western civilization by emphasizing centralization and the necessity of a concern with continuity. The bias of communication in paper and the printing industry was destined to be offset by the bias of the radio. (Innis 1982: 60)

However, Innis (1972) was at pains to express that this capacity does not stem exclusively from media-as-technologies (i.e., the internal properties of matter and form), but from their practical, functional, operational and above all social embedding (i.e., use and know-how). For example, the rise of print media, such as newspapers, facilitated the rise of a new monopoly of knowledge. They undermined the deeply time biased nature of religious life immersed in communal, oral communication and face-to-face mediation, and instead infused possibilities for more abstract and individuated, spatialized forms of nationhood (Anderson 1983). This did not happen because the internal properties of print (on paper) created one, but because they enabled a shift in bias away from one completely focused on a collective ritual of repetitive presencing (e.g., as in the sacrifice of the mass) to a much looser organization of time and space (as the printed word was believed to preserve its content, Luther's notion of *sola scriptura*: scripture only), enabling forms of spatial governance that favoured central control (and, hence, the rise of absolutist sovereignty in sixteenth-century Europe).

However, less than 200 years later, the space bias of print (which, for example, enabled the formation of the idea of the nation as an imagined community) gave way to a print culture that re-enabled a sense of time and continuity (which was more conducive to industrial capitalism). Aided by a rise in literacy, the printed word lost its militant protestant edge, and became an instrument of consolidation and standardization. That is to say, when immersed in a struggle with non-literary mediation, print facilitated a different kind of bias than when it enjoyed a more monopolistic position. Indeed, Innis argues that only for a (very) short period in the early twentieth century, a 'balance' had been achieved between space and time bias with the emergence of radio (and perhaps only in North America; Innis 1972: 81). Indeed, Innis (1982: 88) himself recognizes that:

> the monopoly of equilibrium was ultimately destroyed in the great depression and gave way to the beginnings of the monopoly of the centralized state. The disappearance of time monopolies facilitated the rapid extension of control by the state and the development of new religions evident in fascism, communism and our way of life.

It should be clear that Innis (1972) was very critical of intentionalist views of history in which crucial turning points were being reduced to the deliberate and willed actions of individuals. Instead, his historical analyses show how thought itself was being produced and conditioned, focusing on the intersections between communication and transportation, and bringing this in relation to military, political, economic and religious forces. Bias in communication then, should first of all be seen as the way in which particular orientations in thought are being structured. Hence, bias is not an inherent quality of particular media, but stems from the way a mediation is 'set into work', involving a constellation of form, matter, use and know-how.

Bias is that which media-technologies reveal and conceal at the same time. In doing so, mediation produces a sense of truth and of reality that appears as fully self-transparent, yet highly biased and partial (Vattimo 1992). Innis' concept of bias is perhaps the most effective way of exposing this double-edged sword. For Innis, the revealing/concealing relates not simply to the 'matter' of communication, that is, the internal properties of the medium, but to the way in which the medium becomes operational.

Bias highlights that media-technology is constituted by an interplay between the technological artefact (the tool or better 'matter' and 'form'), its practical applications (usage), as well as the knowledge and skills that are necessary to make it work (know-how). This is why it is wrong to interpret Innis' concept of bias *solely* from the perspective of the 'matter' of communication; bias is not a simply consequence of the internal properties of a medium, but of the articulation between matter, form, binding-use, and know-how with which this use is deployed, modified and transferred.

For example, if electronic media are seen to be biased towards space (e.g., Meyrowitz 1985; Postman 1987), it is not because of the internal properties of television or radio, but because they provide selective and functional advantages to space biased societies, such as those of western modernity (i.e., the territorialized concept of the nation state).

In space biased societies, the control over knowledge, wealth and power is derived from the territorialization of information flows, including what McLuhan would refer to as their 'neurological' extensions. The space bias of (nation-orientated) televisual communication is developed through the selectiveness of particular applications: those related to the way in which broadcasting is made to function with regard to political and military action, as well as the formation of a set of particular skills and know-how over time (e.g., propaganda, strategic disinformation, public relations, spin, etc.).

From political economy to biophilosophy

McLuhan was clearly inspired by Innis' mode of analysis. The sweeping essayistic style with which Innis painted a historical overview of western civilization with extremely broad strokes was often interspersed with detailed comments about how particular media-technologies played a crucial role by facilitating changes and shifts. It was this combination of detail and generalization which McLuhan took on in his own work.

However, although he followed the basic premises of Innis' analysis of media-technological evolution, McLuhan was much less keen on providing a political-economic account as the foundation from which to explain the logic of historical change. That is to say, Innis' model, which placed bias as an intermediate device (a translator, as well as an engine) between natural environment and particular social formations based on flows of wealth, knowledge and power, heavily relied on the assumption that the driving force of history is a *socio*-logic. It is related to the way in which human, social constellations are always geared towards increasing control over the accumulation and distribution of wealth, knowledge and power. Innis acknowledge himself that this 'bias' towards a concern for monopolization stems from his interest in political economy.

In contrast, McLuhan adapted Innis' understanding and moved away from political economy by arguing that it is more closely connected to the very nature of the human being, both in terms of its physiological, as well as its psychological sense. We can identify the (invisible) hand of Nietzsche here. McLuhan shares with Nietzsche a suspicion towards particular elements of modernity: its instrumentalization of life, its linear paradigms (mainly due to print induced forms of literacy), its pathological glorification of reason, and its relentless industrialization of social life with its associated effects of commodification and alienation.

Like Nietzsche, the crux of McLuhan's thinking rests on the insistence that thought itself is intricately connected to the physical embodiment of the human being (the 'clever beast that once upon a time invented knowing'; Nietzsche 2006: 114). He understands the human being as a living, thinking creature whose motivations and desires are endlessly diverse, and never reducible to either the accumulation of wealth, knowledge or force. In other words, whereas McLuhan kept the analytical method of dialectical materialism, he connected to it a more vitalistic ethos, rather than a Marxist one.

For a McLuhanist reading of Innis, bias of communication would not be a primarily political phenomenon, but one that encompasses the whole of the human condition.

As a result, the driving force of historical processes is neither an abstract, disembodied 'force' of nature, nor a socially reproduced desire for the monopolization of wealth, knowledge and power, but a non-reducible 'will' that is bound up with the meaning of being human. Any further attempt to qualify this will, as the will to power (Nietzsche 1992) or the will to know (Foucault 1979) violates the inherent non-reducibility of this will. In line with McLuhan's implicit philosophy, 'the will' has to be a multiplicity; it can be cynical, as well as charitable, egoistic as well as altruistic, geared to the gratification of needs, as well as to the fulfilment of ideals.

The tetrad

The problem with McLuhan's writing is that he never reflected on the epistemic and ontological underpinnings of his arguments. He does not offer any explicit reflections on the philosophical assumptions that inform the logic of his writing. This has generated a lot of confusion, misunderstanding and – from the outset – a rather hostile reception of his ideas by a large section of the academic establishment who – needless to say perhaps – took issue with what they believed to be a radically antirationalist stance (Miller 1971; also see the discussion in Levinson 1998).

Levinson argues that the major reason why this was the case is that McLuhan's writings are primarily assertions of new ideas. He was not a scholar; rarely did he develop his work by commenting on his predecessors or contemporaries. He never offered a 'critique' in the traditional sense of the word, i.e., one that engages with what other, usually well-known and established, thinkers and writers had argued or thought. As already mentioned, he did not explain his assertions and claims by elaborating on the logic of the argument, particular concepts used or developing propositions that could be empirically verified or falsified by means of a simple test. Finally, he rarely engaged with his critics, either by defending his claims or modifying them.

Instead, McLuhan's main interest was to explore (Levinson 1998: 24). His explorations were generally based on a particular *modus operand;* which he only explicated towards the end of his life. Levinson (1998: 15) has summarized what he argues is the most succinct definition of this *modus operand;* and termed it 'the tetrad'. McLuhan's tetrad consists of four particular questions with which any medium could be analysed:

> What does it enhance or amplify in the culture? What does it obsolesce or push out of prominence? What does it retrieve from the past, from the realm of the previously obsolesced? And – and here the tetrad projects into the future – what does the medium reverse or flip into when it reaches the limits of its potential? (Levinson 1998: 16)

These are the elementary analytical dimensions of McLuhan's unique version of medium theory. They constitute the pallet by means of which McLuhan painted particular pictures of media life cycles, which were always intertwined with social and cultural (as well as political) processes. At the heart of it lies the notion that the medium is an actor and that its actions are themselves influenced by (perhaps even conditioned by) the environment in which they operate.

A major misunderstanding in interpreting McLuhan's medium theory is a conflation of the media-as-actors perspective with the idea that media are *therefore* the primary force of historical change. This, in effect, would be a straightforward version of techno-logical determinism, which has indeed been a major accusation filed against McLuhan and his followers (Morley 2007). Technological determinism is the assertion that all changes are caused by technological forces.

Technological determinism is an unfortunate label in many respects. First, its use is always negative. It is a label to denounce a perspective or point of view as inad-equate. The inadequacy is expressed by the postfix 'ism' in a very similar vein as many ideologies have been labelled before their dismissal. What the critics using the label 'technological determin*ism*' attack, is the view that hypostatizes that technology *alone* is the driving force (determinant) of history. Apart from the problem that very few serious thinkers would ever endorse such a reductionist, one-dimensional view of his-tory, it also introduces a rather problematic form of theorizing history (as being determined), within which the critique and its response must operate to make sense.

A second problem emerges in relation to this determination. As very few scholars would ever dare to suggest that technology alone *fully* determines history, critics of technological determinism use the label more often as a variable: those associated with it place *too much* emphasis on the impact of technology as a historical force. As a result, we enter into the deeply problematic question of what kind of weighting of technological determination of history would be accurate? This kind of misplaced concreteness mystifies the deeply speculative nature of discussions over technological determinism because what is considered to be significant remains itself purely arbitrary and based on the subjective preferences of the adjudicator.

There is in the social sciences and humanities quite a widespread consensus that technology *alone* determines very little and that technology itself is socially and cul-turally embedded (Mackenzie and Wajcman 1985). Such views correspond with a more widespread ethos of liberal humanism, which marks the prevailing intellectual climate of contemporary social thought and by placing considerable emphasis on human agency, deliberate intervention and narrating history through the prism of social struggle and intentions.

There are, however, a few problems with this as well. First of all, just because technology *alone* is not a significant determinant of history does not mean that it has no impact whatsoever. Second, not all forms of agency are necessarily human, ani-mals, for example, have agency too, and the same could be said of technological devices [e.g., Latour's (1988a) famous case of the automatic door closer as an actor]. Third, it makes perfect phenomenological sense to distinguish between an analysis of routine practices and extraordinary events, as well as between forms of agency that act out of their own volition and those that respond to (or are conditioned by) perceived necessities. It is not accurate to only ascribe agency to the first category; actions out of necessity are conditioned or may be even determined by other forces, this does not mean that they are *therefore* beyond intentionality. Both unconditioned and conditioned forms of action entail particular motivations; agency is the particular mode of articulation of motivations and actions.

In the routine practices of everyday life, we invoke technology as a set of tools. That is, we relate to these tools in terms of how they are supposed to work. It is exactly in such ordinary circumstances, when things that are ready-to-hand perform as expected, that technology is taken-for-granted and most effective in its enframing of the world. In contrast, when technology no longer functions as expected; when a danger (or risk) is being revealed, when we are confronted with discomfort and inconvenience, the *enframing* is no longer 'taken-for-granted' and technology no longer 'holds sway' (Van Loon 2002).

By allowing us to think that media are capable of action, Innis and McLuhan became the straw puppets for arguments against the thesis that social changes were the simple (intentional or unintentional) effect of technological innovations. However, a closer reading of Innis and McLuhan suggests that this is a logical mistake on two essential counts. First, the capacity to act, which media undoubtedly have, should not be confused by the capacity to determine. Second, even if media-technologies have the capacity to determine, this does not mean that they can do so unconditionally themselves, let alone on their own. In simpler terms, the fact that media are capable of acting, and perhaps even conditioning, does not mean that other forces (e.g., social, economic, cultural, political, physiological, psychological) are therefore irrelevant.

Focusing on media-forms within a historical context, makes it possible for us to side-step the entire stalemate between technological determinism and instrumentalism as itself a rather unhelpful red herring caused by intellectual poverty and a rather sheepish herd-mentality within the academic establishment. Technological processes are never inconsequential and rarely correspond with the intentionalities of the actors (agencies) that set them into work.

Critical media analysis

McLuhan has often been associated with a form of technological determinism that fails to adequately account for the way in which mediation functions in service of power (for a recent reiteration of this position, see Morley 2007). That is, McLuhan's work is often accused of being uncritical. The question is whether the tetrad, which is arguably McLuhan's least known theoretical notion, has the potential to facilitate a more critical media analysis; that is to say, whether it is capable of contributing to the development of a critical purchase that affects the basic principles of mediation itself. The answer to that is a firm 'yes'. The tetrad cuts into the very essence of mediation; it explores its limits and exposes its transgressions.

This may sound a little odd, especially to those who generally associate radical critique with a critique of ideology, because McLuhan's tetrad is certainly not intended to facilitate an ideology critique in the traditional (Marxist) sense of the word. Indeed, whereas most media theory is, indeed, merely a substratum of political theory, McLuhan's certainly is not. His writings have never been explicitly concerned with issues related to political ideologies; instead, he preferred to comment on the communication style of politicians, and how they were better (or worse) adapted to particular media types.

However, McLuhan's tetrad does provide a strong critique of two particular ideological positions, which – if unaddressed – may become huge obstacles to any particular political pursuit of radical media critique as well. The link between media critique and ideology critique is perhaps less straightforward in McLuhan's work than in other writings, and therefore this chapter should be read first of all, as an attempt to explore the political nature of McLuhan's tetrad.

The first ideological position that McLuhan's tetrad problematizes is instrumentalism. Apart from the theoretically misguided fallacy that treats media as neutral vehicles for any political pursuit, instrumentalism also mystifies how media actually work, naturalizes their specific conditioning, misunderstands agency and thus obscures the power differentials at work in them. Instrumentalism feeds into the political ideology of liberal pluralism and its various offshoots (including so-called 'democratic socialism'). It endorses the aforementioned false assumption that communication is a process by which a sender sends a message in the form of a code, which the receiver merely has to unpack to obtain the message. Neither the messenger nor the code, nor the means by which the sending takes place, are of any real concern in this approach beyond the issue of whether or not they enable effective communication (which may itself be misleadingly associated with 'absence of bias').

The second ideological position that is radically undermined by the tetrad is linear evolutionism. This is a position closely associated with technological determinism in that it portrays social, cultural, political, even biological change [e.g., see for a critical demolition of such simplistic concepts as the 'post-human'; Ansell-Pearson (1997), Hayles (1999) and Doyle (2003); also Chapters 4 and 5] as an inevitable outcome of technology (Curtis 1977). Linear evolutionism, however, is more than a misguided theory of technology and media. It also affects political thought. Fascism (and its corollary in, for example, Spencer's version of Darwinism) is one extreme example, but so is the kind of more moderate pragmatism behind politics that seeks to justify itself by referring to 'market forces' or 'economic principles'. Thatcherism and Reaganomics both are particularly vivid examples of forms of thought based on the proposition that one cannot change the direction of history, but merely amplify or exploit it for one's own benefit.

Both positions are intrinsically connected to modernism and the Enlightenment. They are, indeed, part of the 'grand narratives' that Lyotard (1979) suggested have lost much of their credibility, simply because they suffer from a performative deficit. That is to say, they are not well attuned to provide for the far more pragmatic demands of science, governance, commerce, law, the military and, of course, the media industries [or as Postman (1987) called it 'show business']. It is with this in mind, that a close analysis of the tetrad enables us to see the radical potential of McLuhanism beyond a mere opportunistic celebration or cynical denunciation of media change.

s 'Extensions of Man' [sic]

The first dimension of the tetrad points towards the cultural amplification effects of particular media. The idea that media amplify aspects of our 'being-in-the-world' is nothing new. The radical potential of a courier-based postal service was already discovered in early Qin dynasty (221–206 BC) in China (Zhang 2007). It enabled a centralization of military command structures, as well as forms of governance and enhanced bureaucratic forms of control. The postal service itself depended on written communication – in this case carvings on bamboo sticks, which were subsequently replaced by ink-based writings on papyrus. Innis called the latter space biased and the former time biased because bamboo carvings were far more immutable, they would endure over time, would resist mutations, are better 'kept in place'. The latter thrive on speed (a good indication of space bias), travel well across distances in shorter time spans and enable more intertextual links because they could contain more information with less material dependence. However, they are also more perishable and therefore less effective in securing permanence.

Whereas McLuhan did not use space or time bias as central categories of his media analysis – and, instead, preferred to use the metaphors of hot and cool media – the underlying thematic is rather similar. Inspired by Innis, McLuhan sought to provide a detailed analysis of how media affect the modern human world. For example, in the *Gutenberg Galaxy* (1962), he argued that, in the twentieth century, we have entered a completely new era in which our emphasis on print and literacy has been replaced by the emergence of electronic media. This is not a matter of the simple replacement of one medium with another; instead, in the tradition set out by Innis, McLuhan first stressed that this shift has had profound spatiotemporal implications by which our entire world is being altered irreversibly. However, he radicalized this idea further by arguing that these alterations not only affect our environment, but the very nature of the human species itself.

Another example may shed a bit more light on this. One might argue that the use of radio for public broadcasting in Germany was a major contributor to the rise of fascism, because through radio, messages could be transmitted with a high level of emotional attachment, which in turn circumvent the more rational and detached 'literacy'-based culture of western civilization. Hitler's radio speeches were an infamous reminder of a preliteracy culture in which tribal sentiments [e.g., a philosophy of *Blut und Boden* (blood and soil)] prevailed. This could explain why in the US, radio did not have the same effect, because when it was introduced as a public broadcasting medium (having been primarily a military technology before), it was received in a cultural climate already widely immersed in literacy, and without a strong attachment to either blood or soil as these had been severely weakened by print (and immigration!).

One might see this argument [which is a truncated version of McLuhan's (1964) essay entitled 'Radio: the Tribal Drum'] as technologically deterministic because it places a combination of radio and print as the principal devices for the ordering of two distinct cultures: those of Germany, which was susceptible to fascism, and the USA, which was not. Such a critique may prefer to point towards distinctive economic climates, or to a different psychosocial make up of these cultures, or perhaps just to serendipity (with a strong emphasis in the personality of Hitler).

However, these critiques can only provide radical alternatives to McLuhan's version if they exclude print and radio as constitutive actors. This is deeply problematic because it would forge an artificial separation of, for example, the print industry and capitalism (in fact, print was the first domain of production where capitalism manifested itself in Europe) and radio, the modern military and a residual sense of belonging [which Smith (1990) calls 'Ethne'] that preceded its instrumentalization by the nation state in the nineteenth century (Gellner 1983; Giddens 1985). In this sense, any explanation of the rise of fascism in 1920s and 1930s Germany, without inclusion of the role of radio, suffers from an inability to understand the way in which a 'mass movement' could be manufactured in a popular culture that has a weak grounding in literacy.

Furthermore, it must be stressed that the purpose of McLuhan's essay was not to explain the rise of fascism in Nazi Germany as the effect of the rise of radio. Instead, he merely reflected on the internal properties of the radio as a medium and to show how its cultural embedding in wider social and political structures was radically differentiated according to its relationship with print and a culture of literacy. In this sense it also provides an excellent critique of linear evolutionism.

An example: print in China and Europe

For McLuhan, language is obviously a medium; its content is already something else, e.g., a thought or an object. Indeed, the notion of 'immediate' communication that forms the archetype of, for example, communication studies or the sociology of interaction, is always already mediated and, thus, a contradiction in terms.

In a literal sense, media provide a 'coming-in-between'. That is, they provide an intercession that marks the essence of communication. Media bring into being a 'third' term, making it impossible for dialogue to remain totally 'private'. For example, any interaction using speech invokes the 'lexicogrammar' of a distinctive cultural system that includes semantics and thus structures of meaning that go well beyond the interlocutors within the dialogue.

By taking language for granted, those who forget that language is a medium, have created theoretical models in which all other subsequent 'media' are seen as 'add-ons', causes of possible miscommunication, bias and perhaps even deliberate distortions. Simultaneously, such views have also fuelled a particular kind of communication politics, namely of idealizing 'pure communication' as one that is either without media, or with media that are wholly transparent and immediate.

It is by forgetting the mediated nature of human being that theoretical speculations have spun off into diatribes about the apocalyptic consequences of mass mediation as fuelling alienation, hyperindividualization (the death of the social), indifference and inauthenticity. Such cyberphobia often invoke an extremely romantic and humanist notion of human existence at the helm of their political utopia (against which the real world offers a very dark contrast).

By contrast, those that have not forgotten the mediated origins of human being, are often far less pessimistic about the future. McLuhan was one of them. For McLuhan, media are intrinsically connected to the unfolding of human history. The spoken word, writing, the pictogram, the alphabet and numbers, were all crucial communications media that have helped to shape human history. More controversially, perhaps, he also included the wheel – and its inevitable corollary the road – as media in this history (also see Mumford 1961; May 2003). The latter were, of course, of crucial importance as functioning alongside horses as means of transmitting messages.

Linking communication and transportation from the beginning, McLuhan's mentor, Innis (inspired by Lewis Mumford) saw in the joining of writing and horse riding the emergence of the postal system that, in turn, enabled the formation of the first bureaucratically governed empire, that of China. The ability to send messages across an established network of couriers created new possibilities to extend the imperial office into a much wider geographic domain than what was possible via traditional messengers. It is certainly no coincidence that the imperial civilization of China attained such hegemonic dominance in East Asia; its internal stability fostered not just a balanced political ordering, but also a means to accumulate wealth, as well as knowledge. Perhaps Confucianism was the first school to adopt modes of Distance Learning as key means of disseminating their curriculum in the form of written texts.

Obviously, ancient China and medieval Europe were two completely different societies, with very distinct cultures, social structures, religious formations, political systems, structures of governance and economic organizations. Moreover, the particular historical conjunctures surrounding the introduction of print were very different. Whereas there was relative stability and peace when print arrived in China, its arrival in Europe took place in the back of the Black Death, which decimated its population by an estimated 35 per cent and in some places even by over 60 per cent (McNeill 1976; Herlihy 1977) and a series of internal wars as well as on its borders with, for example, the Tartars, the Moors and the Ottomans. Such instability and population decline had a profound impact on the political, social and economic organization of medieval Europe.

Until then, European society was organized as a feudal system at the centre of which was a political-economic arrangement of dependency and reciprocity (Wolf 1982). Political and economic power were combined, and although there was no monopoly of either wealth or power (feudal society was very decentralized, consisting of many small 'fiefdoms' ruled by local lords), there was a monopoly of knowledge that was in the hands of the Church that controlled most of the then dominant media of writing and preaching, and had a strong bearing on maintaining a close relationship between literacy and the practising of Christianity (Winter 1996).

The European feudal system was finely balanced around exchange relationships, interpersonal fidelity and a face-to-face mode of communication. When reflecting on the role of print in the rise of modern Western civilization, Innis (1972) stressed the industrial nature of printing as an early form of mass production, which also depended on the mass production of paper, as well as the mechanization of the printing press. This theme returns in McLuhan's earlier work when he critically associates the birth of the print industry with the collapse of knowledge systems that depend on a combination of visual and oral forms of communication.

Here, we can clearly see the strong guiding hand of Innis' notion of bias. It is unlikely that the print revolution would have succeeded without radical changes in the social, economic and political organization of medieval European society. After all, it did not produce a radical change in Chinese civilization 700 years earlier (Zhang 2007). In China, the space biased modus operandi of centralized bureaucratic control that was initiated under the Qin dynasty (221–206 BC) and expanded during the Han dynasties (206 BC–184 AD), was merely extended by a transformation of media.

By contrast, the European feudal system relied strongly on oral communication and visual images, in which patronage was an entitlement related to the value of one's word, which in turn determined one's status of honour. After the arrival of print, one's word of honour became transformed into the signature and the contract, whose value was not dependent on a moral anchoring of the face-to-face encounter, but on the strength of law enforcement, based on objective, immutable, but mobile 'evidence'.

Because the Chinese empire had attained a relatively high level of internal stability, the arrival of print in the eighth Century was not such a dramatic event as it turned out to be in Europe some 700 years later. The latter certainly did not enjoy that internal stability regarding the distribution of power machinations of governance and the accumulation of wealth which characterized eighth-century China. The final of the Innisian triad, i.e., the accumulation of knowledge, was perhaps a different matter as Catholicism provided a stronghold – even monopoly – of scholarly knowledge and investigation that could certainly be compared with the position held by Confucianism in China (Winter 1996). Yet, without the integration into monopolies of power and wealth, a monopoly of knowledge is rather vulnerable on its own.

As we have seen, understanding the distinctive nature of the print revolution in Europe, requires a close analysis of the *social context* in which this particular medium became operative. This context was marked by:

- an absence of a monopoly of wealth;
- an absence of a monopoly of power;
- a vulnerable monopoly of knowledge;
- the decimation of the population following the Black Death;
- rapid technological innovations;
- the rise of cities and mercantile capital.

However, a more phenomenological concern for *media-form* reveals that the print revolution in Europe was also marked by a distinctive *media content*. Print did not arrive cold in Europe, but in a culture already steeped in distinctive traditions of mediation, for example, involving the following media:

- language;
- the alphabet;
- writing;
- iconography;
- street theatre;
- preaching;
- bardic narrativity (minstrels using song to narrate sagas, myths and legends of heroic deeds).

It was particularly the moveable typesetter's use of the alphabet that made print such a useful and radical innovation within Europe. With only 26 different characters, the alphabet was easily incorporated into printing techniques. The combination of an alphabet and moveable typeset printing was radically different from the pictogrammatic form of writing in China; which still required high levels of skill to be linked up to print.

Another distinctive feature of the print revolution in Europe was its association with the Protestant Revolution (Eisenstein 1983; Winter 1996; Briggs and Burke 2002), which marked a radical transformation in terms of social, existential, as well as epistemological terms (Innis 1972). In terms of social lineages, which define the social, political, as well as economic context in which print emerged, we should point to:

- the emergence of protocapitalism with print as the first mass medium (the birth of the mass as a political force);
- the standardization of vernacular languages;
- the rise of nationalism (Anderson 1983).

It was the breakdown of the feudal economy in Europe that provided another significant 'rupture' in media evolution (White 1962). In Europe, print became a labour-saving device and an early form of industrialized mass production. Hence, European print was from the start an industry because its very logic became tied in with the mass production and dissemination of material (Briggs and Burke 2002). In order to accomplish this, it required a radically new form of organization, both in terms of labour relations as well as logistics (Eisenstein 1983). There would be no print without a print industry and there would be no print industry without the mass production of paper.

It is with regard to the role of paper that Innis' early work on Canadian staples economies proved vital. Innis' grounding in history and political economy, granted his approach to communications and media a strong materialist emphasis. Yet, the role of paper is remarkably absent in reflections on print communications. It is as if 'there is nothing beyond the text', to paraphrase Derrida (1974: 158).

In contrast, existential lineages refer to the way in which perception and interpretation were structured and organised. As Ong (1982) has shown, literacy, and in particular print, enable us to *think* differently, in compartmentalized blocks that can be independently stored. This has had the following aspects:

- the textualization of perception (see Chapter 1);
- the merging of Euclidian geometry of (empty) space and linear (empty) time (Newton's approach to physics is perhaps the best known example of this, see Adam 1990);
- the return of linear perspectivism (especially renaissance art);
- the interiorization of conscience (e.g., the work of Descartes (1960)).

Finally, epistemic lineages relate to the ordering and organization of knowledge (Foucault 1969). Here, we can simply refer to:

- the segregation of spheres of life (secularization);
- the secularization of religion itself;
- the birth of the 'modern episteme' (Foucault 1970);
- the birth of 'man' as origin and destiny (man over nature, God and history);
- the birth of individualization (Bauman 2001).

The difference between Innis and McLuhan lies simply in the fact that, whereas Innis provides a context-based explanation for the way in which print was able to introduce a new type of bias into European culture, McLuhan instead enables us to focus on the missing links, i.e., the relationships between media-form, sensory perception, and the socioemotional and cognitive constellation of human being. That is, McLuhan developed an approach to understanding media evolution that was derived from the centrality of human-technological interfaciality.

McLuhan's (1962) *The Gutenberg Galaxy* offers an analysis of the impact of the print revolution on European society and culture, and links these transformations to what is always the core of his concerns: that is:

- the relationship between media and the human psyche;
- the sensory perception and the socioemotional and cognitive constellation of human being.

In other words, whereas for Innis' notion of bias the primary mode by which media engage human being is thought, McLuhan shifts attention to sense, and thus to a more affective and less cognitive concept of mediation.

The relationship between the arrival of print and a radical change in the world of art, with the return to perspectivism, but also linearity, was just as important as the rise of Protestantism. Indeed, both are closely intertwined. The return to linear perspectivism during the Renaissance fostered with it a revival of an ethos of indifference, pragmatism, objectivism, distance and separation. This resonates strongly with the emphasis of Protestantism on *sola scriptura*. This Lutheran doctrine insisted that only sacred scripture gives us access to God; we can only know God by reading 'His Word' and by contemplating, interpreting and reflecting on it.

Print and linear perspectivism engendered a new, alternative paradigm to that of medieval scholasticism and Thomism. This paradigm would not come into the fullness of its being, and a new monopoly of knowledge, until after the two other crucial pillars of any social organization – wealth and power – were also sorted out. That is, as Foucault showed in *Les Mots et les Choses* (translated as *The Order of Things* 1970), the new paradigm, that is modern science, only came into being after the settlement of a dominant regime for the accumulation of wealth, i.e., industrial capitalism (the Industrial Revolution) and the settlement of the functioning of power in terms of governance, i.e., parliamentary democracy (e.g., the American and French Revolutions; de Tocqueville 2000).

Decentred subjects

Indeed, the same McLuhanist paradigm can be used to show why we now experience a crisis in modern thought. Our culture no longer depends on a monopoly of print. Instead, electronic mediation has dispersed subjectivity by externalizing its cognitive and emotional neurological operations. Radio and television are powerful mood engines that break with linear perspectivism and guide us towards an 'instantaneous all-at-onceness' (see Chapter 5).

For McLuhan, media are never purely technical apparatus, pieces of hardware with particular functions, instruments of communication. Media are always already socially embedded, imbued with particular (human) values and, as such, preconstituted by social forms. For example, he emphasized the difference between a 'hot' medium, such as the radio and a 'cool' medium such as television, as based on a difference in values attributed to the implication of the social.

Radio is hot because it involves people; its assemblage is intensive, instantaneuous and volatile. For example, think here of listening to a football (soccer) match on the radio; the commentator's voice is often loud, high-pitched, full of excitement; the audience is depending on this voice alone and unable to anticipate what was going to happen. The screaming of the word 'goal' is then what makes all the difference between a significant and an insignificant moment.

On television, commentators are generally more laid back and controlled; they have less to say, talk about things other than the proceedings of the match, drift off into small talk. The audience are less dependent upon the televised voice and, instead, more passively involved as the images allow greater predictability, and can easily wash over the viewers, who can use the images to generate their own commentary, discussions, associations, in a way that radio cannot.

McLuhan's analyses of different media shows that they often imply different social forms – hence, print media, such as newspapers and novels, have been associated with the rise of nationhood and nationalism (Anderson 1983), radio with the rise of fascism (McLuhan 1964), terrestrial television with the rise of mass society (McLuhan 1964; Williams 1990), satellite television with the rise of the Global Village (McLuhan and Fiore 1967) and telematics with the rise of virtual communities and cyberspace (Levinson 1998).

In *Understanding Media*, McLuhan (1964: 90) writes: 'It was not until the advent of the telegraph that messages could travel faster than a messenger . . . [and] that information has detached itself from such solid commodities as stone and papyrus.' Like Virilio (1977), McLuhan did not perceive speed to be merely a quantitative phenomenon that was somehow indifferent to the quality of matter; instead, increased speed (like power) 'is itself a disruption that causes a change of organization' (McLuhan 1964: 91).

Speed and acceleration are central themes in McLuhan's framework of media analysis because they highlight the limits of what media are able to accomplish as a form of agency. Acceleration is a particular trope of media; one that points towards attempts to transform time bias into space bias. It is telling that, in the modern age, space biased media have prevailed and time biased media have been subdued. As a result, our culture thrives on perpetual renewal, that is, modernity endorses the cult of 'the new' (Vattimo 1988). Marxists would, of course, point towards the logic of capitalism, and rightly so, for capitalism requires ever increasing turnovers of products and thus waste, to maintain growth. The very language of capitalism is that of acceleration, destruction, wasting and renewal (Baudrillard 1993).

However, what McLuhan rejected is that media are merely instrumental in carrying out that logic as if automatically ordered to do so. Instead, he insisted on analysing the interactions between media properties and media functions in the context of the particular forms of selection that characterize the evolution of all media-technologies. This approach enables a far more critical understanding of the technological underpinnings of social change exactly because it avoids simplistic notions of functional instrumentation (e.g., media as mere tools). It allows us to analyse media-technologies as having their own dynamic, which is not necessarily conducive to the logic of capital and may, for example, enable forms of resistance that became marked expressions of class struggle.

Indeed, McLuhan himself never endorsed a mono-dimensional theory of social and cultural change. Instead, he perceived media-technologies not as somehow outside of the realm of human being and action, but part of it. Indeed, he argued, that media are 'extensions of man' with which he meant that the potential scope and effects of human perception and intervention increases with the application of media (McLuhan 1964). In the advent of electronic media, such as television, the homogeneity of literary (textual) print cultures was broken up. With it, imagined communities (Anderson 1983) were no longer primarily defined in terms of the nation, but more and more linked to emergent, tribal and even nomadic social forms (Mafessoli 1996). An example of this is the rise of community television. This is a form of hyperlocal television production in which audiences have a greater role in the production of content. The fact that in the UK, the BBC is very active on this front suggests that even media corporations, most closely tied to imagining communities through the concept of nationhood, are now diversifying their social spaces.

The technological environment which we have created (with media) in turn generates the context in which we can make sense of this world and engender our own present-future existence. This is reflected in another famous expression: '*the medium is the message*'. With this famous statement, McLuhan envisaged a world in which the content of a medium was always another medium, hence, obliterating the notions of 'pure' form and 'pure' content:

> [T]he personal and social consequences of every medium – that is of the extension of ourselves – result from the new scale that is introduced into our affairs by each extension of ourselves, or by any new technology. (McLuhan 1964: 23)

Whenever the alliance between medium and mediator is complete, the difference ceases to be noticed, and the medium seems to become devoid of any content. In this sense, mediators (human beings, for example) become 'numb' to the technology that extends a particular function. This numbness, caused by the self-referentiality of the medium, engenders a particular form of narcosis for which McLuhan (1964: 33, 51–6) used the term 'narcissistic' – embroiled in love of and for a self that is mistaken for an other. It is the mistaking of the self for another that causes the numbing trap of self-referentiality. Hence, it is not a case of autoeroticism, but of autoamputation; one is no longer capable of recognizing the self as self.

Prosthetic numbness is a common feeling for those whose bodies have been supplemented by prostheses; we forget that we wear glasses (spectacles) or contact lenses perhaps as easily as we can be drawn into a movie on a big screen. When driving a car, it is necessary to become one with the machine, for most responses require embodied reflexivity, that is, instantaneous reaction without mediation by cognition, a know-how-without-knowing ('know' how to brake, change gear, use indicators, use mirrors).

From the notion of prosthetic numbness, one might get the impression that the connectivities are always smooth and operationally functional, as for example has become the case with the telephone-computers-cable television assemblage. However, such smoothness is not immanent to media as their compatibility is never to be taken for granted. For example, hot and cold media might balance each other, but they might also constitute a far more explosive mix or media-hybrid.

Hybrid media

> The hybrid of the meeting of two media is a moment of truth and revelation from which new form is born. For the parallel between two media holds us on the frontiers between forms that snap us out of the Narcissus-narcosis. The moment of the meeting of media is a moment of freedom and release from the ordinary trance and numbness imposed by them on our senses. (McLuhan 1964: 63)

McLuhan has a specific purpose for using the notion of hybrid media. He deployed it to describe highly particular and unusual instances of media evolution ('ruptures' such as the arrival of print in Europe) when the technological embedding of mediation can no longer be taken for granted and becomes exposed. This exposure [which is very similar to Virilio's (1997) notion of escape velocity, see Chapter 6] is a moment of revelation in the sense that the essence of technology as ordering is being revealed.

Elsewhere (Van Loon 1999), I have already applied McLuhan's notion of hybrid media to the case of the beating of Rodney King, the acquittal of the four police-officers and the subsequent L.A. riots of 1992. This was a highly unusual and violent event; unique in many ways. It showed a moment in which a relatively new technology (a domesticated video camera, i.e., the camcorder) had been adopted into the wider structures of both television and judicial systems, resulting in an explosive confronta-tion of realities (also see Butler 1993a; Fiske 1994; Thompson 1995). Today, the use of camcorders in television making and courts is extensive and does not lead to much controversy. The digital era has facilitated many media-hybrids but few of them have produced 'moments of truth and revelation . . . that snap us out of the Narcissus-Narcosis'.

Significant recent exceptions are '9/11' and the bombings of the London transport network of 7 July 2005. These can be seen as particular media-hybrids. The combi-nation of hand-held recording devices and television expanded the work of terrorism. In the case of 9/11, the terrorism was, indeed, itself already a media-hybrid of its own, as plastic knives, airplanes, and kerosene were combined to create a whole new type of ruthless, precision ballistic, gigantic Molotov cocktail with devastating consequences. Such media-hybrids produced a radical rupture in perceptions of how we relate to our being in the world, for example, in terms of security and risk.

Such unique, but relatively rare media-hybrids perform a mode of ordering that does not sit comfortably within the ordinary everydayness of the modern television (an)aes-thetics. On too many occasions mediation was itself brought into the spotlight as the message (for example, the role of television as a medium of terrorism). Our percep-tions were constantly called into question as images do not speak for themselves and the multiplicity of (digital) video recordings could be transformed into instruments for both terrorist and 'security'-orientated military operations. Our (Western?) sense of alienation was brought into presence in a dramatic and crude fashion, exposed as the numbness of being held accountable for global world politics for which we have had very little responsibility.

Technologies allow us to understand our environment, act upon it and recreate it (also destroy it). This is what Heidegger (1977) meant by enframing. Every medium creates its own structures/codes of understanding and relation to the environment (Van Loon 2000). Media embody specific concepts of time and space. For example, newspapers are locally and territorially focused, but involve a time-lag (always reporting after the fact), whereas television and radio are inherently designed to cross boundaries, focus on institutional centres, and try to overcome a time-lag in an ongoing flow (covering events while they are happening). New (satellite-linked) electronic media go one step further: they actualize events, create events, they deplete our sense of place and instead create 'ubiquitous presence'. The problems we have with new media are usually not related to knowing which buttons to press, but to the concepts of space and time that are embedded in such technologies.

Media, such as cinema, radio, television and camcorders, have particular characteristics that help us create and understand messages in particular ways. They become part of the structure of a message: a photographic image does not work in the same way as a television image. A voice on the radio functions differently from a voice on television. They require different skills from their respective audiences – audiences are drawn into the technology in different ways.

McLuhan as a cyborg theorist?

The idea of media as 'extensions of man' has found a strong renewal in the late 1980s with the emergence of cyborg theory and post-humanism (Featherstone and Burrows 1996). From Donna Haraway's (1990) subtle, but provocative suggestion that the cyborg could function as a metaphor of a renewed sense of radical political agency – in a world overdetermined by forms of communication and intelligence, geared towards the maximization of command and control (the military industrial complex is a good example of this) – to the much more reductionist popular assertions that we will all become cyborgs, contemporary theorists have sought to come to terms with the radical explosion of technological appropriations of human functions (see Chapter 5). McLuhan's early writings, however, were often ignored in this, and as a result much of cyborg theory lacked the intellectual and analytical rigour it needed to become more than a cheap fad (Robins 1996).

If all media are extensions of human functions, then – at least metaphorically speaking – we have always been cyborgs. Hence, cyborgs predate the information society. The only new aspect of cyborgs in the information society is that human beings have become aware of their cyborgian (or perhaps better: cyboriginal) nature. This, however, should not be seen as a minor event. It is exactly this interplay, between the changing nature of our material being as organisms and our ability to reflect on this in terms of consciousness, that marks the radical political potential of 'being a cyborg'. It highlights an evolutionary rupture. The externalization of our own neurological system by electronic media has enabled us to become at once reflexive and reflective on our media extended being. Our cyborg reflexivity is not some deep philosophical achievement, but a feature of our comportment as technologically extended bodies; our cyborg-reflectivity is not a primary achievement of our own intellect either, but comes to us from the outside, from media cultures that have absorbed human consciousness through the externalised neural networks of electronic communications (e.g., as in the film *The Matrix*).

This interplay is the crux of media evolution. It is neither technologically determined nor intentionally accomplished by the human will, either with or without struggle. McLuhan's work could be seen as a type of media evolutionism that was geared towards analysing the past, commenting on the present and sketching the future in a seemingly seamless stream of metaphorical associations. This forms the unique basis of his radical media critique.

Media evolutions

The first and second dimensions of the tetrad are closely associated with the specific amplification functions of media as 'extensions of man' [sic]. They form the basis of McLuhan's evolutionist approach to understanding media change. In *The Soft Edge*, Paul Levinson (1997) appropriates a highly interesting symbiosis of Darwin's theory of evolution with Popper's philosophy of science, to suggest that without the social and cultural embedding of media as part of human life, we would not be able to talk about, let alone understand, how media develop in the first place.

The development of media over time – one could call this the longe durée of media – is primarily (albeit not exclusively) a history of media usage. The selection process, by means of which one medium (e.g., television) ascends, while another (e.g., radio) descends is to a large extend facilitated by the fact that these specific media relate to different human faculties and thereby amplify different human capabilities (of course, often at the expense of others).

Just as in natural selection, the development of species is never simply the effect of the species' internal properties, media selection is not exclusively driven by the medium's internal technical features either. Instead, both are entirely dependent on the interaction between the particular medium and its environment. In the world of media-technologies, this interaction is primarily facilitated by human agents: inventors, engineers, managers, marketers, operators, administrators, regulators, consumers, etc.

However, the third and fourth axes of the aforementioned tetrad complicate this line of thought and highlight that McLuhan's approach was far from a linear evolutionist, but a proponent of the non-linearity or complexity of sociotechnological change. When media are said to revive an older form or function of our human being, it means that something is being retrieved from the past that until then had been subdued.

Electronic media have revived 'oral communications'. Levinson (1998) shows how online writing, for example, has taken the form of speech and retrieved a sense of active dialogue in electronically mediated communications, as exemplified by, for example, chat rooms, messengers, MUDs, *Second Life* and multi-user platform games, such as *Runescape* (see Chapter 5). In these media, we notice that the language appropriated is remarkably similar to that of SMS texting (phonetic writing). In fact, the creative combination of phonetics, numbers and emoticons has caused many difficulties in terms of censoring inappropriate language, with the users being able to circumvent censorship by reinventing spelling and grammar.

The fourth axis of the tetrad is one that seeks to describe the future turning of a particular emergent media technology. It asks us to seek and develop analytical tools for projecting how a particular medium is likely to evolve by analysing its characteristics, not in a descriptive mode, but by means of metaphorical association. I suggest that to do this, a return to Innis might provide some crucial insights.

In Innis' terms, the revival of speech coincides with a return to a more space biased form of communication. Speech is so ephemeral that its traces are easily erased as if nothing had ever passed. Electronic speech of online communication may leave more enduring traces except that they usually get swamped by the overload of data that typifies the Internet. Yet, there are forms of electronic communication whose storage and detection is becoming of central importance, for example, to scrutinize public officials or track down child pornography traffic (Loader 1997). The latter are part of technologies of 'securing' that are thriving particularly well in the post-9/11 risk society that is now run by the (anti-)terror war machine (Van Loon 2002).

The completion of total space bias is thus generating fundamental problems for securing and social ordering that now return to us in most extreme forms, terrorism, violent crime, pandemic outbreaks of electronic viruses, pornographic excesses, etc. History teaches us that these extreme conditions are unlikely to endure for the very mechanisms of selection are at risk of dissipating into oblivion. The most probable, turning into which the digital media mix is most likely to 'flip', is that of a more time biased character. Alongside a new impetus to enhance storage facilities, we should expect greater investments into data retrieval, data aggregation, data mining and pattern matching. Against the apocalyptic tendencies of acceleration, we should expect an enhancement of memory, a revival of particular traditions of inscription (but perhaps not those of writing), a reinvention of rituals. We should expect greater emphasis to be placed on the acoustic functions of resonance and echo; stressing the more enduring aspects of aphoristic communication, rather than the sloganism which currently predominates.

An alternative critique

This is a more optimistic reading than the one provided by Neil Postman who saw the disappearance of writing and the ascendance of image-based telecommunications as an irretrievable loss of civilisation. His *Technopoly* (1992) is a social system driven by a wasteful excess of non-information or entertainment. The excessive nature of space biased media reduces all information to ephemeral pulp whose function is not representational but merely seductive (also see Baudrillard 1990). This echoes an assertion made by Innis:

> The influence of mechanization on the printing industry had been evident in the increasing importance of the ephemeral. Superficiality became essential to meet the various demands of larger numbers of people and was developed as an art by those compelled to meet the demands. The radio accentuated the importance of the ephemeral and of the superficial. In the cinema and in the broadcast it became necessary to search for entertainment and amusement. (Innis 1982: 82)

Postman notes how modern culture is formed on the basis of an evacuation of meaningful communication. Making a strong association between linear perspectivism, written discourse and rational deliberation, Postman's views of the arrival of electronic media are profoundly negative and pessimistic. Like McLuhan, he understands electronic media, especially television to be an extension of our nervous systems. However, unlike McLuhan (and McLuhanists, such as Levinson and De Kerckhove), he does not view this as a potential enhancement of our capacity to process information [what de Kerckhove (1996) calls 'articulated intelligence'], but as a means by which our central nervous systems can be further externally manipulated in service of an ever expanding entertainment industry. This sounds remarkably similar to the work of Jacques Ellul (1964, 1965; Karim 2003; Porquet 2003).

A central role in this process is played by what Meyrowitz (1985: 74) calls 'access codes' (the ways in which media 'impinge' on our senses). Access codes entail the logic of operation of the usage of a medium, it is in effect the 'know-how' that transforms a tool into a *useful* technology. The innovation of electronic media lies in the radical lowering of the threshold of access codes:

> In contrast to reading and writing, television viewing involves an access code that is barely a code at all. Television by no means presents 'reality', but television looks and sounds much more like reality than sentences and paragraphs do . . . Television's code of electronic signals, which produces facsimiles of everyday sights and sounds, has basically one degree of complexity. (Meyrowitz 1985: 75–6)

The radical simplification of access codes also entails the emergence of a new kind of sign-value (see Chapter 3), one that is no longer dominated by the learned skills of literacy (with a rather restricted access code), but by one's capacity (or willingness) to be 'impinged upon' by the medium itself. This is why, for Meyrowitz, the advent of electronic communication media also heralded an age of blurring boundaries; distinctions between public and private, masculine and feminine, childhood and adulthood (Disney!), etc., all started to wane. Television has, indeed, been a tremendous leveller of cultural values and tastes. Unlike Postman, however, Meyrowitz does not espouse a prophecy of doom, but insists on the transformative potential of the new social landscape.

Far from suggesting that content does not matter, Postman and Meyrowitz highlight the interconnectedness between the logical, operational aspects of media and their (historical, philosophical and interpersonal) significance. Hence, it is because the medium cannot be dissociated from its messaging that Postman's more negative analysis of contemporary culture should not be dismissed with a sleight of hand. It is undoubtedly true, for example, that the political process with which modern western societies seek to legitimate their own ordering, no longer rests on logic, argumentation and persuasion, but on a capacity to generate loose (one might even say random) associations with a potentially endless number of 'trivia' (junk data), which are set to work on the senses by means of affectivity. In the words of William Connolly (2002), our world is now largely run by 'neuropolitics'. In this sense, the medium is also the massage (rather than the message) – it works on our senses without having to make sense first.

In *Amusing Ourselves To Death*, Postman (1987) contemplates the loss of oral debate as the means to do politics, with the joint arrival of the telegraph and the photograph. Similar to Meyrowitz (1985), Postman identifies this as a loss of the 'placeness' of communication. Electronic communications obliterate our sense of place because it presents information in a decontextualised fashion – as if it emerged 'from nowhere' because it entails a separation of social place from physical place (Meyrowitz 1985: 115).

The crisis (which Innis identifies as the breeding ground for media-technological innovation) of our world is the annihilation of place – a bias to spatial control that is no longer territorially confined; rather than the elimination of space it is the elimination of place (Augé 1995; Castells 1996; Hardt and Negri 2000). Place becomes devoid of sense; it no longer matters where on is; as a result communication loses its historical sense, and becomes abstract and individuated.

The crisis, however, also extends to the personal level. Without place it becomes more difficult to attain a sense of integrity; one's comportment – and the interpersonal responsibilities that go with it – becomes loosened and disconnected from faces and from face-to-face encounters. In the interfaciality of electronic communications, those who are involved are invited to suspend claims to authentic being in favour of playful and performative assertions. This is what Castells (1996) calls 'the space of flows' which becomes radically separate from the 'space of places'. The first are only temporarily spatialized – usually in non-places (Augé 1995), e.g., transit hubs, such as airports and dense electronic networks – the second are spatially confined in zones of exclusion, marginalized as worthless (Charlesworth 2000).

Conclusion

In this chapter, I have presented an analysis of Medium Theory (or Media-Ecology) as a primary example of critical media-analysis. It argues that the issue of technology should be at the centre of media theory, since the very nature of media is technological. Anyone seriously reflecting on mediation as a phenomenon, must take into account the nature and logic of different media.

Media-Ecology provides a strong antidote against the reductionist assumption that technology has to be understood as a facilitator, a device or tool, in service of something else. This 'something else' is deemed more fundamental and, as a result, the process of mediation is reduced to an epiphenomenon. It is quite remarkable that even if this 'something else' takes the form of a social, cultural or communicative process, ultimately it is always the political that surfaces as the supreme 'force' of motivation. While the political is by no means irrelevant, a case has been made for understanding media 'as such', that is to say, not as instruments or tools, but as 'agents' of social and cultural processes.

Heidegger (1977) once stated that 'the essence of technology is revealing'. Nothing could be more true of media-technologies whose reason of existence is exactly that they 'reveal' the world, by transforming events (encounters) into 'representations'. This comes before any specific interest in the accumulation of power or wealth, for example. However, this revealing is also a specific 'ordering' or 'enframing' of the world – in the double sense of providing a structure and commanding specific actions. This applies to every media technology; although different media-technologies will have different (spatiotemporal) parameters of how they reveal and enframe (that is 'order'). However, without a generic phenomenological understanding of media technology, distinctions between different media are easily exaggerated to the point of fetishism.

Using Medium Theory or Media Ecology has generated a view of media technology as historically evolving. McLuhan's concept of the tetrad is an effective way of analysing how media evolve in terms of specific relationships between media and particular sensibilities. Indeed, linking back to Innis, the tetrad can be further operationalised to reveal that media evolutions are constituted by the interplay between four aspects: matter, form, use and know-how. It is the specific articulations between these aspects that generate distinctive technologies of mediation. These articulations enable us to talk about 'media histories'.

More specifically, we have seen that the historicity of mediation can be analysed in two distinctive ways:

- in terms of specific political-economic contexts (such as those of China and Europe which led to radically different articulations of print technology);
- as specific forms of connecting sensibilities (e.g., feelings, sense, meaning).

Whereas the former is closely linked to Innis' work, the latter was more central to McLuhan. How we perceive, make sense and interact is directly linked to the way in which distinctive media extend our faculties of perception, thought and communication. The figure of the cyborg is just one example of how such an approach may help to illuminate the current predicament of living in a world of ubiquitous mediation.

Finally, a sustained focus on media technology enables us to revisit the political field. We cannot ignore that media are contested sites and can provide means and instruments, as well as agency for the development and organization of collective action, tactical intervention and forms of 'resistance'. However, these terms can now be reconsidered as part of the technological assemblage, rather than outside of it; forces such as 'stakes', 'interests' and 'motives' then become similarly part of the process of enframing-revealing that constitutes the essence of media. This focus will also help us to reconsider the critique of 'technological determinism', which nowadays is used too often rather carelessly to dismiss any form of criticism that seeks to attribute some active and creative power to the technology itself.

Suggested further reading

Babe, R.E. (2000) *Canadian Communication Thought: Ten Foundational Writers*. Toronto: University of Toronto Press.

A comprehensive account of key figures in North American Media Theory, including Innis and McLuhan.

Briggs, A. and Burke, P. (2002) *A Social History of the Media. From Gutenberg to the Internet*. Cambridge: Polity Press.

A wide-ranging historical analysis of media.

Heyer, P. (2003) *Harold Innis*. Lanham, MD: Rowman and Littlefield.

A thorough and critical introduction to one of the twentieth century's leading media theorists.

Levinson, P. (1998) *Digital McLuhan. A Guide to the Information Millennium*. London: Routledge.

Perhaps the best analysis of McLuhan's work; it is critical, but remains close to McLuhan's own unique approach.

3 | ALTERNATIVE TRAJECTORIES: TECHNOLOGY AS CULTURE

A technological rationale is the language of domination itself. It is the coercive nature of society alienated from itself ... It has made the technology of the culture industry no more than the achievement of standardization and mass production, sacrificing whatever involved a distinction between the logic of the work and that of the social system. This is the result not of a law of movement in technology as such but of its function in today's economy. (Adorno and Horkheimer 1979: 121)

In the previous chapter, we have mainly focused on some of the most sophisticated exponents of North American media theory; in this chapter we will explore some manifestations of a European tradition, which – for the sake of clarity – have been divided into geographically distinct trajectories: German, British and French. What binds the different European trajectories together is the idea that media technology does not simply or even primarily transmit culture, but that it *is* culture (Carey 1992).

When photography emerged in the nineteenth century, it posed some fundamental questions about how modern human beings perceives the world (Barthes 1993a; Lury 1998). Initially, these questions primarily related to matters of perception; however, as the *use* of photography spread, it also started to affect fundamental cultural processes, such as narration, memorizing and identification. In this sense, photography as a technology *becomes* a specific 'cultural form' itself through particular practical engagements (forms of use). As we have seen in the previous chapter, use is fundamental to what a technology is. It is through use that media-technologies take on specific forms. Indeed, use 'binds' technological matter and form to specific purposes. Use is culturally embedded. Therefore, we need to explore how technological use can be analysed.

The German trajectory: the work of Benjamin

One of the earliest attempts to read technology as culture, has been provided by the German theorist Walter Benjamin. Benjamin lived in the earlier part of the previous century and died as the Second World War started in 1939. Benjamin is a highly controversial but influential thinker, who has retained a significant popularity as one of the twentieth century's leading cultural theorists (Franklin 2003). His ideas had an ambivalent and, therefore, often underestimated influence on the Frankfurt School, primarily through his personal friendship with Theodore Adorno. Although, in his collaborations with Max Horkheimer, Adorno took a rather different and evidently more pessimistic turn in media analysis than Benjamin's, there are also interesting continuities that have been largely overlooked in media studies because of a neglect of the more critical undertones of Benjamin's (1969) work (Leslie 2001).

Throughout his work, Benjamin was mainly concerned with the question of modernity and how it affected human society. He was strongly influenced by Marx, but unlike Marx, he did not attempt to provide a synthetic approach to historical materialism through dialectics. Instead, he opted for a more eclectic 'snapshot' as the basis of his cultural analyses.

Benjamin's writings are a strange and unique mixture of melancholy and optimism. In 'Work of Art in an Age of Mechanical Reproduction', he argues that in the age of mechanical reproduction (of which he takes photography and cinema as prime examples), the nature of 'art' changes. Before mechanical reproduction, especially since the Renaissance, the nature of art evolved around what he called 'its aura'. Aura is what gives a work of art its aesthetic value. Since the Renaissance (and unlike medieval iconography), this entailed a strong emphasis on the 'genius' of the artist, which could only be encountered in the presence of a work of art. This idea of 'presence' made the experience of a work of art a highly specific, time-space contingent, event. Needless to say, it was usually the privilege of the (aristocratic) elites.

With mechanical reproduction, the balance shifted away from an emphasis on 'presence', i.e., on being in the (exclusive) vicinity of meaning-production, to that of 'representation' in terms of 'reproduction'. What happens as a result is that the unique specificity of space and time disappears, and perception and interpretation become displaced (and privatized); the location of aesthetic experience becomes everywhere and nowhere at the same time (Shields 1991). Technology is no longer connected to any artistic ability, craft or artisanship (Heidegger 1977); as a result values start to shift away from the intrinsic qualities of the work of art, to its external qualities [what Baudrillard (1993) referred to as exchange value and sign value].

Benjamin's historical materialism

As mentioned, Benjamin was closely associated with two other German theorists: Adorno and Horkheimer. Their most famous work is 'the Cultural Industries: Enlightenment as Mass Deception' (1979), which is a criticism of the way in which mass media generates a mass culture based on deception and alienation. They instigate standardization and 'obedience to the rhythm' (as in today's dance music), and generate a sort of brainwashing by replacing human relationships with object relationships as social interaction is displaced by consumption:

> Real life is becoming indistinguishable from the movies. The sound film, far surpassing the theatre of illusion, leaves no room for imagination or reflection on the part of the audience, who is [sic] unable to respond within the structure of the film, yet deviate from its precise detail without losing the thread of the story; hence the film forces its victims to equate it directly with reality. (Adorno and Horkheimer 1979: 126)

Those associated with the Frankfurt School were, indeed, quite univalent and negative in their perceptions of the way in which modernity was likely to unfold. For Adorno and Horkheimer (1979), as well as Marcuse (1964, 1974), modernity provided little within its own unfolding that could be seen as enabling human emancipation. Especially in the realms of media and popular culture, potentially radical and liberating cultural interventions were being marginalized by a continuous expansion of commodification and a subordination of meaningful sensibilities to the crude demands of social reproduction.

In contrast, Benjamin's reflections on the cultural implications of technology were highly ambivalent in terms of their political consequences. He stressed that within the means with which mass culture was being forged, there were already openings for new, and perhaps more authentic and less alienating, sensibilities (Leslie 2001). To fully appreciate Benjamin's approach to understanding the role of media technology in the development of modern western culture (in a way that significantly differs from the Culture Industries thesis), we need to contextualize his work both in terms of the historical period in which he was writing, but also in terms of Benjamin's wider concerns over the relationship between critical thought and cultural (re)production.

In Benjamin's (2006) early writings, especially in his reflections on his own childhood in Berlin, one can already distil a heightened sensibility towards the way in which meaning is deeply intertwined with artefacts. That is, his childhood memories testify of the ephemeral nature of sensibility itself. Reminiscing can be seen as an attempt to reconfigure these ephemeral traces into meaningful representations. To a large extent, twentieth-century 'man' has developed devices to enable a more 'convenient' (and visual) anchoring of memory; it is called photography (Lury 1998).

However, you only have to step into a room that has the same unusual smell as one you were in when you were a child to realize that photography only provides a very partial (visual) anchoring. For example, the smell of my grandparents house, the taste of the lemonade my sisters and I were given when we visited them, even the sound of their cuckoo clock, have specific resonances for me as I contemplate some of the more pleasurable traces of my own early childhood. These traces are, however, also mediated and they can be retrieved, even if only as smithereens of momentary existential awakenings. Because they are mediated, I am still able to recover some of the moods and sentiments; their ephemerality has not completely vanished into thin air.

One aspect to which Benjamin devoted considerable attention was that of 'perception' (Caygill 1998). Benjamin follows the Marxist paradigm in that he implicitly accepts that perception is structured by the mode of production. The fact that Marx did not really elaborate on how the capitalist mode of production affected perception, representation and other 'super-structural' phenomena was primarily because when Marx (1990) was writing his most elaborate critique of capitalism in *Das Kapital* (originally published in 1867), the capitalist mode of production was still in its infancy.

Benjamin's motivation to write a historical materialist critique of art was certainly politically motivated and primarily directed against the then emergent ideology of fascism, which strongly relied on concepts of art, such as 'creativity and genius, eternal value and mystery' (1969: 212). Without taking into account this motivation, that is, without seeing it as primarily politically motivated, Benjamin's essay is easily misunderstood.

'The Work of Art' in an age of mechanical reproduction

The central thesis of 'The Work of Art' is that with mechanical reproduction, the nature of artistic representation shifts from one being based on genius, orientated towards maintaining authenticity (its unique existence or 'presence') and asserting the authority of its creation, to a 'liquidation of the traditional value of the cultural heritage' (Benjamin 1969: 215). Benjamin uses the term 'aura' to refer to this traditional value of a unique presence, which is often identified as the 'genius' or 'authority' of its creator, that is, the author (Franklin 2003).

Similar to McLuhan (30 years later), Benjamin notices how 'media' (as technologies of reproduction), affect the modes of human sense perception. Benjamin stresses the role of historical context in changing the nature of media. His most profound contribution lies in the suggestion that the age of mechanical reproduction has brought something historically unique, namely that it has engendered, within the very essence of human sense perception, the capacity to perceive its own historically contingent and conditioned being. That is, the ability to perceive both the world and the conditions of perception (Benjamin refers to this as 'analogous insight') is greatly enhanced by the annihilation of a naturalized relationship between perception and 'immediate presence' (e.g., the unique presence of an original work of art). This is the main consequence of 'the decay of aura' (Benjamin 1969: 216).

It can be argued that, for Benjamin, the presence of aura imposes upon sense perception a naturalization of the signification process (the attribution of meaning). Marxists would perhaps call this 'ideology'. However, the decay of aura undermines this naturalization as signification is made available to 'the masses' by means of mechanical reproduction that, in turn, is favoured by mass movements (Benjamin was writing at a time which witnessed the rise of two powerful non-literary 'mass' media: cinema and radio). '[M]ass movements, including war, constitute a form of human behaviour which particularly favours mechanical equipment' (Benjamin 1969: 244). In other words, for Benjamin the impact of mechanical reproduction upon human sense perception and modes of subjectivity is not only relevant in itself, but also matters in its impact on transforming the 'mode of participation' and, more specifically, the inauguration of 'mass culture' (Benjamin 1969: 232).

The logic of mass media is to 'bring things closer to home'. Through mechanical reproduction, people no longer have to be in the presence of a work of art to 'see it'. That is, photographic images can make identical copies of original paintings and movies can make near-identical copies of stage performances, such as theatre, opera and ballet. While it is impossible for the masses to all go to museums, theatres and concert halls at the same time, mechanical reproduction (and soon thereafter electronic mediation) enables a dissemination of artistic works into the everyday life worlds of the masses:

> To pry an object from its shell, to destroy its aura, is the mark of a perception whose 'sense of the universal quality of things' has increased to such a degree that it extracts it even from a unique object by means of reproduction. (Benjamin 1969: 217)

There are parallels between Benjamin's and McLuhan's analyses in that both insist on the primacy of form. That is, both try to direct the reader away from leaping into content analysis, overlooking the subtleties of the medium itself. Indeed, in more poststructuralist terms we could say that 'aura' inaugurates what Derrida (1982) called 'a metaphysics of presence' not because of the nature of its content, but because of its own 'media matter'. The metaphysics of presence is the forgetting of mediation; a forgetting that nothing is ever present to us 'as such' (immediacy), but always re/presented (Van Loon 1996a). The forgetting of mediation [or what Vattimo (1992) calls 'the illusion of transparency'] is what enables, for example, journalists to claim that their news 'really happened' in exactly the same way as it is being reported. The conflation of the event and its mediation, however, is not just a consequence of 'poor thinking', but as Virilio (1997) has argued in *Open Sky* (and Heidegger has implied long before that), an objective condition inherent in modern technology itself.

Unlike McLuhan, however, the matter for Benjamin is exclusively determined by 'its use', that is, for Benjamin the essence of historical context is social, political and cultural, rather than 'technological'. For example, in Greek antiquity, as in Christian medieval culture, the unique value of a work of art, its aura, is determined by (religious) ritual. Religion thus provides the location of its original 'use value'. Although subsequently secularized, the 'sacred' nature of aura persisted through the Renaissance and early modernity because the work of art continued to be evaluated in terms of a mystical sense of 'beauty'. It was only with the advent of mechanical reproduction in the industrial age that a 'negative theology' of art became possible in the form of the idea of 'pure art' (art for its own sake). The matter of the medium changed because its use changed. Art lost both its social function (ritual), as well as its representational one (beauty):

> Mechanical reproduction emancipates the work of art from its parasitical dependence on ritual. To an ever greater degree the work of art reproduced becomes the work of art designed for reproducibility . . . But the instant the criterion of authenticity ceases to be applicable to artistic production, the total function of art is reversed. Instead of being based on ritual, it begins to be based on another practice – politics. (Benjamin 1969: 218)

Media-technologies in the modern age have become *primarily* instruments of politics. This view has become so pervasive in media-analyses that the field of media studies is often seen as a mere branch of political studies (see Chapter 1). In the 'Work of Art' essay, this becomes most clear in the epilogue that was added at a later stage, presumably to provide a more direct response to the rise of fascism (Leslie 2001):

> Fascism seeks to give [the masses] an expression while preserving property. The logical result of Fascism is the introduction of aesthetics into political life. (Benjamin, 1969: 234)

Benjamin explained this shift of politics to aesthetics in terms of the logic of mediation (i.e., mechanical reproduction) itself. This gives his analysis the enormous advantage of not having to endorse a circular and tautological mode of explanation that sees the shift of the politicization of media as itself an effect of politics (or political economy). Consequently, his analysis can remain more truthful to historical materialism than many forms of 'Marxist analysis' as it does not need to smuggle incognito forms of intentionalism and idealism, such as the plans of bourgeois elites to deliberately use media to expand their rule (related to their 'reasons', 'motives', 'desires', 'consciousness', etc.).

Cult value and exhibition value

In other words, Benjamin is important to media analysis exactly because he offers an account of the increasingly political nature of mediation without reducing media to mere instruments. It is particularly his concern for the role of 'value' as the logical principle underlying the particular forms of usage that makes his work so relevant to us today. Separating cult value from exhibition value, he argues that mechanical reproduction shifted the main currency of art from the former to the latter. Cult value is essentially maintained through ritual and remains place bound, whereas exhibition value is a function of accessibility and is increased by mobility and displacement. For Benjamin, this shift in turn brought about a transformation of the work of art itself; its value generation was no longer dependent on its creation but became an effect of its consumption, thus constituting a market (Benjamin 1969: 224).

For example, in film, the audience's identification with the actor is really identification with the camera. Consequently, the audience takes the position of the camera; its approach is that of testing (Benjamin 1969: 222). A wider social effect of this has been a blurring between production and consumption, which is perhaps most emphatically represented by the Internet that, for the first time, has completely levelled the discrepancies (at least in terms of signifying potential) between producers and consumers as the first many-to-many 'mass' medium.

The central role of consumption in determining the value of a work of art should not be understood in terms of arbitrary configurations of taste, but are an effect of the particular 'appeal' of specific art forms to sense perceptions. Benjamin notes that film, for example, has enriched our methods of perception by externalizing modalities of retrieval (he gives the example of the Freudian 'slip of the tongue'). It has thereby deepened our perceptivity of 'hidden motives' that can be isolated more easily. McLuhan has made similar observations regarding the origins of film as a series of photographs taken to show in detail the exact movements of a galloping horse. This experiment of taking a sequence of pictures to record movement stemmed from a bet between photographer Edward Muybridge and horse owner Leland Stanford in 1889. The bet was about whether all four feet of the horse were sometimes off the ground at the same time. 'The movie camera and the projector were evolved from the idea of reconstructing mechanically the movement of feet' (McLuhan 1964: 165).

The extraordinary ability to increase visibility beyond natural limits created by moving images and photographs have also had an enormous impact on science, including the behavioural sciences, among which psychoanalysis has perhaps been the most avid consumer of movies. Fifty years after Benjamin, Baudrillard (1990) would invoke the term 'hyper-reality' to argue that the main consequence of the vast expansion of technologies of signification has been an implosion of reality; in the sense that the 'real' is no longer conditioned by our own sense perception, but instead has become itself either an abstraction (for science) or virtuality (for commonsense) and thereby 'reveals entirely new structural formations of the subject' (Benjamin 1969: 230):

> By close-ups of the things around us, by focusing on hidden details of familiar objects, by exploring commonplace milieus under the ingenious guidance of the camera, the film, on the one hand, extends our comprehension of the necessities which rule our lives; on the other hand, it manages to assure us of an immense and unexpected field of action. (Benjamin 1969: 229)

A British trajectory: Cultural Studies

In contrast to the German leanings towards pessimism (although Benjamin was a noticeable exception to this), the relationship between technology and culture was worked out in a rather different ambience within British cultural theory. The essence of this difference relates to the core of how culture was conceived in both intellectual traditions. For German intellectuals, *Kultur Kritik* was a form of engagement with cultural forms in which the subjective-aesthetic experience was the pinnacle. The investment of *Kritik* was to establish a logical continuity between subjective experience, aesthetic sense and artistic expression in encounters with cultural products.

In contrast, in the British tradition of literary criticism, the main focus was on the interactions between the cultural product and collective experience, whose primary value lies in its sociomoral articulations. Hence, British criticism of popular culture, such as that of F.R. and Q.D. Leavis (Storey 1993), was primarily concerned with the consequences of particular forms of 'culture-usage' that are enabled or disabled by specific cultural products.

However, apart from the untenable generalizations that are inherent to naming diverse intellectual activities by means of a label derived from the nation state (such as 'German' or 'British'), we should also be careful not to exaggerate the differences. Both German and British trajectories are inspired by a 'romantic spirit' that emerged in the nineteenth century as an alternative to the more dispassionate rationalism (both in its Cartesian and Kantian variants) of the modern enlightenment movement. This spirit emerges in an ethos, shared between German and British intellectuals, that there are properties inherent to specific cultural forms that cannot be manufactured or engineered by means of the application of scientific reason. As a result, both have a built-in aversion to particular modernist aesthetics, especially those that associate change with progress.

Unlike many of their contemporary intellectual movements, especially those in the fine arts, British and German cultural criticisms were not unequivocally supportive of modernism. Hence, intellectuals of the Frankfurt School, although closely associated with particular modernist *avant garde* art, such as Bauhaus and cubism, were primarily concerned with a dialectical exploration of modern art, rather than providing a linear celebration of the progress it proclaimed. Their main motivation was to analyse alienation, and this has begotten deeply romanticist connotations derived from the 'darker' and more mystical moments of Marx' historical materialism in combination with a Nietzschean disavowal of philosophical moralism and a distinct Freudian inspiration regarding the workings of the unconscious (Connell 1998).

The British academy was far more suspicious towards Freudian thought and did not share their continental European counterparts' fascination for radical romanticism, including hermeneutics. Unlike the Frankfurt School (which remained relatively marginal), the British approach to Cultural Criticism became the central intellectual focus of a new field which was later to be labelled as 'Cultural Studies'. The earlier conservativism of F. R. and Q. D. Leavis, or the more radical literary critique of modern culture by G. K. Chesterton (or, more implicitly, by J. R. R. Tolkien and C. S. Lewis), were rooted in a more generic appreciation of the role of 'intuition' in relation to reason. Hence, against the dual charge of elitism and subjectivism, such cultural critics would point towards the historical continuity between their own more intuitive critical observations and a long-standing *heritage*, often firmly based in commonsense, which linked value with endurance.

Raymond Williams' cultural history of television

Similar to the German tradition, British cultural criticism was from the outset concerned with the emergence of 'mass' or 'popular' culture. While originally an expression of an quasi-aristocratic disapproval of 'the popular' (as, for example, in the critical tone of the BBC Charter of 1923, which specified that the BBC had a role in promoting and preserving the best of British culture), a unique turn occurred after the Second World War, when several writers started to combine literary criticism with a more Marxist inspired social critique.

This turning has been located with the writings of Richard Hoggart, E. P. Thompson and Raymond Williams. Through their works, this emphasis on the value of historicity became rearticulated in relation to a critique of *popular* culture. It is from this intellectual tradition that Raymond Williams' analysis of television stems and this also explains why he pitched his intervention much more against a phenomenological reading of media technology in favour of a historical-materialist one. It may also explain why after Williams, no one within the tradition of Cultural Studies sought to undertake a serious analysis of media technology (at least until the late 1990s).

Williams' particular approach to media-technologies cannot be understood without recourse to his more generic work on culture. For Williams (1983: 87), culture has three layers: (a) lived culture, (b) recorded culture and (c) selective tradition. The latter is what Marxists would refer to as 'ideology', as it entails the transformation of specific symbolic associations into culturally dominant ones. The more we move from (a) to (c), the more limited the scope of the cultural becomes and the more closely its meaningfulness becomes tied to the interests of the dominant groups in society.

As Williams was interested in popular culture, it is not surprising that his concern with technology was mainly limited to broadcasting media and, in particular, television. In his main analysis of television, Williams focuses on how specific genres ('cultural forms'), such as news, discussion, education, drama, films, variety, sport, advertising and pastimes, as well as new 'mixed forms', structure and order particular understandings of the world, not primarily at the level of ideology, but at the level of ordinary and everyday banal expectations, which – he argues – are the primary processes of the technology itself.

However, Williams goes beyond the forms of particular programmes and discusses the distribution and flow of television programming, which indeed have taken over to structure much of what goes on in the domestic sphere of modern western societies (Moores 2005). The flow of television is an ongoing set of alternative sequences without intervals other than flows of advertising.

Williams is critical of views that separate technology from society. Instead, he proposes a view that restores 'intention' at the heart of analyses of technological development (Freedman 2003). Technologies, such as television, were intentionally developed with certain purposes and objectives in mind; whereas television might have other unintended consequences, this should not blinker us from the understanding that very little technoscientific Research and Development actually takes place without any preconceived objectives.

This immediately makes clear why Williams favours a historical approach. It enables him to retrace the unfolding of a specific technology such as television over time, as a culmination of intentions, actions and consequences. In the case of television, its history is closely intertwined with the history of electricity, which itself is linked to the history of industrial capitalism. His analysis, thus focuses on the interaction between different kinds of 'needs' meeting around specific technoscientific practices (e.g., very few forms of communication have been developed without a direct military-based motivation, Virilio 1977). Alongside electricity, the development of television was also linked to three other technological innovations; telegraphy, photography and later radio (which was already closely linked with telegraphy).

Alongside the development of television as a technology, Williams also stresses that one needs to take a historical approach in the analysis of television usage. Here, again, he stresses the importance of the association between technologically generated possibilities and needs. What started off as primarily motivated by the military and to a lesser extent commercial systems of communication, developed into what was deceptively called 'mass communication' by means of its association with (primarily) the nation state and its specific system of 'representational politics' of parliamentary democracy.

Williams also points towards the increasing need for regulation and control. As an institution, mass media had a clear advantage over other 'ideological state apparatuses' (Althusser 1971) in the dissemination of 'ideology' because of their near universal reach to entire populations in their own private, domesticated settings. More than an echo of Benjamin can be heard in the following quote:

> Unlike all previous communication technologies, radio and television were systems primarily devised for transmission and reception as abstract processes, with little or no definition of preceding content . . . It is not only that the supply of broadcasting facilities preceded the demand; it is that the means of communication preceded their content. (Williams 1990: 25)

Against technological determinism

From the outset, Williams' analysis of television is pitched against various versions of 'technological determinism', which he simplifies to the phrase 'television has altered our world'. Under this heading, he gathers a wide scope of viewpoints, varying from the strong intentionalist idea that television was designed to alter our entire way of perceiving and thinking, to far more weakly formulated views that television interacted with other social forces to produce particular cultural shifts. He then calls one end of this axis 'technological determinism' and the other 'the view of symptomatic technology'. In the latter, television was merely an accidental occurrence or effect of particular social forces that were already in place and which merely co-opt any technological device (Williams 1990: 13). This view is referred to elsewhere in this book as 'instrumentalism' and is – unlike Williams' own suggestion – not less deterministic (and reductionist) than its technological variant.

However, Williams aimed to develop his own 'middle ground', which he described in the following way:

> To change these emphases would require prolonged and co-operative intellectual effort. But in the particular case of television it may be possible to outline a different kind of interpretation, which would allow us to see not only its history but also its uses in a more radical way. Such an interpretation would differ from technological determinism in that it would restore intention to the process of research and development. The technology would be seen, that is to say, as being looked for and developed with certain purposes and practices already in mind. At the same time the interpretation would differ from symptomatic technology in that these purposes and practices would be seen as direct: as known social needs, purposes and practices to which technology is not marginal but central. (Williams 1990: 14)

Williams starts this investigation with an historical analysis of the emergence of television in relation to a number of other crucial technologies, such as electricity (which was central to a more generic reorganization of both industrial production and everyday life), telegraphy (which, in turn, was central to developments in international transportation and trade), telephony (itself a product of a combination of electricity and telegraphy), photography and the mechanical reproduction, transmission and projection of still and moving images. This enables him to argue that television technology is itself a product of a series of interconnected 'technological histories', and not a self-standing invention.

Despite his polemical opposition to McLuhan, Williams' insistence on historicity and the central role of media-use as a key selective device in media evolution provide strong testimonies to McLuhan's thesis that 'the medium is the message'. Moreover, the idea that a medium always involves multiple lineages of evolution is highly adept and closely fits McLuhan's tetrad on media evolution. However, it is less convincing as an argument against technological determinism, simply because replacing singular with multiple causality does not in itself negate the possibility of some form of determination.

A weakness in his particular genealogy of television is that Williams restricts himself to names of famous inventors and dates of their invention. Although this enables him to state that the development of television was not accidental, but by and large 'foreseen and its means were being actively sought' (Williams 1990: 17), it does pose the question to what extent this intentionality is not itself a product of historical reconstruction (if only because we know nothing about the failures and red herrings, Latour 1996). More importantly, however, is his conclusion that this historical account shows that there was very little 'social investment to bring the scattered work together', which marked a significant difference between the technological systems of television, on the one hand, and telegraphy, photography and telephony, on the other. He resorts to an economic explanation for this. Whereas the latter systems of communication had an economic viability, forms of social communication (such as television) had not.

One element in the technological genealogy that Williams singles out as a decisive factor in the changing nature of the fortunes of television was radio. Initially, the technological genealogy of radio was seen in the same vein as telegraphy, as a form of person-to-person communication whose main value was related to commerce and politics. This would change after the First World War, when – for the first time – broadcasting became associated with social communications.

At each decisive moment of technological innovation, Williams sees an already exist-ing set of socially produced needs as generating the conditions and possibilities. This is why in Williams' analysis, the social history of the uses of television technology is primary to that of the development of technology as such. This clearly reveals Williams' Marxist roots, but it is a specific (idealist) version of Marxism that is central here: one that sees social forms (as articulations of ideas or 'culturally generated representations') as the key to understanding the logic of technological innovation:

> It is especially a characteristic of the communication systems that all were foreseen – not in utopian but in technical ways – before the crucial components of the developed systems had been discovered and refined. In no way is this a history of communication systems creating a new society or new social conditions. The decisive and earlier transformation of industrial production, and its new social forms, which had grown out of a long history of capital accumulation and work-ing technical improvements, created new needs but also new possibilities, and the communication systems, down to television, were their intrinsic outcomes. (Williams 1990: 19)

Need and technological innovation

The relationship between a socially and culturally (re)produced 'need' and technologi-cal innovation is an historical one, in the sense that both needs and the incentives they give to technological innovations are contingent upon particular circumstances. This makes it impossible to present a generic account of socially produced technological innovations.

However, Williams does provide some generalized ideas about how certain needs, namely those corresponding to the interests of powerful groups (e.g., economic, political or military elites), are more likely to generate technological innovations, because they are more likely to attract investments and funding. Hence, this might explain why radio technology was not seen as having much *social* use in the first place, because wireless communication was primarily designed for *strategic* military use.

Indeed, the intersection between state, capitalism and the military as providing the context for the way in which the technology was shaped through its use is the most fascinating and insightful aspect of Williams' analysis. It is a remarkable foreshadowing of contemporary analyses of the way in which the military are intricately connected to entertainment industries (what James Der Derian has called the 'Military Information Media and Entertainment Network' or MIMENET, cited in Curtis 2006). It is here that media really bite. This is the frontier of 'pure war': the continuous mobilization of resources to support the preparation for and conducting of war, outside battlegrounds (Virilio 1993). It is here that we can see the role of the US military in the development of war simulation computer and video games to get young teenagers to appreciate the world of military warfare. It is also here that we can see a fusion between simulation media in the preparation of military personnel for combat and the way in which such simulations can be fed into news production systems as images to 'evidence' news events around 'precision bombing' and 'clean warfare' (Clark 1997).

By bringing the role of the military into an analyses of the development of media systems, particularly with reference to technological innovations and the structuring of dissemination and reception of media-use, Williams argues that the relationship between 'technological innovations' and sociocultural consequences is deeply contextualized by both institutional and more 'opportunistic' (contingent) forces, which at once act deliberately, yet generate many unforeseen consequences. It is the deliberate nature of technological innovations that points to sociological and psychological questions about motivation and need.

The key issue in this model is how to understand the translations between motivations, needs and technological innovations. Williams' own example is that of the press, which – according to him – only became an influential social form with the advent of 'news'. The press would not itself have existed without print and print emerged long before there was any social use for 'news'. In fact, the social use of print related to something that was distinctly not economic, but religious; that is to say, the primary motivation behind the successful introduction of print technology was not to intensify the monopolization of wealth, but to enhance the production and dissemination of knowledge.

Although the first mass printed *product* was a leaflet written by Luther, and this was sold for profit (Winter 1996), the economics of print were by and large an unforeseen consequence of the ability to mass produce written texts. Yet, the development of print was always already tied to the development of industry and it is clear why Williams' emphasis on the social embedding of technology is so effective. As the fundamental desire behind the introduction of print was not to make a profit, but to change the nature of the dissemination of knowledge, we also have to accept that the subsequent use of print technology was enabled by what the technology itself revealed (e.g., the relative valuelessness of paper compared with printed paper).

As we have seen in the previous chapter, this was seized upon by religious reformists as a means to break the monopoly of knowledge held by the Catholic Church, and this resonated with radical changes in the social, economic and political organization of both the mode of production and the state. The link between Protestantism and the print industry was not a coincidence of ethos, but at least partly driven by the technological agency of print media that enabled, at once, an articulation between mediation and the accumulation of wealth (from the start, print has been a form of proto-capitalism), *and* a transformation of how to link perception, thought and communication (from orality to literacy).

One of the problems with (orthodox) Marxism is that such motivations always need to be reduced to the logic of economic forces if it is to fit the model of historical materialism. That is to say, even if not all motivations are seen as directly economic, historical materialism tends to interpret all forms of motivation as rational calculations geared towards the actualization of self-interests.

Perhaps because he recognizes the limitations of economic reductionism, Williams' version of technological genealogy is not entirely 'social determinist'. He does acknowledge that there are technological limitations to the way in which technologies can respond to needs. If technology can set limitations, it is undeniably itself an actor.

Anglo-Germanic synergies?

Williams remained a rationalist and was not willing to make a more radical leap of faith to accept non-human agency. In this sense, he could not enter into the kind of political ethos that Benjamin professed, simply because for Williams, social needs are the main driving force of history. However, in terms of ethos, there are some clear connections between nineteenth-century German Romanticism, as for example expressed in the form of *Kultur Kritik*, and British approaches to understanding culture. Williams shared some of these connections.

The loss of aura of the work of art, which Benjamin saw as the key consequence of mechanical reproduction is not necessarily an unequivocal 'bad thing'. The aura, after all, was also an excluding device; as the experience of it required the privilege of gaining access, and – in the words of Bourdieu (1984) – the know-how (*savoir-faire*) of interpretation, which was derived from specific forms of cultural capital.

Mechanical and electronic reproduction enabled new forms of cultural production and dissemination. Williams points out that whereas in the first instance, what was being shown on television closely resembled the world views and interests of cultural elites (for example, as enabled by the BBC's Lord Reith's extremely paternalistic definition of culture), the rapid expansion of commercial forms of cultural production provided a strong levelling device. An increase in interest in non-elite forms of culture, which were to a significant extent facilitated by the rise in prominence of the USA as the world's leading exporter of cultural products, became commercially viable. In its wake, European cultural industries, such as the British one, rediscovered its own subaltern cultural heritage. In Britain this was evident in the rise of working-class literature; in Germany, it was, for example, exemplified in the growth of *Heimat* films, which showed an interest in the common cultural thematic of the rural life of ordinary people.

In the 1950s, a number of British academics started to focus on the specific heritage of the English working class as part of an analysis of literature. Richard Hoggart's (1990) *The Uses of Literacy* was the first example of this new type of literary criticism, Raymond Williams (1965) *The Long Revolution* was a similarly foundational text in this emergent tradition which later would be associated with the birth of Cultural Studies (Storey 1993). The rising interest in 'popular culture' cannot be explained without understanding the role of media-technologies, especially radio and television. Williams argues that from the outset, the dissemination of these media-technologies preceded content. The process was driven by the manufacturers of receivers rather than programme makers. They, thus, tuned into to the emergent system of 'mass production' which, in the twentieth century, became the hallmark of industrial capitalism (also known as 'Fordism'). The mechanical reproduction of culture was, thus, not limited to the production side, but expanded to the dissemination and consumption of media-technologies that themselves became commodities.

It was perhaps still too early for Benjamin to include this in his 'Work of Art' essay, but it is certainly not incompatible with its main observations and Williams provides an interesting account of this with reference to television. Williams argued that television preceded its content. In order to sell television sets, companies like Philips had to create programmes in order to generate 'consumer need'. This perfectly supported his thesis that media-technologies are primarily defined by their use. However, television technology was already defined before the television set had been commodified. That is, Williams' model is unable to explain what the content was of the medium of television before it was 'given its programmes'. It is as if there are two different types of television: the medium-as-such and the medium-as-used. The former is the invention, the latter the commodity. For Williams, television is thus a bifurcated medium.

By linking media-technologies to mass culture (and commodification) via transformations in sense perception, subjectivity and modes of participation (and probably in this logical order), Benjamin's approach has a clear logical advantage here because it does not seek to allocate primacy with use. Moreover, whereas Williams 'bifurcated medium' requires a strategic intervention by entrepreneurs to transform a machine into a commodity, Benjamin allows us to see how commodification and the creation of 'mass' is also an intrinsic quality of the media-technologies he associates with 'mechanical reproduction'.

Williams was mistaken in assuming that television preceded its content. As McLuhan has shown, the content of (early) television was already another medium, namely radio, combined with 'see through' media, such as stained-glass windows and, of course, electric lights. Before producing television sets, the Philips company had made a fortune in producing electric light bulbs. For them, there was a logical connection between light bulbs and cathode-ray tubes.

However, from Williams, we can learn how television became a cultural industry and how its domestication was partly informed by a process of commodification (while also being directed by deliberate political and military strategies). However, we need to add to this Benjamin's insight regarding mechanical reproduction as transforming the nature of sense perception and, thus, the nature of use itself. This shows us that, whereas the television set was not a commodity from the outset, because it was not yet defined by particular modes of consumption or use, the logic of commodification was encapsulated in the way it relates to human sense perceptions and modes of subjectivity, as well as participation, that were themselves already radically reconfigured by both mechanical reproduction and electronic communications (such as telegraphy, telephony and radio).

Aura and structure of feeling

There is another peculiar connection between Benjamin's and Williams' work, namely Benjamin's notion of aura and Williams' notion of 'structure of feeling'. Both embody an attempt to label something that is at once ephemeral, yet contain a sense of logic or internal organization [a bit like Freud's (1989) Unconscious or Lacan's (1977) Imaginary). As we have seen, the aura of a work of art is like an index pointing towards the singular genius of the artist, the creator. However, modern media-technologies have shown that singularity of the genius is no longer isolated, but a multiplicity, in which a range of traditions are merged into a stream of mythical associations.

Whereas Benjamin was not averse to a more mystic ethos of interpretation (while remaining faithful to a non-idealist historical materialism), Williams clearly favoured a more materialist theoretical ambience (while relying on an implicit idealism). For Williams, the domains of mythical associations that could be bestowed upon cultural products were not exclusive to 'works of art', because they were not necessarily tied to the genius of its creator (creativity). Unlike Benjamin, mechanical reproduction for Williams does not radically alter the existential ontology of human perception, but merely reconfigured it, historically, in a new relationship with the capitalist mode of production, its embedding within particular nation states and its possible wider functions for social ordering (including those of a military strategic nature).

However, Williams concept of culture was not simply an epiphenomenon of capitalism, but – in its historicity – had a significant (relative?) autonomy from the mode of production. He deployed the particular concept of 'structure of feeling' to theorize the relationship between cultural historicity and its material effects. Structure of feeling is, as the term suggests, not a tangible phenomenon in itself but is as a second order reconstruction of particular patterns and sensibilities. For Williams, these were historically formed in relation to particular collective experiences of people which were themselves dependent on the material conditions of existence in which these people find themselves. However, unlike Althusser's notion of ideology as 'the imaginary relationship of human beings to their real conditions of existence' (1971: 162); structure of feeling is less cognitive and more embodied, less tied to language, but by and large emotive.

Structures of feeling are embedded in the material practices through which cultures are historically actualized. They are then reflected by specific media products as well as in the sequencing and programming. They are reinforced by media-institutional strategies and decisions, and provide the basis upon which these take on an appearance of commonsense logic. Because of their overall historical specificity, structure of feeling is much more closely aligned with Gramsci's (1971) concept of 'commonsense' than with the various concepts of structure used in structuralism. The closest concept to structure of feeling, however, is Bourdieu's *habitus*: 'a system of shared social dispositions and cognitive structures which generates perceptions, appreciations and actions' (Bourdieu 1988: 279).

Like the habitus, structures of feeling mediate between individual and collective experiences and expressions. They enable people to make sense of events collectively without this assuming the form of an imposition. Because their embodiment nature is the product of an historical process, structures of feeling are not fixed, but dynamic. Especially in the face of dramatic events (such as a huge calamity), one encounters a sudden rupture in structures of feeling, which reveals itself in a generic inability of people to make sense. The only thing people are able to express in such circumstances is that they are devastated – literally, this means that their structures of feeling have collapsed.

Mediated cultural production can be seen as an attempt to streamline structures of feeling. In a sense, they are generic forms of 'neuropolitics' (Connolly 2002) in that they shape sense-making processes not at the level of deliberate reasoning or persuasion, but through the embodied sensuality of experiences. The 'new' aura of works of art in an age of mechanical (and electronic) reproduction is thus no longer tied to the *creativity* of the product, but to its *affectivity*: its capacity to induce affective relationships between media and their consumption. In a more McLuhanist slant, one could say that the aura is no longer a primary attachment to the meaningful signification of particular content, but to the work of the medium itself.

The most significant contribution of Williams to theorizing media technology is his insistence on the central importance of technology use for the way in which particular media become intertwined with distinctive social and cultural forms. The development of specific 'flows' and sequences that mark television content are, indeed, directly related to the specific and often deliberate interventions in programming and organization. Williams has shown that the practical appropriation and usage of media takes place, not in a vacuous social space, devoid of interests and desires, but *through* them. However, this does not mean that we should exclude the possibility that media-as-technologies have their own forms of engagement (binding-use), which cannot be reduced to either the intentions of their inventors, designers, developers, disseminators, regulators, users or consumers.

French trajectories: Barthes and Baudrillard

With the exception of Jaques Ellul (1964, 1965), French theorists were relative late-comers to forms of media analysis that sought to explore media-as-culture (Mattelart and Mattelart 1992). This is quite remarkable because in virtually all other domains of cultural theory, the French were the leading thinkers. Owing much of their intellectual strength and influence to the seminal teachings of Alexandre Kojève, as well as to the highly original inspirations of Georges Bataille, French cultural theory took the intellectual world by storm in the 1950s and 1960s (Descombes, 1980). However, despite the shift in attention to the role of language and culture, electronic media were hardly deemed worthy of concern in this philosophical revolution.

Although electronic media have a clear role to play in understanding how language and culture could be understood as constituting significance and experience, the realm of the technological was not generally seen as worthy of distinctive critical analysis. Yet Foucault's (1977b) analysis of discipline and surveillance, for example, provides a classic medium analysis of 'the panopticon' as a technology of surveillance and incarceration; showing that understanding subjectivity in the modern age also necessitated a concern for the modes by which subjects were brought into being (Poster 1984).

Barthes: text and image

In approaching media-technologies, phenomenologists will always seek to explore the forms or modalities through which media manifest themselves. Roland Barthes' work is an excellent example of this. One of the key contributions he has made to cultural theory and – although less recognizable – media theory has been his conceptualization of the logic of particular forms of signification, most notable text, image and music. In this section, we will mainly focus on the first two.

Barthes's writing on culture and media is extensive (Allen 2003). In one of his most famous writings, *Mythologies* (Barthes 1993b), he discusses popular media products, such as wrestling and commercials, and the way in which they have a tendency to generate very specific perceptions and interpretations that echo William's concept of 'structures of feeling' in relation to understanding how the world works. In this sense, myths are technologically enframed because technology reveals the world in very specific ways. Barthes emphasizes this revealing in terms of the symbolic realm, that is, how their meaning is culturally established. He thus seeks to develop a methodological analogy between literary analyses and medium analysis. In this sense, his approach is concerned with the transformation of cultural practices into texts, which enabled him to engage in a systematic analysis of their inherent modes of signification.

However, whereas Barthes' writings often used literature and literary forms as their main objects of analysis, which makes him perhaps a less-than-obvious candidate within media analysis, his interventions have had wide-ranging implications for how we understand the role of media and communication in modern culture (Allen 2003). In order to understand his general approach however, it is perhaps useful to first take a closer look at how he defines 'the textual'.

Text

For Barthes (1977: 157) 'Text' is a universal trope or 'methodological field' governing a paradigmatic shift in thinking about the process of signification. Based on the example of literature, he distinguishes 'the text' from 'the work' in that the latter is what is being displayed as, for example, objects (products) of writing, while the former is 'a process of demonstration that speaks according to certain rules' (Barthes 1977). This intervention is crucial when contemplating the nature of 'media products'. It suggests that the media product is always doubled in terms of 'work' and 'text'. The first is primarily concerned with meaning as derived from exegesis, the second with signification as an active, dynamic mediated process.

The literary trope, however, is not inconsequential. Following McLuhan (1962), and Ong (1982) we can see how this invokes the centrality of 'linear perspective' and a serial logic. However, fully aware of the limitations of the literary trope, Barthes stresses that the text, the signifier, is not simply the first stage of signification and that the work, the signified, is not simply its completion. Instead, he refers to the text as 'deferred action' that emerges from the infinity of the signifier. Hence, using mathematical figures, we could describe this as a noticeable shift from the serial 'line' of literary (or literal) signification to an open 'fractal' of metonymical shifts and multiple displacements. The latter is what characterizes, for example, 'hypertext'. Indeed, 'the metaphor of the text is that of the *network*' (Barthes 1977: 161).

Barthes' insights point towards the importance of form and highlight that form itself can engender ambivalence. The form of text binds a multiplicity of signifiers. Although these bindings do not allow straightforward deductions; they also do not imply an 'anything goes' type of diversity. The 'polyphony' of technological revealing is not anarchic, but ambivalent:

> The Text is not a co-existence of meanings but a passage, an overcrossing; thus it answers not to an interpretation, even a liberal one, but to an explosion, a dis-

semination. The plural of the text depends, that is, not on the ambiguity of its contents but on what might be called the stereographic plurality of its weave of signifiers (etymologically, the text is a tissue, a woven fabric). The reader of the Text may be compared to someone at a loose end . . . what he perceives is multiple, irreducible, coming from a disconnected, heterogeneous variety of sub-stances and perspectives: lights, colours, vegetation, heat, air, slender explosions of noises, scant cries of birds, children's voices from over the other side, passages, gestures, clothes of inhabitants near or far away. (Barthes 1977: 159)

This is further explored in the relationship between writing (inscription) and reading. Written works are consumed; whereas the reading of texts is itself a form of re-inscription. Weblogs and Wikis (a specific form of Internet-based technology that allows users to freely create and edit web page content; e.g., Wikipedia) are good examples of this; they are not to be read (consumed) as 'works', but as a continuous flow of inscriptions and reinscriptions.

Hence, whereas the work is confined to the linear logic of literacy embodied in the standardization of the alphabet and of grammar; texts resemble much more closely the more primordial conditions of 'speech' as 'it asks of the reader a practical collabora-tion (Barthes 1977: 163). Barthes refers to this practical collaboration as '*jouissance*' or 'a pleasure without separation'. It is the embodiment of one's involvement in texts, being drawn into the medium. 'The Text is that social space which leaves no language safe, outside, nor any subject of enunciation in a position as judge, master, analyst, confessor, decoder' (Barthes 1977: 164). This resembles Derrida's (1974: 158) famous aphorism that 'there is nothing outside of the text: *il n'y a pas de hors-text*'. This is in effect a tautological truism, for signification is a prerequisite to being ('there is') in so far as 'what is', is only revealed to us in terms of 'what is perceived', and what is perceived is given to us via our senses, and what is given to us via our senses is what 'makes sense', i.e., signification.

Barthes' insights indicate that far from an accomplishment of recent technological innovation, hypertext is a mere reiteration of the very essence of textuality itself. Through hypertext, we are encouraged to rediscover the primordial being of the Text not as written words (of 'the work'), but as the inauguration of significance. This primordial essence of textuality is not the linear chain of signs and referents to which the written word has accustomed us in a drive towards 'civilization', but a fragmented, multiple, unstable series of shifts, displacements, bifurcations, ambivalences, paradoxes and ambiguities.

Image

Barthes' approach to textuality, however, becomes most readily recognizable as an intervention into media analysis if we consider his particular writings on photography. From the outset, he stipulates that whereas the photographic image and the text are separate entities, they must be analytically juxtaposed. A good starting point for this is perhaps his distinction between textual (code) and photographic (analogon) modes of representation (Barthes 1977: 17). These two modes institute different notions of time and space. Textual representation evolves around a notion of a reading path – a sequence that extends over time ('being-there'). In contrast, the photographic image is instantaneous, it presents a frozen moment by representing the 'having-been-there'. As Benjamin noted, the photograph turns the image into a political field when he referred to the key roles of film and photography in the Nazi propaganda machinery.

Yet, for Barthes it is essential that one should always analyse images in conjunction with texts:

> These two structures are co-operative but, since their units are heterogeneous, necessarily remain separate from one another: here (in the text) the substance of the message is made of words; there (in the photograph) of lines, surfaces, shades. Moreover, the two structures of the message each occupy their own defined spaces, these being continuous but not 'homogenized', as they are for example in the rebus which fuses words and images in a single line of reading. (Barthes 1977: 16)

For Barthes the content of the photograph is 'reality'. The photograph does not transform reality by breaking it up into units (as a literary text would, by means of the alphabet). Instead the relationship is based on an analogy. Hence, it is a 'message without a code' (Barthes 1977: 17) and, moreover, a 'continuous message'.

Images signify not through differentiation, but through resemblance. As they are not dependent upon a code, and thus require no division of its mode of representation into 'units', they provide continuity between signifier and referent. The message without a code is typically realized via 'denotation', which works through iconic signs. The analogy is a non-transformative relationship of equivalence between signifier and referent, i.e., a statement of 'quasi-identity' (Barthes 1977: 36). The analogon transmits (literal) reality through resemblance; that is, it does not have a code.

Denotation and connotation

Despite the impossibility of an absolute difference between the *analogon* and the *code*, Barthes' deduction of a double signifying effect, however, remains a very useful way of opening the image for critical analysis. The basis of Barthes' semiotics of the image is the assumption that all images consist of a *denoted* message (the *analogon* itself) and a *connoted* message: 'the manner in which the society to a certain extent communicates what it thinks of it' (Barthes 1977: 18). The *code* of transformation, then, always takes place via *connotation*. One can never begin to make sense (in 'descriptive language') of an image in its *purely analogical state*. This constitutes 'the photographic paradox':

> In front of a photograph, the feeling of 'denotation', or, if one prefers, of analogical plenitude, is so great that the description of a photograph is literally

impossible; to *describe* consist precisely in joining to the denoted message a relay or second-order message derived from a code which is that of language and constituting in relation to the photographic analogue, however much care one takes to be exact, a connotation: to describe is thus not simply to be imprecise or incomplete, it is to change structures, to signify something different to what is shown. (Barthes 1977: 18–19)

The paradox is not that denotation and connotation are different structures, but that the process of *making sense* (description) is a coded practice, which itself takes place on the basis of a message *without a code*. Although this paradox is itself a structural inevitability, it engenders an 'ethical paradox' in which the denotation is understood as neutral and objective, but can only be understood via coding practices which (by the same definition) are themselves neither neutral nor objective (Barthes 1977: 20). This is why for Barthes signification is always political.

Baudrillard on electronic hyper-visualization

For Barthes, photography reveals a 'literal reality'; there is no need for a relay or code that mediates between them. This apparent immediacy thus diminishes the issue of 'representation'. In this sense, the photograph signifies a 'having been there' in the presence of what really happened. It thus generates the possibility of the idea [or as Bolter and Grusin (2000) called an 'illusion'] of immediacy (a non-mediated relationship) between the real and the representational. This has proven to be an exceptionally effective technological device in the proliferation of mythologies.

This theme has been picked up by another French thinker Jean Baudrillard, who has extended Barthes' analysis of textuality and photographic technology to that of electronic media. For Baudrillard, the distinctive characteristic of post-war media culture is that there is an explosion of signs to such an extent that everything has become a signifier (Gottdiener 1995). While having been widely dismissed in social theory for his fantastical exaggerations (Merrin 2005: 4), Baudrillard's assertion perhaps irritates exactly because there is some truth in it.

Baudrillard asserts that mass media, such as television, are 'anti-communicative'; that is to say, they do not engage in what he terms 'symbolic exchange' (Baudrillard 1993), but instead in 'simulation'. The concept of symbolic exchange is associated with the transformative event that results from 'gift giving' (Mauss 1990), which is never simple reciprocity, but a 'social engine' consisting of both interdependence and agonistic confrontation (Derrida 1992; Merrin 2005). Mauss saw the '*hau*' or 'spirit of the gift' as that from which the transformative capacity of the gift emerges. As Sahlins (1997) explained, the *hau* always inhabits the process of giving and receiving, and comes as a moral obligation to 'return' profits gained from the gift to its original source.

For Mauss (and Baudrillard), modernization entails a loss of *hau*. The sacred nature of the gift has been absorbed into rational calculations of the *homo economicus*. This echoes Durkheim's (1984, 2001) critique of modernity as a loss of the sacred and conversely organic solidarity, which in turn manifests itself in a loss of sociality or what one might want to call 'communion'. As Carey (1992) has suggested, the Durkheimian tradition has been largely ignored in media and communication studies. With this neglect also comes a lack of appreciation for the shared connections between communication, community and communion and the 'ritual' functions of communication.

Branding

Baudrillard extends his understanding of communication to the practice of consumption:

> Consumption is the appropriation of a signifier: the idea and meaning of the object or message ... For Baudrillard the sign is born when this relationship [between human beings in a 'directly experienced situation'] is broken, a process of the transformation of all relations and meaning into signs to be combined, appropriated and consumed that has become, he says 'a defining mode of our civilization'. (Merrin 2005: 16–17)

Branding is perhaps the most acute affirmation of this insight. The referent of a brand is nothing tangible; brands denote nothing; they are 'pure connotations' that only become real in so far as they can solidify their status as 'myth'. In Latour's (1987) terms (see Chapter 5), brands are designed to become 'immutable mobiles'. Brands are signs that can be attached to anything.

The brand does not signify in the sense of denotation, it is pure connotation (Lash 2002). Analysing the use of branding in Best Western Hotels, Yaklef (2004) has argued that branding works like signage: it spatializes familiarity and indexes a sense of 'having already been there'. Brands thus provide indexicality. They do not signify as symbols and thereby defy the basic operations of text-based semiotics. Brands only connote; they are, to speak again with Barthes, myths *pur sang*. Using Peirce (1940) one might say that they signify indexically by pointing towards something else that lies beyond our immediate perception and bringing into presence a resonance, a shadow, of the intangible. Brand culture testifies to the victory of the *simulacrum* (see below).

As replicas without originals (simulacra), brands are like the shadows on the cultural tapestries of the urban landscape. What they stand for is never tangible. So whereas a make-up manufacturer may produce 'make-up', their brand sells 'hope'. Because our world has now been fully commodified, commodification no longer provides the main thrust of cultural innovation as it did in the heyday of industrial modernity. Instead, the primary site of material conquest has become the immaterial itself. The very idea that hope is now something that can be sold (and thus bought) testifies to this massive shift in the economics of western modernity.

Popular valorization

Baudrillard (1993) argues that instead of the symbolic, our culture is now dominated by the semiotic. The semiotic has marginalized the 'sacred' nature of sociality and, instead, invites us to engage in a series of sign relations, which results in a perpetuation of the circulation of messages, but without any corresponding 'communion'. It is the separation of object from the concrete relation in which it is exchanged, that the semiotic 'gathers' its primary mode of signification. The shift from symbolic exchange to semiotics, however, is not just social, but also economic. It stems from a merger between a range of processes: the rise of retail and cultural industries, the emergence of consumerism as a significant social movement, etc., all played their part.

However, one major force should be singled out as having played a particularly prominent role: the rise of visual and electronic media. It is through electronic and visual media that literacy lost its hegemonic status as the main engine of signification. In the twentieth century, it had to compete with photography, telephony, cinema, radio and television, and later, this all merged into a digitized universe of 'electronic visual/ textual virtuality' with the spread of ICTs.

Whereas Briggs and Burke (2002) rightly point out that 'print culture' never really entailed a total monopoly over communication media, their historical analysis does show that it attained a near-hegemonic status already at the early stages of the 'Great Transformation' (Industrial plus American and French Revolutions). That is to say, print by and large defined what were to be seen as leading modes of thought and thus what could be considered 'meaningful', 'significant' and 'culturally valuable' (Eisenstein 1983).

A good example of this is visual art. What is considered valuable art in the modern age did not stem from the iconicity of the work of art itself, but from what was written about it in the form of 'critique'. Moreover, it was not simply what was written, but what was written in print that determined its value.

Again, this does not mean that such hegemonic forms completely overrun popular commonsense. As Bourdieu has shown in *Distinction* (1984), the working classes have remained sceptical towards the values of high art regardless of what was valorized in print. However, what the working classes thought about art never mattered in terms of its valuation; perhaps it was even the opposite. Because the working classes did not value modern art, it became more valuable as an affirmation of the aristocracy of cultural exclusivity. At any rate, it shows that cultural hegemony can exist without a broad basis of popular support.

That the cultural hegemony of print was broken in the second half of the twentieth century was not the consequence of organized popular revolt. There was a sort of revolution, but it was not organized by a party or group of intellectuals. The revolution was far more internal to capitalism itself and entailed a discovery of 'marketing' as a demand-led strategy within industrial production.

The fact that marketing took off as an essential business strategy in the 1950s, cannot be explained without recourse to changes in communication media. It was because of a change in the use of communication media that the nature of 'the popular' started to change. The undermining of print hegemony affected how meaning could be attributed, and how signification and valorization could be anchored socially, culturally, politically and economically. The return to prominence of modes of signification that were rendered marginal by print, namely the icon and the index, also entailed a radical undermining of the elite culture that had found a relatively stable balance between the aristocratic (primarily political) and the bourgeois (predominantly economic) modes of valorization in the nineteenth century.

That the USA were to be the place where this revolution would begin is also logical. After all, this country had become extremely powerful in terms of economic and military capacity; it also did not have a strong aristocratic tradition. The aristocratic roots of elite culture (which in the USA were mainly as a result of European colonialism and later immigration, as well as of its own neofeudalist slave economy) were not as deep and hence, relatively easily unearthed by bourgeois capital. We can still notice this distinctive contextual situatedness of media innovations

Telematics and the post-modern

When we reflect on the dramatic changes of media over the last 50 years, we see that they are dramatic exactly because they were not limited to media-technologies and media-use only; they were dramatic because they corresponded with wider social, cultural, political and economic transformations. The rise of the brand, the pure simulacrum so to speak, fits nicely within a culture where the arbitrariness of signs (which is the essence of textual forms) has been transported back onto icons and indexes. We now assume the universal arbitrariness of all signs, including those that – by their very nature – are not arbitrary at all. This is why brands provide a purely abstracted, disembedded indexicality; there is no natural causal relationship between sign and referent (as there is between smoke and fire). Indexical causality is ordered, engineered, cultivated, laboured so to speak, by means of marketing, advertisement, in short by virtue of deliberate signification programmes (technology).

This logic, we could argue, finds its culmination in telematics: the merger between telecommunications and digital processing. It happens when in the communicative event, the availability on demand of large stocks of data, neatly ordered in files, creates an illusion of immediacy, an illusion of 'full presence'. It is at that point that the 'problem' of arbitrariness is overcome; data aggregation, data mining and pattern matching provide the means to transform the value of exchange (of giving and receiving) into sign value, whose valorization remains self-referential and, therefore, arbitrary. This enables acting-at-a-distance. There is no deeper meaning in ensuring the copresence of say, beer and nappies on supermarket shelves than the fact that data show that many people buy them at the same time and that their collocation in space helps to smooth the retail process.

The hybrid of media-technologies have produced a telematic revolution that can be seen as major forces in the creation of what in the late 1980s became known as 'post-modern culture' – a culture without depth (Kroker and Cook 1988; Jameson 1994) – all there is are links between various 'islands' of meaning; sense can only be made if one suspends a belief in a grounded reality and, instead, takes the image as the real thing.

Baudrillard's notion of hyper-reality entails what he referred to as 'an epidemic of simulation'. Everything is generated by imagery, whose context is only sensible in terms of other imagery. Disney World is a prime example of this. There is no origin to Disney, except Disney itself. Disney World turns animation film into a theme park; creating a pseudo-reality that can be projected back onto the representations that were its basis. Indeed, this is the essence of the simulacrum. It is a world in which media have dispersed 'the real' into endless self-reproducing simulations. The world has become a branded theme park.

The so-called post-modern condition, thus means nothing more than a recognition that the arbitrariness of symbols, which is inevitable in textual forms of mediation, has affected all forms of signification. This, however, is not a radical departure from modernity, but a logical extension of it (Berman 1982). It is with this in mind that we must locate Baudrillard's critical contribution.

The simulacrum

As we have seen in our discussion of Walter Benjamin, in the modern age, both iconic and indexical modes of signification have been radically transformed by mechanical reproduction. Texts and images can now be reproduced on a scale and with a speed which is virtually instantaneous. As Baudrillard (1993) has noted, such reproductive force institutes a systemic simultaneity of the multiplying and forgetting of origins.

For example, whereas the photograph implies an origin outside itself, it is, in itself, a new origin. It fixates a fraction of time into an image as it turns the event into a phenomenon. It thus allows for the image to acquire a sense of timeless permanence (of what is always already 'there'). However, simultaneously, photography invites the retelling of narratives, for example, in holiday pictures. It thus becomes an origin in itself for itself. Conversely, the institutionalized systemic forgetting and multiplication of originality has produced a culture (and this is certainly not limited to 'the West') in which 'the simulacrum' plays a formative role (as a copy of which no original exists).

With the advent of television, video and, more recently, digital computer graphics, the distinctions between symbolic, indexical and iconic modes of signification have become rather blurred. The video graphic mode of signification ('moving images' with a more or less analogic relationship to what they represent) installs reading paths onto iconic significations. That is, more than books or films, it has the capacity to integrate iconic modes of signification into narrative forms. Unlike film, which operates on a photographic principle and institutes flows through rapid succession, video graphic signification is electronic and digitalized. One step further, cybernetic modes of representation have allowed these representations to constitute digital forms that can be manipulated and worked on exactly like texts as text and indeed through text (hypertext) and can be generated purely internally.

Three-dimensional computer simulations make it possible for us to interact with and intervene directly into the representational forms it displays. They have acquired the capacity to internalize their environment, to make a (virtual) world of their own in which 'presence' is extended and controlled to a far greater extent than any other mode of representation. This presence is at once spatial (in the sense of being located in a 'coming before' – i.e., 'here') and temporal (in the instantaneous moment of 'now'). The here and now of cybernetic videography is completely decontextualized from the time-spaces of origination as well as reception. They can be filtered, stored and transmitted electronically and, hence, instantaneously brought into a sense of global presence.

In the hyperreal, everything is already simulated. Indeed, the medium provides its own indexicality. The intensity of mediation induces a reality far more powerful than anything that came before it. In this world, authenticity equals death. Only simulations are capable of surviving the intensity of symbolic extermination; that is, only a recognition of the futility (death) of the reality principle is a realistic strategy which, instead of dialectic, is therefore catastrophic (or fatal; Baudrillard 1993: 4–5). This futility resides in 'the metaphysics of the code' – the differential modulation of 'being' – the *simulacrum*. 'Today reality itself is hyperrealist' (Baudrillard 1993: 74). Indeed, no community at all – let alone a global one – seems possible in this hyperreality of the simulacrum. The simulacrum 'transcends' (albeit in a simulated transgression) both the world of the counterfeit and use value, and the world of production and exchange value.

Entropy and self-referential mediation (autopoiesis)

In line with McLuhan and Fiore's (1967: 68) statement that 'print technology created the public, electronic technology created the mass', we might add that digital (and genetic) technology created the simulacrum. As a copy for which no original ever existed, the simulacrum discloses in the void of the lost original the futility of all authenticity. The original is an afterthought of the simulacrum and its authenticity can therefore only be a simulation itself. Self-referential closure finds its completion in the simulacrum as its environment becomes completely internal and its capacity to recognize difference, therefore, totally dependent on the logos of similarity–repetition.

However, as Baudrillard also emphasizes (but apparently very few are listening), the simulacrum is not the 'final solution', it too falls prey to its own negation and implodes. What is left is sheer nothingness or exteriority – *entropy*.

Simulation is a process of cooling down. A cool medium does not simply involve, it also dissociates, displaces, dislocates and (im)mobilizes an *indifference*. Whereas McLuhan was quite positive about the way in which cool media could be used as affective educational devices, his inherent optimism needs to be qualified and it is here where Baudrillard fits in. He states that:

> [t]hrough the reproduction from one medium into another the real becomes vola-
> tile, it becomes the allegory of death, but it also draws strength from its own
> destruction, becoming the real for its own sake, a fetishism for the lost object
> which is no longer the object of representation, but the ecstasy of denegation and
> its own ritual extermination: the hyperreal. (Baudrillard 1993: 71–2)

In the face of television, we watch in awe. This simply means that with a release of energy, i.e., entropy, there always emerges the shadow of death in the background, ready to strike when least expected.

McLuhan's appropriation of thermodynamics in the language of 'hot' and 'cool' is not accidental. Any theory of mediation requires an acute sensitivity towards physics (otherwise it would be metaphysics). The first law of thermodynamics, i.e., that everything strives towards an equilibrium (because energy can never be created or destroyed, but only transformed) is still very central in most contemporary social sciences. This principle constitutes the theories of order, hegemony, function, stability and normalization.

However, what McLuhan ambiguously opens up and Baudrillard clearly shows is that this homeostatic 'law' of movement and permanence of matter cannot adequately account for many of the processes that are currently ongoing. These processes are better described by the second law of thermodynamics: everything strives towards greater entropy (all systems tend towards disorder; Adam 1990: 62). If *autopoiesis* is the tendency towards self-productive and self-referential closure (Maturana and Varela 1980; Luhmann 1982; Zolo 1991; Van Loon 2002), a simultaneity of autopoi-etic tendencies would result in the breakdown of communication between systems: hence, the greater the drive to autopoietic autonomy, the greater the disintegration and entropy.

Entropy exposes the disintegration, loss, death, and elimination of reversibility of social processes, i.e., what Vattimo (1997: 48) has termed 'ontology of decline'. The exchange of the gift (given) is never reciprocal, but always transforms, in an endless repetition, the very matter it seeks to replace (Derrida 1992; Van Loon 2000). There-fore, entropy is not only the disappearance of energy (into heat) and thus the cooling down of mediation, but also the dissolution of matter into the hyperreality of energy. Entropy enlarges the unpredictability of social systems which autopoiesis (e.g., in the forms of surveillance and discipline) seeks to control and manipulate. This is what

McLuhan meant with progress as being the attempt to let new media do the work of the old; progress itself is inertia.

In his seminal work, *The Society of the Spectacle*, Guy Debord (1994a) argues that the emphasis in modern society has been on creating 'spectacles'. Spectacularization is the principle mode of production of contemporary sociality; it renders everything visible [(Foucault's (1977b) panopticon (also see Lyon 2001)]; referent becomes index, index becomes icon, icon becomes symbol, symbol becomes sign, sign becomes signifier, signifier becomes referent. This is the tautology of mediation: it does not eliminate the 'real' in any absolutist fashion, but disseminates the reality principle into a tautological closure (Debord 1994: 17–18), that is, *autopoiesis*.

However, these transformations are irreversible. The gift cannot be returned as the same (an insult terminating a relationship), but requires a transformation of matter. In this sense, in contrast to Baudrillard's sweeping claim that all we have left is reproduction, production still *matters* (albeit in very specific and marginal forms) and remains in excess of its total simulation – as a violent remainder and a reminder of violence.

Conclusion

The accounts by McLuhan of the mediascape, Baudrillard on the simulacrum and Debord on the spectacle all provide a sensitization of mediation as a condition of what others have called 'late modernity' (Lash and Friedman 1992). To put it crudely, they all argue for a consideration of the all-pervasiveness of mediation in sociality. This echoes Vattimo's use of Nietzsche's phrase of the 'fabling of the world', which he argues, constitutes the essence of what he calls 'the transparent society':

> Instead of moving towards self-transparency, the society of the human sciences and generalized communication has moved towards what could, in general, be called the 'fabling of the world'. The images of the world we receive from the media and the human sciences, albeit on different levels, are not simply different interpretations of a 'reality' that is 'given' regardless, but rather constitute the very objectivity of the world. (Vattimo 1992: 24–5)

What the mediascape offers is an illusion of transparency, a forgetting of the mediated nature of being and a conflation of existence to presence.

We must never forget to distinguish between a medium (tool) and a technology. The latter refers to the constellation of practices in which the tool operates; which includes form, matter, usage and know-how. Together they constitute the particular 'framing' of reality as an experience of 'objectivity'. For example, a baton is a tool used in policing, but when connected to rules and regulations, on the one hand, and training and disciplinary practices, on the other hand, it becomes part of a technology of policing as both institutionalized and embodied.

It is quite clear that many, if not most technologies themselves, involve a combination of media [what Bolter and Grusin (2000) referred to as hypermediation]; however, what is more striking perhaps is the increased 'linking' (connectivity) of media: satellites, computers, cable wire, digital telephones, television, etc., which takes place on a global scale. Indeed, this resonates once again with McLuhan's (1964) famous aphorism that the medium is the message.

Moreover, as in the works of Innis and McLuhan (see Chapter 2), we can see that European cultural theory also insists that technologies on their own do not change cultures. It is the specific *selective embedding* of particular technological innovations in a wider context of social, cultural, political and economic change that often enable them to become catalysts of more rapid changes. This is the core of all cultural analyses of technology. It is quite obvious that media *are* themselves social forms and, thus, an essential part of the process of *social formation*.

Binding-use manifests itself in the way in which media articulate specific modes of perception or sensibilities. Benjamin's thesis on the work of art shows that perception is governed by the way in which media enable us to experience the presence of a specific mode of signification (e.g., a work of art). Williams' thesis on the historicity of media forms as generated by the selective fine-tuning of forms of use, is the logical consequence of this. As our sensibilities change, so will our practices of everyday life. His notion of 'television flow' captures this very nicely as the continuous engagement of electronic mediation with structuring the everyday (and thus 'affective modalities of being in the world'). Barthes enables us to see how these affective modalities are 'textured'; his example of the photographic image as producing an intensification of vision is nearly identical to Benjamin's conception of cinema. To label this, Baudrillard's concept of hypermediation comes in handy. In the digital age, hypermediation has led to a proliferation of simulation and to the paradoxical implosion of mediation as both 'autopoiesis' and 'entropy'.

This chapter has tried to show that cultural embedding provides an important dimension to analysing media technology because it helps us focus on the way in which technological practices become meaningful in everyday settings. Media-technologies do not act in isolation from meaningful practices, nor are they simply determined by them. Context and sensibility are both articulated through the interplay of matter, form, use and know-how, and these are themselves realized in distinctive cultural practices. The notion of 'binding-use', which can be distilled from a close analysis of the specific cultural-historical ways in which media come into being provides a useful conceptual safeguard against simplistic mono-dimensional notions of causation.

Perhaps one domain where 'binding-use' becomes extremely evident in a physical sense is the body. It is through our embodiment of specific forms of mediation, in acquiring distinctive means for how we perceive, think and communicate, that use becomes binding physiologically. This is the main concern of the next two chapters.

Suggested further reading

Allen, G. (2003) *Roland Barthes*. London: Routledge.

An excellent introduction to the work of Roland Barthes, which enables the reader to engage with some of his most critical and illuminating concepts.

Leslie, E. (2001) *Walter Benjamin, Overpowering Conformism*. London: Pluto.

One of the most authoritative accounts of Walter Benjamin's work. It also offers a critique of the way in which some contemporary authors have aimed to reinterpret Benjamin to suit their own specific versions of history.

May, C. (ed.) (2003) *Key Thinkers of the Information Society*. London: Routledge.

A very useful collection of essays on various eminent theorists of mediation, among others Benjamin, Williams, Innis and Ellul.

Merrin, W. (2005) *Baudrillard and the Media*. Cambridge: Polity Press.

A key constructive and critical introduction to Baudrillard's work on media and communication.

O'Connor, A. (1989) *Raymond Williams on Television*. London: Routledge.

An insightful and sympathetic assessment of Williams' analysis of television as a cultural form.

Storey, J. (1993) *An Introductory Guide to Cultural Theory and Popular Culture*. Hemel Hempstead: Harvester Wheatsheaf.

One of the key introductory texts to cultural studies. It provides an extensive overview of most important streams and developments. One of the texts to read if one is new to the subject.

'MEDIA AS EXTENSIONS OF WO/MAN': FEMINIST PERSPECTIVES ON MEDIATION AND TECHNOLOGICAL EMBODIMENT

If we accept McLuhan's axiom that 'media are extensions of man' then one obvious question is whether he was referring to 'man' as an ungendered human being (mankind?), or more particularly, as those human beings of the male sex? Obviously, this question is as much borne out of the peculiarities of the English language in which both referents are conflated into one word as it is a reflection on the changing nature of sociopolitical thought in the western world where the issue of gender is now at the forefront of many critical interventions grouped under the label 'feminism'.

The idea that media are instruments of male domination is widely accepted within media studies and forms the backbone of many (but not all) feminist approaches within the field (van Zoonen 1994; Boyle 2005). For example, most of the critiques of male domination, cited in van Zoonen's extensive overview, have focused on either the contextual aspects of corporate control and ownership, or on specific gender-ideologies and stereotypes one finds in the content of many media products. The technological aspects of gendered mediation have received far less attention. However, they have been central to some of the most innovative contributions to feminist theory of the last two decades.

As we have seen in the introduction, the notion of embodiment is central to any phenomenological understanding of media technology. In this chapter, embodiment will be dealt with in terms of a critique of its anthropocentric bias. That is, it is modelled on the form of 'human embodiment'. However, this will be problematized at the same time by a concern for 'difference'.

The gendered body is always already differentiated and this fundamentally upsets any 'homological' approach to understanding media as 'extensions of "man"'. Instead, the difference within enables us to consider the body not as a self-enclosed, self-contained 'unit' of action, but as unfinished, open, contested, dependent, vulnerable. This chapter explores a particular branch of feminist theory, most notably reflected in the works of Haraway, Plant and Hayles, as an important, but often ignored dimension of analysing media technology.

The key concept that makes this possible is 'embodiment'. Whereas the notion of embodiment is at the heart of McLuhanism (media as extensions of physical and psychic human faculties), McLuhan's ungendered (and anthropocentric) concept of embodiment has made his analytical apparatus rather vulnerable to understanding the sociopolitical conditions and consequences of differentiation. By pointing towards 'gender' (i.e., as derived from 'genre') as a marker of differentiation, feminist conceptions of embodiment have also enabled greater sensitivity to other forms of differential embodiment, most notably those of race, ethnicity, disability and last but certainly not least, social class (Martin 1987; Haraway 1991; Van Loon 1996b). Finally, a focus on technological embodiment through feminist analyses of media-technologies will further underwrite the thesis that technological constellations of media cannot be analysed independently from their use.

This point, which was so strongly advocated by culturalists, such as Raymond Williams (see Chapter 3), however, is easily misunderstood for suggesting that use itself *determines* the nature of technology. Using more sophisticated forms of feminist analysis however reveals that the technological embodiment of mediation is not limited to the abstracted 'social' aspects of 'use', but more significantly involves a sense of 'binding-use' in close association with the form, matter and know-how that constitute particular media-technologies.

Technological fixation: engendering the gaze

Perhaps the most widespread form of feminist critique has been with reference to media content, and more specifically the representation of women both in various forms of fiction, as well as 'factual' programmes, such as the news (van Zoonen 1994). In terms of the latter, feminism has affected journalism studies in terms of analyses of who does what within news organizations, such as – for example – the division of labour in terms of editorial decision-making versus presentation, managerial positions, career trajectories (Chambers *et al.* 2004).

Analyses of media content do have an important bearing on our understanding of media technology once we accept that 'the medium is the message'. Feminist critiques of media content, however, have not been particularly strong in linking content issues with those of technological arrangements. Like many other thinkers in the tradition of the non-linear paradigm (Curtis 1977), McLuhan's work is generally not seen as conducive to feminist analyses (with the exception of post-structuralist strands). Most feminisms have far more in common with the emancipatory drive central to a modernist linear paradigm, because they are united in a politically motivated critique of patriarchy.

The less-than-loose associations between patriarchy, modernity, capitalism and technoscience (Wajcman 2004), however, should enable us to provide a more sustained critique of medium-as-content. One domain within feminism where one can find a body of critical work that involves analyses of media-as-technologies is that of film studies. In film studies, from the outset, cinematic technology was seen as a key factor in the organization of film content. The arrangement of the cinema, the large screen, the high volume PA system, the near-total darkness, the arrangements of the seating, these all contribute to a particular positioning of the viewing subject as an individuated spectator cum participant in the cinematic experience. The spectator is invited to at once lose him/herself in the real world and find him/herself again in the world of (narrative) cinematic representation (Mulvey 1975; Copjec 1989; Ellis 1992).

Film studies have contributed greatly to our understanding of the importance of the use dimension of media technology. Cinematic technology without this use dimension is poorly understood because it is incomplete. However, it would be just as mistaken to only read its technological features from the perspective of the user as the following case illustrates.

The pornography issue

Perhaps the best example to illustrate the value of feminist analysis for understanding the relationship between media technology and media content is pornography. Pornography is here defined simply as a representational apparatus of sexual practices (Boyle 2005), but we should always bear in mind that the apparatus is itself also a sexual practice. This definition of pornography is rather inclusive and would also contain what some people might call 'eroticism' or 'glamour culture'. It entails elements of mainstream media that are themselves not classified as 'pornographic'. A good example of this would be the famous 'Page 3 girl' who features in British tabloids, such as the *Sun* and the *Daily Star*, and thus appears as a daily (banal) presence at the breakfast table of many otherwise 'ordinary' households in Britain as an innocent and harmless 'bit of fun' (Holland 1983).

For many feminists, the dilemma of how to understand media-technologies in relation to content, was painfully exposed in the so-called 'pornography debate' of the 1970s, which dramatically split the women's rights movement into severely antagonistic camps. The key issue here was whether pornography should be censored. On the one hand, 'radical' feminists wanted to shore up the legal basis to endorse moral principles that would curb individual sexual freedoms; on the other hand, 'liberal' feminists saw such censorship by means of a legal/moral alliance between feminists and the state as an extension of patriarchal incorporation.

Many feminists have criticized pornography for its exploitation of women. Whereas, for some, the main emphasis was on the effects of porn consumption by men ['porn is the ideology, rape is the practice', Morgan (1978: 128)], others have emphasized that the very nature of pornographic portrayal is already offensive to women.

Regardless of particular questions of taste, feminist analyses of pornographic content will not fail to point out that the vast majority of pornographic material involves representations of women's bodies performing various sexual actions that affirm male sexual desires (Church Gibson 2004). Although strictly speaking, content-based analyses can only speculate about audience reception, it is not more than commonsense to assume that pornographic representations conform to particular standards because they feed into expectations around what is deemed erotic. In simpler terms, porn exists because there is a demand for porn and the demand for porn is primarily from men. Indeed, only a casual glance at mainstream heterosexual pornographic material, whether visual or textual, reveals that, as a rule, women and their sexual desires are put on display for male consumption.

However, on the other side of the coin, some feminists have criticized opponents of porn for endorsing a moral conservative agenda that is geared towards keeping women incarcerated in patriarchal, heterosexist structures, such as marriage and the family (Millet 1970). Such opposition often entails alliances with various gay movements for whom (queer) pornography is often seen as an opportunity to express their identity, a form of rebellion against the hegemony of heterosexist patriarchy. For these critics, pornography is a necessary corollary of the freedom of expression and a means to expose the hypocritical basis of patriarchal culture. This, in turn, was associated with a feminist critique that identified opposition to sexually explicit cultural manifestations as expressions of fear of the threat of female sexuality and thus turned into a matter of taste (e.g., Bristow 1997; Segal 2004).

A critical analysis of pornography as a media technology (mediated sex), would pinpoint two basic facts, namely:

- that porn is an industry (e.g., the so-called 'adult entertainment industry');
- that pornography is a technology.

These two are not separate in the sense that the organization of production, distribution and consumption of media, is an essential part of the media technology as well. After all, technology should not be reduced to mere tools, but include the social embedding of how it comes into being, and is being set-into-work as matter, form, binding-use and know-how.

The porn industry is a well-funded, well-organized branch of the culture industries (Adorno and Horkheimer 1979) and perhaps *the* ideal/typical exponent of the thesis that the main purpose of the cultural industries is to the engineer the psychocultural incorporation of society into the logic of capitalism. It is so powerful because it requires little or no persuasive power to function.

The main drive of pornography is the commodification of sex. Whereas sex has always been associated with some form of commodity nexus, the porn industry engages in a more radical assimilation of human sexuality into the logic of capital. It thereby destroys the very possibility of a relationship between sex and commodification, because sex itself becomes a mere commodity.

The organization of the porn industry, generally, follows traditional gender lines. Men often (but by no means exclusively) occupy the positions of entrepreneurs, financiers, distributors, directors, editors, producers, scriptwriters, cameramen, photographers, choreographers, while women are mainly involved in acting, modelling and support work, such as hairstyling and make-up, as well as catering, etc. However, it is well-known that women are increasingly taking more leading roles in the organization of the production and distribution of pornography (for example, Christie Hefner is now the chairman and CEO of Playboy Enterprises, which has a worldwide circulation of 4.5 million copies each month; also see Gallen 2006).

As Marx (1990) stressed in *Capital*, capitalism entails modes of exploitation that appropriate commodity forms as means to incorporate social relationships within capitalist relations of production. Exploitation is systemic and never reducible to the intentions of 'bad' capitalists. Apart from the fact that exploitation is a key feature of all capitalist enterprises and permeates all forms of wage labour and – following Marcuse (1964) – forms of consumption, all forms of pornography entail a mode of objectification as it turns human subjects into vehicles (instruments) for the gratification of sexual desires and this is regardless of whether it is done *by* women or men, or *for* women or men. That is, pornography provides an excellent example of what Marx (1990) defined as 'commodity fetish'.

Pornography as a technology of mediation

However, this exploitation goes further than the content or organization of pornography and it is here that we need to turn our attention back to media technology. From the outset, the logic of porn [which is in essence a myth in Barthes' (1993b) sense of a signifier without signified] has infiltrated mainstream popular culture. The creation of 'sexual situations' has been a main sidetrack in the formation of many narrative plots in literature and film, and as Barthes has shown, photography (like striptease) is an inherently voyeuristic medium that feeds our desire by means of the potential (not actualization) of exposure and the suggestiveness of anticipation. Indeed, technology itself plays a part in the logical formation of pornography. In this respect, Heidegger's (1977) phrase 'the essence of technology is revealing', could also be taken literally.

Pornography and media-technologies have been intertwined in a highly sophisticated symbiosis, enabled by the expansion of sexual commodification into nearly all realms of popular culture. For example, in photography, the 'pornograph', that is, the sign (*graphe*) of sex (*pornea*), is intrinsically bound to the logic of 'exposure' through which the photograph comes into existence. Photography's ability to create a hyperreality, by freeze-framing a moment and enabling an continuous, detailed scrutiny of every detail that would normally bypass the eye (Chapter 3), is conducive to the formation of 'the gaze'. It not only enables one to look more closely, it invites 'the gaze'; it turns everything, every bit of material, into a potential object of our gaze.

The articulation between exposure and the gaze is a fundamental feature of modern visual culture (Mulvey 1975). It also entails a destruction of narrative. Comparing the photographic/pornographic image to a piece of pornographic writing, one will notice that the former effortlessly accomplishes what the latter struggles to achieve – pure description. Through its capacity to denote, the photographic image enables the destruction of narrative exactly because a picture is worth a thousand words. However, it would be foolish to assume that images speak for themselves; the reason why photography and pornography form such a smooth symbiosis is because through connotation, photographic images enable a multiplication of narratives; each one inviting another gaze to create a new story; each one capitalizing on energy unleashed by sexual desire.

This again affirms that media form matters. Photography, while supposedly 'leaving nothing to the imagination', enables a multiplicity of interpretations through connotations that narratives close down. Writing enables the invocation of 'thoughts' and verbal articulations of desire; instead photography enables a juxtapositioning of interpretations. Narratives enable the inclusion of motivations, a comparison of different subjective positions, an invocation of different considerations and a build-up of suspense towards the climax. Narratives, thus enable a justification of the pornographic moment, i.e., the 'exposure' of a transgressive sexual encounter to a medium and thus, a third party. Photography does not. All it offers are snapshots; confrontations, testimonies of transgressions that have already taken place.

The moving image of the film, however, combines both and enables a juxtapositioning of both aspects. Yet, an often heard comment about pornographic films is the lack of narrative depth, dialogues and setups (the foreplay), are often seen as 'getting in the way' of 'the real stuff'. This suggests that the photo*graphic* logic of mediation dominates the porno*grammar* of the narrative.

It shows, however, that the medium matters and that one cannot simply assume one logic to apply to all forms of mediation. What is peculiar about porn in the modern age is the association with visual media and electronic media: photography, film, television, video and last, but not least, the Internet. First, as main representatives of the media machinery of mechanical reproduction, photography and film destroyed the 'aura' of the unique work of art or performance (to reiterate Benjamin 1969). In simple terms, it facilitated a debasement of the artistic object. It thereby created an immediate sense of continuity between highly sophisticated, artistic expressions and extremely basic primary instincts. Sex, having the peculiar inherent quality of associating both affirmations of 'divine imprints' (the orgasm, *jouissance*, ecstasy) and animalistic drives (lust), suddenly becomes a common, if not universal, signified.

However, as Benjamin argued, mechanical reproduction did more than that. By making a work of art commonly available, it blurred the boundaries between public and private consumption of artistic objects, thereby enabling a loosening of the workings of external social control (Freud's super-ego), and shame. The vast majority of porn is consumed in private (the home) or semiprivate settings, such as clubs (Juffer 2004).

Electronic reproduction added something unique as well. Being primarily extensions of a more tactile nature, electronic media engendered a direct association between visual and sentient stimuli. This is most clearly expressed in what was once hailed as the major breakthrough in eroticism – cyberdildonics (Featherstone and Burrows 1996; Gillis 2004). Here, an attempt was made to create a direct connection between electronic forms of communication and corporeal sexual intercourse. Although nowadays no longer a hype, the promise of cyberdildonics clearly fits a completely pornographic culture in which sexual fantasies can be realized without any investment in narrative or personal involvement. Indeed, cyberdildonics represents the final erasure of a difference between sex and consumption, which advertisers have strived to achieve for a century:

> With cybersexuality, you no longer divorce, you disintegrate. Proprioceptive reality suddenly becomes improper; it is all done with reciprocal distancing. So what is being set up is a discreet, furtive conjunction not based on attraction but more on mutual rejection and repulsion. Thanks to copulation between partners who are already no longer 'joined together', the aesthetics of disappearance is in turn vanishing in the face of the ethics of the essential disappearance of one's 'nearest and dearest' – the spouse, the lover – to the benefit of the 'furthest' (and not so dear) that Nietzsche once urged us to love. (Virilio 1997: 103)

The fact that pornography is the first and still most lucrative form of e-commerce, shows its uncanny ability to adapt to electronic media. Internet porn is perhaps the purest form of pornography. It consists of a seemingly endless and inexhaustible database of narrative-less fragments of still images, pieces of texts, videoclips, sound bytes, which are assembled in browser-friendly archives that can be searched according to a seemingly endless set of 'preferences'. The logic of pornography is perhaps most emphatically exposed in the systems of classification and categorization it deploys to attract customers (facilitating an endless multiplication of hyperlinks, e.g, Manovitch 2001). Internet pornography is a boundless emporium of sexual signifiers that engineers tastes according to particular fetishes. All sex is fetishized because all sex has become a commodity. In the world of Internet porn, there is no sex outside the commodity nexus.

As a generic phenomenon, Internet pornography does not primarily engage in narratives (although it does contain a lot of storytelling), but only snippets; it thereby affirms that all sex is a myth (a signifier without a signified). It is the pure tactile machine of ephemeral sexual desire – it can never satisfy those desires because they are limitless. Internet pornography has turned the mythical 'girl next door' into a universal glamorous porn-star. Wives, girlfriends, nieces, daughters, all are offered up for sexual commodification as everyone becomes a potential porn-star. Indeed, both *Playboy* and the British tabloid *The Sun* have universalized and naturalized 'glamour modelling' as simply an exposition of the most 'beautiful women in the world'. After all, 'everyone (who is beautiful) can be a Page 3 girl' (Holland 1983).

In its electronic form, pornography has taken the next logical step to mechanical reproduction. Not only is the consumption of the 'work of art' made common, but the debasement of the 'object of art' has been accomplished in a complete collapse of art itself. This is why Andy Warhol's work is highly conducive to the logic of porn. If everything is sacred (because a potential object of art) then nothing is:

> After the seduction of simulation comes the disappointment of substitution: the woman-object of all desire, all fantasy, suddenly yields to the *object-woman*. (Virilio 1997: 103)

Virilio argues that the aesthetics of disappearance that marks cybersexuality in which the objectification of women is no longer a process, but a *fait accompli* (of the *object-woman*) because it is:

> merely the effect of crossing the "time barrier"; the barrier of this limit-time of the speed of electromagnetic light-waves that disqualifies not only the relative speed of the living being but all matter, all effective presence of other people. (Virilio 1997: 103)

Virilio argues that the speeding up that is facilitated by electronic mediation entails a transformation not only of perception but of the matter of being itself. It also clearly resonates with Baudrillard (see Chapter 3) who associates mediation with the decline of 'ritual' or 'sacred' symbolism in exchange for 'pure simulation'. If feminist analysis is, indeed, inextricably connected with the matter of embodiment (Butler 1993b), then it logically follows that digital mediation is a feminist issue.

Hence, a feminist critique of pornography that fails to engage with the organization of the 'adult entertainment industry' and with its media-technological facilitation, remains a superficial commentary on representation. As it seeks for clues in the superficial manifestations, it will remain unable to decide whether pornography is exploitative or liberating (Segal 2004). Such a blinkered view on the nature of pornography has led to facile statements that there can be such a thing as 'feminist pornography'. It suggests that pornography is pure content and thereby affirms by this very gesture the logic of pornography itself.

Simulation revisited: manipulating needs

Pornography is thus a particular, albeit somewhat extreme, culture industry that, nonetheless, displays all the characteristic traits of the latter (as identified by Adorno and Horkheimer 1979) to the extent that it has not been difficult for particular aspects of porn to become mainstreamed and relabelled 'eroticism' or 'adult entertainment'.

An adequate feminist approach to a critique of pornography would need to connect issues of content, organization, production, consumption, as well as technology in terms of matter, form, use and know-how, to provide a philosophically and politically convincing case that a consideration of gender makes a substantive contribution to media analysis. As the case of pornography so clearly shows, it is not sufficient to pinpoint modalities of male domination as the *sine qua non* of the logic of mediation.

It is the technological facilitation of gazing, of reducing the symbolic 'gift economy' of sex, i.e., of giving oneself and receiving another human being, to simulation, which defines the nature of pornography. The essence of pornography as a technology is the revealing of this gift exchange to a third party, entailing a transgression of the intimacy of the encounter by subjecting it to the logic of the spectacle. As Debord (1994) has argued, in the spectacle everything becomes a mere commodity. As a form of 'pure mediation', it thus stands out in articulating technological embodiment in a most emphatic and unambiguous manner. Pornography is capitalism's ultimate desiring machine. In this sense, it is not an exception, but a norm.

The mediation of desire is, of course, not limited to pornography, but permeates nearly all activities of the cultural industries. As Marcuse (1964) has noted, the working class have been invited to 'join' the capitalist settlement through consumption. Consumption, which itself can be best understood as an organized and engineered form of manipulation of needs (Lodziak 2001), has become a means of *incorporating* the working class into the capitalist economy. This invitation to privilege what Marcuse (1964) calls 'false needs' is a form of seduction. It is for this reason that in *Eros and Civilization*, Marcuse (1974) links capitalism to a redefinition of sexual desire; to a reconfiguration of the Oedipus Complex. Indeed, the very act of consumption could be understood as having a sexual resonance. Marcuse's own analytical framework is, to a large extent, derived from a critical reworking of Freudian psychoanalysis with a historical materialist turn.

Lodziak's (1995) manipulation of needs thesis stands as a stark reminder of the way in which capitalism requires incorporation into the everyday lives of people and its mechanisms of reproduction are inherently tied to what are (rightly or wrongly) perceived to be necessities. Following Marcuse and Lodziak, one could rephrase the coming into being of consumerism as a consequence of a radical manipulation of needs. Drawing on Baudrillard (1993), one could extend this thesis by arguing that this manipulation of needs strongly relied on forms of mediation, which engendered new modes of technological embodiment. Far from being mere instruments in the creation of 'false needs', all needs are a consequence of mediation. They emerge with the frictions of embodied interfaciality; the excess of flows of extensions and connectivities.

The use of sexual innuendo in advertising is a simple example of how the simulation of desire can be used to manipulate needs. The manipulation is far from ideological; it is physiological. This is why the sexual reformists of the 1960s got it so wrong. They conceptualized sexual repression as ideological; they thought that by being more explicit about sex, people would be happier. That is, they perceived sexual liberation to be a mental process and their proposed sexual reform was therefore perceived to be taking place in the minds of people.

However, rather than liberating people from sexual repression, the reform ideology became an advocacy of the destruction of sex; sex became reduced to pure signs. In other words, the 'success' of the sexual revolution was not based on ideational factors, but material ones. Instead of intimate relationships based on love, sexual reform entailed a process of commodification of sex as disconnected from love, commitment, solidarity. The manipulation of needs that has been dubbed 'the sexual revolution' thrives on a far more mystical nature of sexual desire, namely its embodiment. The 'urges' and 'cravings' created by means of sexual desire are far stronger than any rational deliberation of beliefs.

For example, advertising as a manipulation of needs, thrives on the myth of secrecy of sex, it needs to perpetuate (by simulation) its sacred aura or *hau* in order to continue to have real effects. Desire is not ideational but embodied; it is not 'in the mind', but visceral, material, externalized (Deleuze and Guattari 1983). In Baudrillard's (1993) terms, the symbols of sex, which entail a unity between mediation and giving (communication) have been replaced by a simulation of sex, where pleasure is derived from the sign only.

Only as a form of seduction, as a duplicity of simulation and 'sacred' symbolism, can advertising continue to work as a manipulation of needs, as a desiring machine. And it is in this duplicity that gender difference is caught up in as well. Gender difference makes it impossible to completely ignore embodiment; gender difference undermines the homology of simulation. That is to say, the gendered body is a prerequisite for the simulation of sex. As Haraway (1988) argued, gender difference reminds of our particularity, our situatedness, our partiality (Van Loon 1996b). Without a reminder of this particularity, mediation would indeed be nothing but a free flowing circulation of signs; desire would be obliterated, sex would become meaningless, advertising would become obsolete, seduction would be impossible. It is the inertia of the body that grants simulation a connection with desire; it is from this inertia that pleasure emanates.

If we return then to the phrase 'media as extensions of man' and emphasize that this extension is not just metaphorical, but also psycho-socio-physiological, we are able to see mediation as having the potential to mean a lot more than simulation. The fact that we often fail to see beyond semiotics is itself a testimony to the success of its seduction and manipulation of needs. However, this success comes with its own price. By severing all links with embodiment, seduction loses its own pertinence and force. Sexual desire without embodiment, as pure simulation, is devoid of life and vitality (Kroker and Cook 1988).

It is on this basis that we might be able to sketch the contours of a more viable feminist politics. Instead of an ideological critique of patriarchy and heterosexual desire, feminist politics becomes truly radical when it turns against simulation. It is only by opposing sex-as-simulation that it can attain an affirmation of gender difference as constitutive of all forms of desire [and not just (hetero-)sexual ones]. Feminist politics can only hope to end patriarchal hegemony by overturning the devil's trick (making people believe that it does not exist) that underlines the manipulation of needs; by exposing not only embodiment as the primary 'matter' of mediation, but also by showing how this matter is being manipulated through objectified, instrumentalized and commodified forms of engineered desire that operate at the service of capitalism (which itself is a simulation of a particular form of male desire).

Feminist medium analyses

In feminism, there are generally two different types of critique of patriarchy: (1) political, for which patriarchy is intentional and (2) philosophical, for which patriarchy is more structural and intertwined with epistemic considerations. Whereas the earlier flirtations with Marcuse and Baudrillard already suggest that the two explanations of patriarchy (as intentional versus structural) can be effectively combined, an undifferentiated use of the term 'feminism' obscures the fundamental philosophical differences between these two positions and as a result provide a rather muddled understanding of the ways in which feminist theory can be deployed for political interventions.

As we have seen in previous chapters, the dualism between context and content cannot be resolved by simply 'adding' them up. We need a more sophisticated phenomenological account of the 'interfacing' device that translates contexts into contents and *vice versa*. Indeed, we need to focus on the embodiment of mediation, which in this book has been primarily understood through the concept of 'media technology', to try and figure out how media may contribute to social reproduction beyond the stalemate of intentionalism versus structuralism.

In order to do this, we will turn to feminist analyses of technological processes to establish a more comprehensive intellectual and political agenda. Barring a few exceptions, feminist analyses of media technology are mainly derived from what is generally known as 'science and technology studies' (STS). Within the field of STS, there has been a strong tradition of feminist research into reproductive technologies (e.g., Franklin 1997; Saetnan *et al.* 2000).

In this field, substantial inspiration has been drawn from the work of Marilyn Strathern (1992) on the interface of nature and culture through which conceptions of gender and sexuality have come into being. Clearly, sexual reproduction is of essential importance for understanding patriarchal society. However, the link with media-technologies is rarely at the centre of these concerns. When media are mentioned at all, they are seen as mere vehicles for discourse. That is to say, despite the fact that STS has been extremely critical of any form of instrumentalism this, has, by and large, not been extended to the analysis of media.

Domestication

There are, however, notable exceptions and these are definitely worth a closer look. A well-established branch of feminist media analysis that has associated itself with a particular approach, within British cultural studies (see Chapter 3), by focusing on the centrality of technology-use as a means for understanding of media work, is the work on domesticity (e.g., Cockburn and Fürst-Dilic 1994; Spigel 2001). Indeed, the seemingly banal example of who controls the remote (Morley 1986; Seiter *et al*. 1989) could be seen as the starting point of an approach within the sociology of culture concerned with 'material culture' (Miller 1987), which in turn strongly influenced cultural studies of technology, such as those of Silverstone and Hirsch (1992). Within this field, feminists have highlighted from the outset that technology-use was deeply affected by gender relations and played a significant role in the organization and structuring of domesticity (also see Wajcman 1991, 2004; Ang 1992; Cockburn 1992; Bakardjieva 2005; Berker *et al*. 2006;).

Berker *et al*. (2006) develop the concept of 'domestication' as a particular way of framing the social nature of technology. Bringing to the fore the ways in which specific modalities of 'technology-use', especially in the realm of ICTs, have impacted on the very nature of technological processes, serves as a welcome reminder of the value MacKenzie and Wajcman's (1985) seminal piece on the social shaping of technology.

Domestication is an interesting concept exactly because of its etymological associations with 'taming' wild animals, making them 'house-trained', allowing them to integrate into the everyday routines of 'family life'. Domestication is thus a process in which (potentially volatile and dangerous) technological agency is incorporated ('made safe' or 'secured') into the 'ordinary everydayness' (or 'safe' mediocrity) of the home.

Although Berker *et al*. do not spend much time reflecting on the implicit genderedness of domestication, it is not difficult to see how this very process of 'house-training' echoes a gendered division of labour in which the *oikos* – the primordial flow of matter (economy; ecology) – comes into being as the ground zero of the *socialization* of technological agency. It is for this reason that Silverstone and Haddon (1996) conceptualize the household as a 'moral economy' (a 'transactional system of economic and social relations', cited in Berker *et al*. 2006: 6). Again, we can see that there are close connections between communication and what one might call the giving and receiving of gifts, highlighting once more the dualistic nature of communication as (a) a transmission of messages (the semiotic) and (b) a modality of association (the symbolic).

In western culture, domestication – like socialization – is traditionally seen as women's work. That is, the social is always already gendered (Wajcman 1991). For this reason, Cockburn and Fürst-Dilic (1994) proposed that the social shaping of technology should be reinterpreted as the mutual shaping of gender and technology. They are particularly concerned about the role of the continued gendered division of labour in the home and how this affects technological development in terms of design and engineering, manufacture and sale, and use and consumption (cf. Wajcman 2004).

Studies such as these have actively adopted a social constructionist approach to understanding technology. Although the primary object of critique for social constructionist accounts of technology is still technological determinism, and this clearly informs the central objective of Mackenzie and Wajcman's (1985) work, the flirtations with actor network theory (Latour and Woolgar 1979; Latour 1987; Law and Hassard 1999) on the one hand, and 'material culture perspectives' (Miller 1987; Silverstone and Hirsch 1992; Silverstone and Haddon 1996), on the other hand, have also generated a more critical awareness of instrumentalism.

Both technological determinism and instrumentalism require a separation of 'the social' (itself a deeply problematic concept, see Latour 2005) and 'the technological', i.e. the human body and the machine. Indeed, social constructionism's major intervention has been to show that sociality and technology are not separate entities, neither engaged in dialectics nor mutualisms, but folded into each other across an intricate and dispersed series of nodes (see Chapter 5).

The attempt to link a feminist critique of patriarchy to social constructionism, however, has been much less straightforward. Social constructions are no longer 'accidental', but structured and purposeful, in service of the strategic needs of the dominant. In order to establish a critical edge in which patriarchal heterosexist structures can be identified as the main powers of social construction, one requires a framework of analysis that either allows for forms of 'determination', often located at the level of 'context' (e.g., capitalism and gendered division of labour, which produce needs that are subsequently imposed onto individuals), or of intentionality, located at the level of the deliberate, wilful, self-interested actions of dominant (male) and subordinate (female) groups that are locked in perpetual struggles over scarce resources and/or autonomy.

The ascendance of 'the Feminine'

Technologies that are incorporated into consumerism often undergo a process of domestication. For example, the success of the Mac, developed by Apple Macintosh in the early-mid 1980s, was predicated upon developing an interface that no longer adhered to the primacy of the perspective of the programmer, but of the user. In popularized versions of this success, the male–female dichotomy was often invoked to argue that MS DOS (the main competitor) was a distinctively male biased operating system because it features abstract, linear commands. Indeed, market research into the use of ICTs at work, often revealed that many women using PCs running on MS DOS found the system illogical (Plant 1995). Apple's success in developing an interface that used icons as buttons was such that Microsoft was forced to develop its own graphic interface, which became MS Windows. Today, visual interfaces are the norm, the mouse has taken over from the keyboard, and most computer users can operate the equipment effortlessly without knowing anything of the operating infrastructures behind it.

Sadie Plant (1995) has used this example to argue that the emergent information and communication technologies adhere much more closely to a 'feminine', rather than 'masculine' ethos. The latter's cumbersome linear rationality becomes outmoded in an economic structure which requires fuzzy logic, multitasking and multilateral thought. Her approach to understanding the emergence of the Internet also places central emphasis on gender. She suggests that there is a long-standing historical connection between women's (subservient) role within patriarchal systems and their relationship to technology. Using the case of weaving (which is etymologically related to the concept of text, e.g., as in textile), which for some (including Margaret Mead) was the one area of technology in which women have always been the main innovators and from which – at least in tribal societies, women drew a lot of social power – she shows how weaving is linked to a register of logical sensibilities that have been largely suppressed by the (masculine) epistemes of early modernity (Plant 1995). Whereas in early modern thought, rationality was linear and sequential, weaving always entails a system of networking.

Plant describes the case of Ada Lovelace (aka Ada Byron) who was an associate of Charles Babbage and mainly responsible for the development of the Analytical Engine – an early form of computer. Plant implies that Ada Lovelace's immense talent and success stems from the fact that she was a women. That is, the analysis presupposes that the logic of networking is feminine because it is formulated in opposition to the linear rationality that was defined as masculine.

Plant's feminism is thus a very optimistic one: as nonlinear (feminine) thought increases in importance, which is without questioning amplified by the rise of digital media and telecommunications, so women's subordination will be reversed because the network society not only needs women as networkers (weavers), but because women will be enabled to reject patriarchal impositions and obtain more autonomy.

Post-humanism and cyberfeminism

The emphasis on networking, interactivity, juxtapositioning, between-ness and open-ness that has characterized feminist analyses of media technology, clearly resonates with nonlinear, nondeterminist and noninstrumentalist understandings of media that we have been exploring in the previous chapters. There, too, the challenge remained whether such an approach to mediation could avoid the allegation of political quietism and indifference. These chapters show that radical forms of media-analyses are inherently political, but not in terms of the politics as we know it (e.g., identity politics). When we pay close attention to the form, historicity, cultural embedding and embodiment of mediation, it becomes clear that the technological dimension is not a separate issue, but interwoven with context and content.

With Donna Haraway (1988, 1989, 1990, 1991, 1997), Katherine Hayles (1999, 2002) has perhaps provided the most sophisticated feminist scholarship regarding analyses of the conjecture of media technology and embodiment. What makes her work so particularly exciting is that, like Haraway (see below) she engages fully with both the literary and scientific registers of understanding the human being (also see Van Loon 1996b).

In contrast to the rather facile complaint that modern technoscience entertains the fallacy of disembodied technology and is therefore wrong, or worse, dangerous, Hayles is far less judgemental about processes of disembodiment that seem to drive cybernetics and information technology. She develops a historically grounded analysis of the increased separation of matter and information, of the molecular and the digital, which resonates not only with Baudrillard's (1993; Merrin 2005) distinction between the symbolic and the semiotic, but also with Virilio's (1997) thesis of escape velocity.

She develops a concept of the post-human to argue that the primacy of cell-based views of life (that one finds in traditional biology as well as the modern 'sciences of man' – Foucault 1970) is withering and making way for a new understanding of life as information processing. Indeed, she argues that matter itself becomes part of an 'accident of history rather than an inevitability of life' (Hayles 1999: 2).

Hayles' crucial contribution lies in her nonmetaphorical association between writing and life. In this sense, her work is a clear example of post-structuralist vitalism (also see Ansell-Pearson 1997). The radical rupture in the nature of writing across the different media of print and computing, is indicative of the close link between virtuality and creativity (Hayles 2002). Digital media enable writing to come to life, to go beyond representation (Kittler 1997). The code of digital media writing is not representative, but performative; it *enacts* being. Being digital only exists because of writing.

However, she does not stop at pointing out that writing is more than semiosis, but actually engages with this 'more than'. For her, it opens up a field of ethical questioning, which in turn can be invoked to develop more politically-orientated interventions. Key to this is to show how gender introduces a difference at the heart of the idea of the human, which in turn undermines a homological concept of human being and opens up a fundamental rupture in the all-too-easy equation between embodiment and self-identity.

This, I would argue, provides a sophisticated turn to Plant's blunt assertion that 'networked being' resonates far better with an ethos of femininity. Cyberfeminism is able to expose not only the deceptive nature of linear thought and the privileges it bestows on 'masculinist rationality', it also shows that this deception is not essential, but historical, that its masculinist ethos is not driven by either testosterone or agnetic solidarity (the brotherhood of men), and that it is unable to maintain its hegemonic position by the sheer drive of media evolution itself. It does not need masculine villains to set itself off against, it merely needed to explore in greater detail the shifting nature of mediation and the excess of semiosis, i.e., embodiment, to reveal that vitality, creativity, virtuality and potentiality are not the principal domain of men, nor of women, in fact, they are not at all the principality of 'man' (in the modernist sense of origin and destiny of history).

Hayles' post-human, therefore, does not locate consciousness in the body, nor does it locate technology outside the body. Instead, the body is always already 'prosthetic' (Lury 1998) and from the beginning engaged in processes of 'extension'. From this, Hayles extrapolates that:

... the post-human view configures human being so that it can be seamlessly articulated with intelligent machines. In the post-human, there are no essential differences or absolute demarcations between bodily existence and computer simulation, cybernetic mechanism and biological organism, robot teleology and human goals. (Hayles 1999: 3)

A statement such as this one invokes perhaps a strong negative response from those who insists that there is something unique about human being. Such views are central to various forms of humanism and suggest that in its natural state, the essence of human being is irreducible to anything else; i.e., completely self-referential. Any claim to the contrary would be defined as misanthropic or nihilistic.

However, the case can be made for a more cautious reading here. What is being rejected by post-humanism is not the existence of a species called 'human being' (or 'man'), but only its modernist version, i.e., the liberal, self-contained, self-referential, autonomous 'individual'. It entails, thus, merely rejection of the (modern humanist) assumption that human being is self-contained. Instead, it posits that this illusion of the self-contained individual is like the devil's trick of consumerism, a product of market capitalism.

Instead of the self-referential humanist individual subject, the post-human subject is a gathering of heterogeneous components, based on a distributed sense of cognition and dispersed consciousness (Ansell-Pearson 1997). This requires that we also radically rethink the issue of embodiment. No longer can it be seen as the ground of all being, but as one of finite embeddedness in a complex material world, one that is not an expression of a unified, centred desire, but rather becomes an expression of an assembly of desires:

A critical practice that ignores materiality, or that reduces it to a narrow range of engagements, cuts itself off from the exuberant possibilities of all the unpredictable things that happen when we as embodied creatures interact with the rich physicality of the world. (Hayles 2002: 107)

It thereby opens the possibility for understanding 'disembodied subjectivities' alongside embodied ones. This, in turn, forms the cornerstone of the concept of 'networked intelligence' (de Kerckhove 1996) and resonates with McLuhan's (1964) understanding of electronic communication as an externalization (disembodiment) of our central nervous system (see Chapter 5).

Embodiment and enframing

Cyberfeminism and post-humanism share a lot of common ground exactly because they are both critical of the particular universalism of modern liberal individualism. As a differentiated being, along both gender and sexual lines, the post-human inhabits a unique position in modern society, because it opens the possibility of imagining forms of being that are not autonomous, but *symbiotic*, i.e., they find their true form not in assertion and domination (power-fetishism) but in sacrifice and giving (and thus revive the symbolic against simulation).

It is perhaps ironic that in emphasizing the primacy of gender difference in a critique of patriarchy, feminist thought has enabled us to reconceptualize not simply masculinity and femininity, but the very notion of human being as something different from that of 'modern man': the self-identical, isomorphic, homological and integral individual. Instead, 'man' is always already differentiated, dispersed, fragmented, vulnerable, open and unfinished. This differentiated notion of human being has become visible again in close association with the dramatic and rapid changes in the nature of mediation with the onslaught of digitalization.

To help understand how a differentiated notion of human being allows us a much better phenomenological understanding of media technology, it is useful to invoke a discussion of technology as enframing/revealing based on Heidegger (1977). The combination of these terms (see Chapter 2) highlights how media-technologies help shape how we perceive the world, how we interpret what we perceive and how we make sense of our perceptions in a wider cultural context of meaningful social interaction. Technology orders (not 'determines') how we perceive and think in the sense that it provides cues, parameters, logical infrastructures, connections, etc., that emerge from a process of a 'setting upon' the world (i.e., technical applications). The four dimensions of technological structuring: matter, form, binding-use and know-how provide distinctive ways of analysing the way in which our world is enframed and revealed.

The technological structuring of mediation concerns the attunement of our existential being (or what Heidegger called *Dasein*), i.e., what we 'are' in a fundamental sense (the 'I'), that is, before we articulate this in terms of a 'self' or 'subjectivity' or 'identity') – to our ordinary, everyday 'being-in-the-world' ('me'). That is, it orders our existential orientation in relation to everyday, ordinary being. We could also refer to this process as 'incorporation'. Incorporation highlights how specific media-technologies become reappropriated as embodied forms. Our everyday operations become 'habits' and 'routines' so that we no longer seem aware of our technologically mediated being in the world. In this respect, what started as an amplification of a specific human faculty, was first presented as an 'external entity' (a medium) through a process of dissociation (which could also be seen as a form of 'estrangement'), and then subsequently reconnected to the body by forms of habitualization and inhabitation, inducing what McLuhan (1964) called 'prosthetic numbness' or 'narcissus narcosis'.

If we complete the movement from technology to enframing, from enframing to incorporation, and from incorporation to embodiment, we come close to an understanding of technology that has been developed by the American feminist scholar and biophilosopher, Donna Haraway. It is perhaps useful here to link the three concepts – incorporation, valorization and discipline (both as a social practice and an organization of academic knowledge) and to situate these in close proximity with the concept of technology as 'ordering'.

In *Primate Visions* (1989), Haraway discusses the field of primatology as a specific discursive formation within which human biology has been developed using the axiomatic distinctions between animal and human, and nature and culture. In this work, Haraway argues that life sciences, such as primatology, work – often implicitly – with concepts of 'man' to structure and organize a 'rational' account of their subject matter. However, this also has direct (and usually unacknowledged) implications for their understanding of human being. Sexual behaviour, notions of domination, of primate strategies, have all been derived from simplistic models of human nature, which in turn, have been reflected back onto it to amplify its account of 'nature-in-general'. At the basis of this criss-crossing of representations and (assumed) realities is a dogmatic, but never tenable distinction between nature and culture.

A distinctive application of this can be seen in the field of reproductive technologies (Franklin 1997). When we consider the role of technology in facilitating human reproductivity, it is difficult to maintain a clear distinction between nature and culture. Nature is more and more a technologically reproduced representation of an origin, which was already a representation, that is, if we accept the primacy of biology, i.e., of DNA as the code of life, then we have to accept that at the core of physiological life, there is a constitutive role for the technological. It is only because of this that life has now become a *political* issue.

Not only is it impossible to maintain any clear distinction between nature and culture on the basis of a singular principle of classification or definition (for there is no way of telling where nature ends and culture begins), but the very logic of making that distinction is self-destructive because there is no way of telling whether this logic is itself natural or cultural.

One of Haraway's (1988) main critical contributions has been to problematize the way in which technologies of visualization create specific partial perspectives while concealing their partiality (e.g., gendered perspectives). In the world of today, visual representation is strongly technologically ordered by various media. At the heart of this is a paradox. As visual technologies become more ubiquitous, they also become more invisible. Yet, at the same time, feminist critiques of 'disembodied' technoscience have turned the technologies of visualization against their invisibility. For example, in *Sexual Visions*, Ludmilla Jordanova (1989) exposes male heterosexist voyeurist desires as being at the heart of representations of anatomy that were used to illustrate 'the discipline'. In a similar vein, Emily Martin (1987) shows how various technologies of visualization in the technoscience of obstetrics reveal their violent and intrusive character in their purposefulness of 'delivering' babies.

Indeed, feminist critique of technoscientific mediation has rendered the visual itself as deeply problematic. The new technological constitution of hypermediation has merely extended the paradox of ubiquity/invisibility by turning the 'illusion of transparency' into a spectacle. In *Prosthetic Culture*, Celia Lury (1998) intensifies this problematization of technological embodiment in visual culture by referring to photography as having the potential implication of a total collapse of any notion of subjective integrity. Photography always orders (enframes and reveals) a 'particular history' of something or someone. Deploying photography to create generic historical narratives, thus implies a denial of the nature of the photograph itself. The 'case' thus exposed loses its own mediated historicity, its singularity becomes 'generic'. By using Virilio's (1997) critical notion of exposure (which in hypermediation becomes 'over-exposure'), Lury argues that the medium of photography works as a radical break of linear representations in the chronological anchoring of memory in linear time, which as the basis of narrative memory, is ruptured.

The 'presence' of memory enframed by the visual image turns it into something else, juxtaposed onto the present as a variation of presence, a repetition and differentiation that exists alongside it. In so doing, the visual is itself 'revealed' as a distortion, a multiplicity of coexisting intensified realities. Visual culture and especially photography entail the loss of 'origin' and the futility of a genealogical tracing that is not, at the same time, a mapping of complexity and indeterminability. Photography captures time by eliminating it.

In 'Manifesto for Cyborgs' (1990), Haraway follows a similar trajectory when considering the technological transformation of embodiment. The idea of an integral, self-sufficient, isomorphic (i.e., nonmediated) human subject is a specifically modernist delusion. Through the process of technological incorporation, the distinction between human being and machine has been shifted and blurred radically. In Haraway's manifesto, the cyborg heralds the end of all originary purity (the *arche* of 'man', i.e., Adam), and of all claims to an indivisible 'origin'. Instead, it asserts that we are all hybrid (i.e., mediated) symbiotic beings. The environments of cyborgs are neither pure reality nor pure representation; they are virtualities. That is to say, what matters to the existence of cyborgs is the multiplication of possibilities (and risks), which – due to their digital informational character – can be reprocessed and reconfigured anywhere, anytime. Cyborgs do not engage in symbolic exchange but engage in simulations. They are, thus, the realization of 'mediated being'.

Cyberfeminism is thus one particular way of attempting to rewrite the present to reclaim the future, and thereby reconnects the political and philosophical strands of the critique of patriarchy. It also establishes a take on power that does not resort to 'a slave morality'. Cyberfeminism does not base its critique on the nature of women as being victims. The process of 'becoming other' is more complicit, it cuts across the divides that create gender, race, humans versus animals, human versus machines, and is therefore never clear cut. The other must, therefore, not be idolized or fixed; the other does not hold a moral superiority. The other cannot be fully incorporated; but we are always invited to appropriate alterity, no 'given' can be taken for granted without some form of violation; the violation of the other is inevitable; the other is within, the violation of the self is inevitable. Partial knowledge is incomplete and it distorts (bias).

Cybertechnologies have exposed the myth of 'pure sociality' and, instead, reveal the multiplicity of associations between human and non-human entities. This means that 'humanism' (or at least its modernist variant) can no longer claim a hegemonic ground in terms of ethics and politics. Ethics now also need to pay attention to other normativities, namely those associated with technologies and animals. Indeed, from the start modern humanism was itself already a technological enframing, based on the denial of alterity and the imposition of the primacy of the idea of the human. However, the other, the inhuman as Lyotard (1991) calls it, is already within; it constitutes the human.

What Haraway originally referred to as the cyborg, that is a form of human being that is integrated with technological mediation, becomes a 'modest witness' in her later work (Haraway 1997). The modest witness is a technologically integrated and genetically manipulated 'information processing unit'; part digital code, part DNA. It exists as a nodal point, connecting a range of (electronic and bio-molecular) networks and flows. The modest witness collects and gathers information and reprocesses these. This reprocessing is what she calls 'diffraction'.

Diffractions are a key part of visual culture and deeply intertwined with photography and the logic of exposure. It is about the process of capturing the slight variations in repetitions that constitute the 'movement-image' of time (Fuller 2005). It is an invitation to meditate on the logical gap between chronology (narrative) and exposure (photography). Visual culture is now determined by overexposure and it has enabled cultural research itself to become an interference, a poetic distortion of the technological enframing of visual technologies; it is a form of writing, of making sense, that intervenes in the technological enframing, to distort its distortions and challenge its ordering. This resonates Benjamin's point on mechanical reproduction, but this time the loss of aura is no longer obscured, but instead (over)exposed.

Conclusion

In this chapter we have discussed the work of some (cyber)feminism in relation to questions over the nature of technological embodiment and mediation. Feminist media analysis is a well established field within media studies and has made particularly strong contributions to understanding the nature of representations, the active role of audiences and consumers, as well as the more intricate complexities of processes of domestication. The latter is of significant interest to analysing media-as-technology and ties in well with Chapter 3 of this book in relation to understanding the role of binding-use.

By focusing on one specific debate, i.e., pornography, which has arguable been the most contentious domain of media studies, it became clear that to be able to move beyond the immediate politics of taste and ethics, we needed to deepen an understanding of some of the more fundamental ontological aspects of feminism as a theoretical and philosophical endeavour (alongside a political one). That is to say, a glaring omission in the mainstay of the pornography debate is a lack of concern over pornography as a cultural industry and as a technology of mediation. By separating media in terms of form and content, it seemed as if feminist media analysis could be safely relegated to content studies only, leaving the gendered nature of technology dangerously exposed to flawed and inherently universalist gender-blind (masculinist) mystification.

It is for that reason that the second half of the chapter looked more specifically at the works of Plant, Hayles and Haraway, as these thinkers have generated important questions about how we could conceptualize the technological nature of gendered embodiment. In contrast to the more identity-politically-orientated mainstream feminists, these feminists have suggested that a stronger political motive for feminism may lie in a conceptualization of a post-gendered, post-human subjectivity, which does not negate the difference within, but abandons the *prima-facie* postulate that the integral, homologous (isomorphic) human body (whether male or female), is the *only* viable and legitimate source of emancipatory politics.

Yet, the importance of embodiment for understanding mediation seems to be annihilated by the very thesis of disembodiment at the heart of cyberfeminism and other forms of post-humanism. However, in this chapter, I have argued otherwise and attempted to show that just because we can expose the notion of a self-contained, integral homologous body to be a myth of liberal individualism that serves a world view sustained by print and materialized by capitalism, does not mean that embodiment does not matter. It simply means that we should understand it as an *effect*, rather than precondition, of our mediated being. As an effect it is, thus, also susceptible to transformation.

I hope to have shown that feminist analyses of media technology go well beyond a critique of male dominated media ownership, content and use, but have a far more profound intellectual calling: to problematize the way we think about the relationship between mediation and embodiment. By systematically calling on the primacy of gender difference it constantly reminds us that processes of mediation may appear to be disembodied, they never really are. Embodiment is the grounding of mediation and ensures that mediation never completely collapses into pure simulation.

The chapter integrated these presuppositions with issues over how we might develop a feminist critique of mediation that does not simply call on either an inversion or on Manichean dualisms (e.g., of good versus bad, i.e., porn for women or porn for men). If we are to see how the context (e.g., as mainly controlled by men) and content (as serving the needs and desires of men) of mediation are connected, we need to focus on the process of mediation as both intentionalism and structuralism fail to provide adequate answers. This, in turn, asked – once again – that we take a closer look at the technological embedding of mediation.

This technological embedding in turn demanded that we consider four aspects: its *form* (e.g., the structuring of the 'male gaze' in pornographic imagery); its *historicity* (e.g., the structuring of pornography as part of the cultural industries), its *cultural embedding* (e.g., the way in which it serves as an engineering and manipulation of needs), and its *embodiment* (e.g., the way in which it appeals to consumption as equivalent to sex, thereby obliterating the difference between desire and objectification). The formation of the male gaze, already explored in the case study of pornography, could also be explored as a consequence of mediated embodiment, one that affirms the 'devil's trick' of the primacy of the individual as the autonomous and private location of semiosis. This assumed primacy of the individual will be critically explored in the next chapter.

Suggested further reading

Church Gibson, P. (ed.) (2004) *More Dirty Looks: Gender, Pornography and Power*. London: BFI.
> A collection of essays addressing the various ways in which the pornography issue has affected critical scholarship and, in particular, feminism.

Cockburn, C. and Fürst- Dilic, R. (eds) (1994) *Bringing Technology Home. Gender and Technology in a Changing Europe*. Buckingham: Open University Press.
> A collection of essays about the gender implications of the domestication of various technologies in everyday household settings.

Gray, A. (1992) *Video Playtime. The Gendering of a Leisure Technology*. London: Routledge.
> This book discusses the experiences of women using VCRs and the social and cultural background to ownership.

Haraway, D. (1991) *Simians, Cyborgs and Women*. London: Free Association Books.
> A collection of Haraway's key essays from the 1980s.

van Zoonen, L. (1994) *Feminist Media Studies*. London: Sage.
One of the first comprehensive overviews of feminist media scholarship.

Wajcman, J. (2004) *Technofeminism*. Cambridge: Polity Press.
> An argument about how technological development is affecting how women think from the point of view that this is primarily the consequence of feminist politics rather than the technology itself.

5 | NEW MEDIA AND NETWORKED (DIS)EMBODIMENT

> This absolute limit is where the history of communication technologies will liter-
> ally come to an end. Theoretically there remains only the question as to what logic
> this completion will have obeyed. From Freud to McLuhan, the classic answer to
> this was a generic subject – humanity which before of an indifferent or interferent
> natural would have externalised first its motor and sensory interface, and finally
> its intelligence, in technical prosthetics . . . Without reference to the individual or
> to mankind, communication technologies will have overhauled each other until
> finally an artificial intelligence proceeds to the interception of possible intelligences
> in space. (Kittler 1996)

It is hard to overestimate the dramatic impact of electronic communication on modern culture. We now expect everything to be turned on or off instantly, with the push
of a button. Albeit somewhat exaggerated, this is evident from how we reveal the world
to our toddlers. Teletubbies, Engie Benji and Micky Mouse Clubhouse are just three
examples of television programmes aimed at the youngest viewers, which are marked
by a fantasy world in which pressing buttons inevitably results into 'things happening'.
Although things do not always happen as expected (which is particularly the case in
Engie Benji), the main idea is that the protagonists of our toddlers' televisual world are
surrounded by convenience in the form of 'black boxes' producing foods (such as tubby
toast and tubby custard), opening doors and performing other 'magical' tasks. (Indeed,
as J.R.R. Tolkien warned in a letter to Milton Waldman in 1951, there is no distinction
between modern technology and magic.)

This chapter explores what it means to 'be virtual'. It will argue that electronic
media have altered how we operate as human beings, both in terms of our social
relationships, as well as in how we perceive and sense time and space. Electronic
mediation engages us in a process of 'partial disembodiment', and this in turn creates

anxieties about the boundaries and integrity of our being. It will explore in some detail how virtuality and networked (partially disembodied) being are intertwined. More specifically, it uses Actor Network Theory (ANT) to analyse the empirical nature of mediation. Particular attention will be paid to the concept of *transduction* as it helps to explain how forms of mediation engage human existence in transformations (Mackenzie 2002). Throughout the chapter these issues will be illustrated by examples of 'virtual being', with a specific reference to 'multi-userdungeons' (MUDs) such as *Second Life* and gaming platforms such as *Runescape*.

Electronic communication media

Electronic communication entailed an overcoming of the relatively fixed relationship between space and time. The first electronic communications medium, the telegraph, already produced a nearly infinite speeding-up of data transmission. This immense acceleration had as a consequence that the linear mode of thought, which is endemic to print culture (see Chapter 2), was being disrupted with the *instantaneity* and *simultaneity* of multiple data flows (the elusive escape velocity of 'seeing time' or the instant-all-at-once-ness). The matter of electronic communication is a rather different kind of materiality than paper; it consists if electrons that in themselves have no real concrete presence, but an abstracted one (Negroponte 1995).

Electronic mediation has enabled a convergence between different types of mediation, particularly visual, aural and tactile. With the arrival of computing this was furthermore extended to forms of data transmission and archiving, which in turn have enabled a greater convergence between data processing and telecommunication (Kittler 1997; Manovitch 2001). This is really what defines the world we inhabit today, a radical rupture between molecular matter that is confined to spatio-temporal specificity and digital, electronic 'matter' whose spatio-temporal configurations are remarkably fluid and adaptable.

This, in turn, deeply affected the nature of 'sociality' or better 'associations' (Latour 2005). It is not that digital technologies themselves change anything on their own, but if we accept that all forms of sociation are by their very nature mediated, then changes in mediation, and especially the *modalities* of mediation, are also likely to affect the *modalities* of association (Wittel 2000). As a reminder of the introduction, association is simply used here as a means to label forms of interaction geared towards establishing or maintaining relationships, or 'ties' between people. In other words, association informs processes of attunement of people (or better, actors) to each other, forms of collaboration, mutual dependency, reciprocity, solidarity, friendship, love, hate, etc. Association is therefore a key element of 'public life' and includes market transactions, law enforcements, institutional procedures, etc. Association also plays an important part in all forms of organization.

This concern with association should be read alongside the previous chapter in which we looked at feminist critiques of technological embodiment. Whereas Chapter 4 geared its concerns over embodiment more directly to issues of (gendered) subjectivity and identity, this chapter shifts to what in a previous area was known as 'intersubjectivity' (Crossley 1996). That is, it questions the often taken-for-granted dichotomy between embodiment and what is often sloppily referred to as sociality, with the first being associated with the interiority of the unit of 'self-hood' and the latter with its (performative) 'exteriority'. As society itself is now articulating a greater awareness of prosthesis and assemblage, the nature of mediation is changing accordingly. The emergent non-linear conception of mediation posits that all forms of mediation are characterized by iterations between embodiment and disembodiment and this iteration can be described as *'the virtual'* (thus entailing a multiplicity of possible actualities). The basic premise of this argument is that whereas the virtual has always been here (Shields 2003), it is only with the onset of digital mediation that 'we' (and not just academics) have been actively invited to reflect on its ontology.

The mass rally

The impact of information and communication technologies, on the ways in which people organize their work and conduct their business, has become a growing field of concern for social scientists and business engineers (de Kerckhove 1996; Jacobs and Yudken 2003). Often, especially outside the social sciences and humanities, such concerns are placed in an optimistic spirit, in which new opportunities open up for organizations to capitalize on the possibilities of increased density, velocity and scope of information flows (Kelly 1998; Florida 2002; Hartley 2004). Issues raised deal with the need to secure a competitive edge and stay 'ahead of the game'. This is certainly also the case for many media organizations who, after the explosive growth of the Internet, have nearly all attempted to branch out into on-line communications and media productions, albeit some with more success than others (Dyer-Witheford 2002).

However, we can also discern a more pessimistic and even nostalgic ambience among theorists and philosophers. For these groups, the critical ethos is that of 'lament'. In this ethos, new media developments generate the loss of self-hood, sociability and communal solidarity, and thus a technocratic world increasingly eroded of human significance. Such a critical ethos of lament posits that the worlds created by digital technologies (often also, but misleading dubbed 'the virtual') are at best an annoying (or perhaps sad?) distraction or at worst a dangerous manipulation of not just our social environment but the very human condition to which we hold so dearly.

Baudrillard (1993), for example, exhumes the spirit of the latter as he seems to condemn all forms of mass mediation for being non-communicative, i.e., non-sociable. It is as if the danger lies in the nature of the technological medium itself. Indeed, this would mean that it is the technological formatting of mediated communication itself that prevents actual communication as a process of sociable, shared involvement.

Setting aside a possible failure to appreciate the deliberately performative subtleties of Baudrillard's critique (Merrin 2005), one could argue that such a view is too essentialist and, indeed, risks becoming another version of technological determinism. It cannot be the *form* of mediation *on its own* that establishes whether association is possible or not. Indeed, it could be argued that many forms of mediated interaction are forms of sociation (as bindings use and know-how).

However, Baudrillard's issue may be more with the prefix 'mass', however, and in that respect he may have a valid point. How does one engage associations with a 'mass'? This, of course, was a central question to Marxism and defined its pedagogical project of propaganda. It equally became a key concern for psychology (Le Bon 1896), psychoanalysis (Freud 1989) and for radical historians, such as Elias Cannetti (1962). It is also of central concern to those who seek to use print, radio or television to convert large numbers of people, i.e., the practitioners of propaganda or what is better known as 'public relations' (Ellul 1965).

The mass rally is an interesting phenomenon in this respect. Here, we have a crowd, gathered in one place, to be in the presence of someone, something or some event. When one extrapolates this to a mass mediated event in print, one immediately loses the notion of spatio-temporal copresence. The mass readership becomes a simulated rally, the 'real presence' of the person or event becomes a pseudo-presence. The mass becomes dispersed and individuated. Although broadcasting has enabled a far closer account of a simulated mass rally (e.g., Hitler's live radio broadcasts), this only extends to a temporal sense of copresentness, rather than the fullness of presence one encounters in non mass mediated rallies.

Perhaps, then, it is the combination of mass and mediation that works against association. Even if this is only conditionally or partially true, then it means that in our world of excessive electronic 'mass' communication, we might find that there is a deficit in terms of modalities of association. It does, however, require some more critical reflection. After all, although the net can be and is being used for broadcasting, many digital forms of mediation are not really 'mass' mediation in the traditional sense. Their 'mass' comes instead from a gathering of many, far more localized, inter-active encounters between mediators: many-to-few (this is what data-aggregators encounter) few-to-few (email, SMS, mobile telephony) and many-to-many (e.g., chat rooms, multi-user dungeons, multi-user gaming platforms), rather than just few-to-many (broadcasting). The latter however, also exist, e.g., weblogs, commercial websites, corporate websites, etc.

It should be clear by now, however, that the analysis presented in this book neither supports the facile celebration nor the full-blown condemnation of a new media-based society, just as it refutes the strong versions of both technological and social determinism. Instead, it aims to cultivate a more sophisticated but critical appreciation of the close and in some instances symbiotic relationships between human-technological *interfaciality* and evolving media-ecologies.

This chapter argues that 'the human' should not be conceived as an integral entity, bound by the flesh of the body, but instead as an open system, a network, or even better, an 'assemblage', imbued with particular values, which has a seemingly infinite capacity to adapt to changing conditions and uncertainty. Hence, it will not be a celebration of the post-human either (as this assumes a concept of the human as an organic entity that coincides with 'the body'). Instead, the question of 'what is human?' will be revisited in the light of contemporary theories that have focused on the impact of the digital revolution on both human subjects and social forms. It will then also develop a few pointers towards developing a more fully integrated framework of 'media theory' that is no longer separate from the major current philosophical debates about technology.

Telematics and disorientation

Media-technologies are operative in the most banal and mundane practices of everyday life; and they affect us all. Hence, it is not the 'mass media' or 'private communication media' on their own that have produced this effect, but their various combinations. The linking has been further enhanced by digitalization which has enabled mediation to become basically another form of information processing, and furthermore by cable-wiring and satellite transmission, which have effectively enabled a world wide integration of telecommunication and data processing, i.e., telematics.

Telematics have vastly transformed the world. First, there has been an enormous increase in our capacity to transcend the physical limitations of space. Indeed, globalization is no longer an abstraction, but a 'fact of life' (Beck 1998); as those who are well connected to telecommunications media can have instant communication with almost any part of the globe. This transformation becomes more apparent when we consider the social forms in which humans exist and give meaning to their being as humans. John B. Thompson (1995: 4), for example, has asserted that:

> In a fundamental way, the use of electronic media transforms the spatial and temporal organization of social life, creating new forms of action and interaction, and new modes of exercising power, which are no longer linked to the sharing of a common locale.

Second, and as a logical consequence of the above, the sense of what it is to be human has changed dramatically as well (Hayles 1999). A human being 'wired up' to global telematics is a rather different organism than a human being that is not connected. The human being, as a social animal, adapts to telematics by adopting different modalities and techniques of association. Moreover, as telematics have changed the nature of our spatial and temporal orientation to the world, this will also affect how we perceive, think and make sense (de Kerckhove 1996; Fuller 2005).

In a world of telematics, the emergent form is that of a 'networked being'. The nature of networked being contains a radically different understanding of 'presence'. It is no longer dominated by the 'face-to-face' encounter, but engages in a 'simultaneity of presences' (a simplistic example of which is the 'telephone conference'), which – when spatialized – entails what Helga Nowotny (1994) has referred to as an 'extended presence'. The extended presence is really a multiplicity of presences that create what McLuhan and Fiore (1967) termed an 'all-at-once-ness'. This is today better known as 'the virtual'.

In such an imagined, virtual, presence, we find it increasingly difficult to locate ourselves as a discrete singularity in space and time. We face constant flows of displacement and desynchronization; and this creates a sense of perpetual disorientation. The combination of instant communication, rapid travel and more volatile interactions between 'microcosmic' (molecular, submolecular) and 'macrocosmic' (global) flows (e.g., HIV/AIDS), have destabilized our orientation to 'the present', manifesting itself, for example, in ubiquitous risk sensibilities (Beck 1997; Van Loon 2002). Indeed, infectious diseases, for instance, can now easily outpace quarantine and – by means of global flows – become 'globally present' almost instantaneously (as the case of SARS has shown us).

This disorientation, exemplified by the heightened risk sensibilities of those who are well-connected, can also be explained as the consequence of a rupture in embodiment by disembodiment. Networked being is partially disembodied in the sense that the nature of networks defies the principle of integral self-enclosed entities. In a state of partial disembodiment, networked beings cannot but engage in a circumspect orientation towards their environment. The boundaries of their being are blurred. The desire for embodiment, however, remains as modernity continues to impose the need for self-identification (as a consequence of individualization, Giddens 1991; Beck and Beck-Gernsheim 2002). To exist in an extended presence means either to give up on a desire for 'wholeness' or to live in a continuous state of anxiety over the possible exposures of a lack of wholeness.

Cyberspace and the interface

McLuhan (1964) consistently reminded us that media are extensions of human faculties and this provides the basis of his phenomenological excursions into analysing different types of media-forms. In this sense, we should perhaps pause for a moment and think about what this 'extension' entails, phenomenologically. First, extension relates to space. By extending human faculties, media spatialize human being as 'being *there*' and particularly the 'there' becomes an extended simultaneous 'networked' presence. Second, extension relates to time, in *being* there becomes 'prolonged' (an extended 'present'). Yet, at the same time, the extensions of human faculties produce increased immediacy and instantaneity. The 'extended present' enables greater synchronization between different flows; hence, McLuhan's concept of 'all-at-once-ness'.

The focus on space and time allows for a more situational specific understanding of mediation. It also allows us to extend concerns over identification and embodiment in media processes with notions of 'movement', 'speed' and 'intensity' that cannot be analysed at the level of 'individual bodies', but force us to take into account the relational-contextual framework of networks.

ICTs involved in realising the Internet have allowed individuals from across the world to hook up to a globally connected network of interactions. The inherent qualities of this system are its diffused, decentralized and non-regulated nature (Castells 1996; Rheingold 2000; Rifkin 2000; Poster 2001). Of course, there have always been attempts to control, centralize and regulate the Internet, but they have thus far continuously and systematically failed to maintain a stronghold of the enclosures of the sprawling digital world, as the net is deliberately designed to bypass the principle of central control (Loader 1997; Elmer 2002). The state system, with its reliance on discursive forms, such as the law, is simply not equipped to deal with the technological challenges imposed by these ICTs.

Brian Martin-Murphy's (2002) critical analysis of the history of the Internet shows that – as with every new technology, especially in the realm of communications – its origins and developments are uneven and diverse. In distinguishing between state, commercial and civic domains (he also adds social movements but they are clearly inseparable from the civic), he points out how a new medium, such as the Internet, contained a whole series of possibilities, opportunities and potentialities, which subsequently evolved into a range of incompatible development strategies.

Moreover, his analysis shows that the Internet owes as much to its military potentiality (and not just the US army's ARPANET) as it does to capitalism. Crucial, however, is that within the state itself, there have been conflicting forces – some driven by concerns over security, some by concerns over freedom of speech and the democratic process, and again others by the possibilities for commercial exploitation. That is, when we are referring to the role of the state in developing specific media-technologies, we should not assume that the state operates as a singular, unitary actor. Instead, it is itself often internally divided. Internet researchers therefore frequently call for more critical empirical analyses to look not only at the motives of those involved in new media technology development and use, but also at the structural contexts within which new media are designed and destined to operate.

One domain Internet research has been quite well established concerns the social interactive forms that new media enable. More specifically, research has focused on issues of identification, sociation and community-formation (Shields 1996; Bakardjieva 2005). The key question here is how humans and new media connect; that is, what is the nature of their interfaciality?

Interfaciality and identification: the case of cyber rape

With interfacially mediated forms of embodiment, we clearly encounter the problematic of identification in a way that traditional sociology and psychology could not have imagined. In cyberspace, 'one' occupies multiple locations at once. 'One' is invited to change identities with every change in connection. 'One' may engage in simulated sex, virtual communities and semiotic reincarnations without ever having to leave one's chair behind the screen. The combination of visual (eyes@screen) and tactile (fingers@keyboard) senses have made participation on the Internet a totally embodied experience (Bakardjieva 2005). However, existence always entails a mode of virtuality which grants it the potential of even being 'better than the real thing'. One cannot contract HIV from virtual sex, but one can contract a computer virus, trojan horse or worm (Lundell 1989; Van Loon 2002). One cannot be physically or sexually abused on the net, although one can be virtually raped or even killed (Dibbel 2001).

Julian Dibbel's (2001) analysis of a rape in cyberspace shows the peculiar nature of 'reality' in an on-line virtual environment. The rape (actually it involved two cases) was committed by an avatar called 'Evil Clown' on a MUD (multi-user dungeon) called LambdaMOO. It is an example of the way in which the virtual manifests itself as both a form of embodiment and disembodiment and it testifies to the radical disorientation that follows from that. In a networked being, where does a body stop being a body?

This is not just an academic question. For victims of cyber rape, these are pertinent issues that at the heart of concerns over embodied integrity, autonomy and entitlements to self-hood. In everyday language, most people use the term 'virtual' as the opposite of real (Virtual Reality or *Second Life* versus Real Life), but the issue of rape shows that there is perhaps little distinction – at least in terms of the psychological damage inflicted – between virtual reality rape and real life rape. The victims of Evil Clown experienced this violation as more than 'mere hypothetical'; their own virtual beings were being violated in the form of simulations. It is already widely accepted by many legal systems in the world that symbolic violence can be legally constituted as causing harm. Threats and verbal abuse, for example, are seen as 'real enough' in legal terms to warrant prosecution if there is sufficient evidence and the cases are extreme enough. Several European countries are now investigating whether forms of symbolic violence, and in particular those of a sexual nature (cyber rape), can be prosecuted if they are committed in multi-user virtual environments, such as *Second Life* (*Sunday Times*, 13 May 2007, p. 10).

Equally important is that Dibbel also shows how the idea of 'community' cannot simply be presupposed, but has to be seen as related to 'action' – it was only because they were actively constituting themselves as a community that the people of LambdaMOO were able to call themselves a community (also see Bromberg 1996). The two things, the virtual nature of social interaction and the constitution of a community, are closely interlinked. Not only did the community effectively come into being through its attempt to deal with the rape, but it was only able to imagine itself *as* a community in the light of the opening up of the question of mediated being. The fact that the community opted to condemn the Evil Clown and to excommunicate him, which is virtually the same as a death sentence, affirmed that the community defined its own virtual realm in very similar terms to what they perceived to be the non-virtual realm of off-line being.

The question remains whether the ghost of the Evil Clown is still haunting LambdaMOO. Dibbel suggests that he is and thus suggests a rather weird twist, namely that the virtual is capable of begetting its own gradations of virtuality within. Shields (2003) has argued that virtuality is not the same as not-real. The opposition between the 'virtual as not-real' and 'the not-virtual as real' is merely a heuristic device that we deploy because we are forgetting that in order to become meaningful, every reality is already mediated. Although it can contain and accommodate fantastical elements, the virtual does not equal pure imagination. Neither can the virtual be defined as that which is not real, nor can the real be defined as that which is not virtual.

The example of rape on the Internet shows this. In pure imagination, the Evil Clown would just be a fictitious creation in someone's rape fantasy. The rape would have been invoked by the victim on her own, as the effect of an application of thought out of her own volition. (This does not mean such imaginations cannot take on the form of external realities, e.g., the phenomenon of addiction provides a clear example where an exteriority starts to impose itself while having been initially inaugurated by the free will of the victim.) Instead, in this particular MUD, the Evil Clown was an exteriority to the imagination; the violation was not imagined, it was enacted in the virtual-social domain of the MUD. The Evil Clown imposed himself, even if only in the form of an avatar (pixel) or a text, and this imposition was experienced as a violation.

Virtual being

As most users of MUDs and multi-user role-play gaming (RPG) platforms will know, one of the great attractions of such on-line events is that they allow one to play with different identities, doubling or even tripling the subjectivities of the disembodied pixel-person (avatar), the self-confessed 'real persona' behind it, and the physical, embodied wired-up person actually enacting both. They enable players to construct elaborate 'fantasy worlds', which are not exclusively controlled by their own imagination, but emerge spontaneously, intersubjectively and with a sense of exteriority that we could call 'virtually real'.

In other words, players depend on each other to construct a triple-layered virtuality as an imagined continuum. My own experience on such platforms is that on many occasions, deliberate conflations are being made between the various layers of virtuality, sometimes also leading to confusion, requiring players to 'step out' of the game and ask about the ontological status of particular statements. There are also instances in which players seem to forget the differences between layers, as has been the case in players confessing to have fallen in love with the avatars themselves.

Playing across these layers of identification, however, is also a great source of pleasure and fun; it provides an excellent opportunity for 'live theatre' (role-playing), in which self-confessed escapism is seen as an antidote against a permanently disappointing reality. This pleasure often does not require one to radically change identities, but simply to create an imagined world with others that is better than the real thing. The pleasure of multiplying identities in RPGs is perhaps even greater when the shifts between the layers are not large, but only subtle, as they can facilitate the actual function of escapism much more effectively, one does not need to pretend to be someone else; one can simple enact a more idealized version of oneself.

It is clear, therefore, that even in the more fantastical elements of virtual reality, mediated being is neither meaningless nor inconsequential. People do experience real pleasure and real pain in virtual worlds, especially in multi-user virtualities, because the enactment of exteriority is never subordinated to the imagination of one player (Argyle 1996). You will have to take the actions of others into account. It is the relay between the three layers of the avatar (representational person), persona (confessional person) and player (acting person) that grants the virtuality of MUDs its distinctive status as neither purely real nor purely imaginary (both, in a way are not that different; both do not really exist but are heuristic devices of binary thinking).

It is therefore wrong to assume that virtuality is meaningless. On the net, electronic intensities work through bodies, connecting the world of meat and chemical currents with that of electronic currents. The differences between 'neurons' and 'chips' are not clear cut. Both are information processing devices that operate independently of a central controlling apparatus. In other words, while being a totally embodied experience, the Internet is just as well a totally disembodied experience. One's presence on the net is always and exclusively virtual.

The social form that accompanies the Internet ICTs is an ambiguous hybrid of individualism and tribalism. The Internet invites tribal formations (e.g., using MySpace.com to set up friendship networks), but the agnatic solidarity upon which these are being engendered, is not derived from a shared ethnic origin or destiny. In this sense, the aesthetic appeal of belonging to a virtual community is a totally individuated experience (Rheingold 2000). The image of a lone cybercowboy, working from a dark attic, operating in isolation from the public sphere, totally hidden from the controlling gaze of the *socius*, is the mythical icon that signifies this symbolic association between individuation and electronic communication. The image is, however, far from that of the typical 'user' (Gauntlett and Horsely 2004; Bakardjieva 2005).

However, because 'one' is forced to occupy an ensemble of simultaneous, multiplied locations and identifications, the 'individual' is always already divided. Its presence is at once 'behind' and 'on' the screen and 'in between'; its being is at once embodied and disembodied. To use the conceptual frame initially developed by George Herbert Mead (1934), the semiotic 'I' of the 'self' is already 'othered' by its counterpart: that which it stands for ('me'). Time-space parameters collapse into a World Wide Web of lines and connections: information disseminated, stored, retrieved, deleted, does not allow for a wholeness of 'one' being. The integrity of a cyberpunk is always already violated by the machine that allows her/him to exist (Featherstone and Burrows

1996). Individuality is a myth that can only be sustained in a none or atemporal universe.

Indeed, the very originating myth of the individual subject, the prisoner in Plato's cave who frees himself from the chains of delusion (the shadows on the wall) and dares to face the bright light of pure ideas, is already divided between mind and body. In other words, while the collapse of the individual cannot be attributed to the Internet, as it has been a founding myth of the entire western metaphysical tradition, it could be argued that ICTs have intensified the implosion of that mythical figure, by pointing backwards to that which was always already part of the myth, albeit under erasure.

Electronic mediation does not support self-standing individuality because it is primarily a tactile form of engagement with the world. McLuhan (1964) wrote about electronic media as extensions of our central nervous system. In this sense, it externalizes our being in every modality of encountering the worlds we inhabit, that is in terms of affect, intuition and cognition.

Touch

> It is a principal aspect of the electric age that it establishes a global network that has much of the character of our central nervous system. Our central nervous system is not merely an electric network, but it constitutes a single unified field of experience. As biologists point out, the brain is the interacting place where all kinds of impressions and experiences can be exchanged and translated, enabling us to *react to the world as a whole*. (McLuhan 1964: 302)

McLuhan's perspective on television is particularly deemed deeply offensive to the dominant streams of media analysis because he refuses to place television under the heading of 'visual media'. Instead, he insisted in *Understanding Media* (1964) that the essence of television is related to that of electricity and the essence of electricity is tactile. Hence, the 'timid giant' as he nicknamed television, was an extension of our central nervous system. In this respect, it shares some of its origins with the telephone and telegraph as two earlier electronic media that were designed to keep people 'in touch', rather than say film, which – being based on a rolling wheel and the analogue that is 'chemical' mechanisms of photography – had, indeed, a far more visual embodiment which was also associated with *movement* and, as Deleuze (1986, 1989) has shown so well, time.

In this sense, the first thing to note about the arrival of digital technology is that it follows the same logic of television, it works on the basis of electricity and 'light-through' modes of visualization (whereas film and photography are 'light-on' media). For McLuhan, television amplified acoustic space (the message of television is in this sense the medium of radio). Amplification is the first of the four laws of media as part of McLuhan's tetrad (see Chapter 2).

The second law of media refers to obsolescence. The history of digital media has shown a remarkable series of media becoming obsolete (e.g., the floppy disk is a great example), while very few of them actually disappeared (e.g., some mainframes still exist and are being used). Becoming obsolete is not the same as disappearing. The fax machine has been made relatively obsolete by the scanner and above all by email, but it still exists. Its role in the network of media systems has been changed into a marginal one.

At the same time, the acoustic all-at-once-ness that marked face-to-face communication has been retrieved. Bolter and Grusin (2000) are right to stress this as an illustration of the fact that all forms of remediation entail a desire for immediacy, as well as hypermediation. The desire to replicate the communal campfire of face-to-face interactions, which enabled prewriting tribal life, reverberates through a massive explosion of media, such as webcams, videoconferencing and mobile Internet telephony. What is being retrieved more specifically is 'the visual'. As Bolter and Grusin (2000) have shown, digital photography entails a remediation of the photographic image, by enabling a combination of the analogous 'chemical' appropriation of light, with the electronic processing of digit flows. Keeping in touch (e.g., as evidenced in the slogans of communication businesses, such as Nokia and Toucan) as become quite literally keeping in touch.

This keeping in touch can be further explored as a system of associations between various actors (human-technological interfaciality). This system of associations is more commonly referred to as a 'network'.

Media as actor networks

> I have sought to offer humanists a detailed analysis of a technology sufficiently magnificent and spiritual to convince them that the machines by which they are surrounded are cultural objects worthy of their attention and respect. They'll find that if they add interpretation of machines to interpretations of texts, their culture will not fall to pieces; instead it will take on an added density. (Latour 1996: viii)

Empirical work in media studies has primarily concentrated on media industries, audiences and texts. Comparatively little empirical work has been directed at understanding processes of mediation. More specifically, it is quite remarkable that media-analyses have not received the same kind of attention that, for example, science and technology have had (in Science and Technology Studies (STS) and its predecessor, the sociology of scientific knowledge). This is the more remarkable since media and technoscience have so much in common (Couldry forthcoming; Hemmingway 2007). In this section, I will explore how one particular version of STS, namely Actor Network Theory (ANT), can help us understand in far greater detail, the empirical relevance of media technology.

Actor Network Theory (ANT) is a specific variation of STS and is primarily based on assumption that 'reality' as we encounter it, is the product of complex interactions between human and non-human actors (e.g., technologies and artefacts). These actors form associations through which certain sensibilities (one might say relationships between forms of embodiment and disembodiment) become stabilized and 'taken-for-granted' so that actors can get 'on with their job' (Latour 1987, 1988b). The concept of network is just an effective means to help us think of human-technological connectivities, convergences and interfaces. It is a more empirical way to conceptualize what was referred to before as 'networked being'.

The primary focus of ANT is on understanding patterns of 'ordering', which we recognize as 'structures' or 'organizations' of ideas and matter without relying on an *a priori* dualism of subjects and objects. To put it bluntly, the key question is how order comes into being? ANT does not presuppose that order, or perhaps better continuity, is a reflection of some reality 'out there', but instead that it is the consequence (a construction) of a (temporary) stabilization of a particular set of forces that can be conceptualised as a *network*. This stabilization is achieved by a temporary closure of possibilities and is highly dependent on the density of the mesh, and thus on the strength of the links and the connectedness of the different nodes (Van Loon 2006).

Rather than focusing on network-as-structures, ANT shifts attention to network*ing* as a continuous practice of enrolment, translation and redefinition. ANT is concerned with analysing action. That is to say, it provides a radical departure from social science approaches that seek to explain social behaviour on the basis of beliefs or opinions. This means that ANT steers analyses towards practical observations, rather than critiques of intentions and motives (beliefs and opinions), and when applying this to media, it means that it is primarily geared to exploring the *significance* of mediation-as-action. This is why it is often seen as a strong theoretical advocacy of ethnographic approaches.

Analysing mediation as action

As one of the early thinkers in this tradition, the French sociologist Bruno Latour, developed a highly influential approach to analysing scientific practices (Latour 1987). As stated, action is different from behaviour in that it focuses more exclusively on what is being revealed by 'doing', rather than what motivates this 'doing' (in terms of 'reasons', 'beliefs' or 'attitudes').

The focus on action asks 'what is brought about by doing?' The performative aspect of action is that it affects relationships between actors; it is through this 'affect' that actions order the particular sociotechnical constellations that uphold a sense of 'order'. Action never takes place in isolation, but through a series of connected points. This is what is referred to as 'actor-networks'. Hence, to understand the nature and impact of certain actions, one must map the networks through which these actions are established. This in turn, however, is only possible by observing how the actions themselves affect networked relationships.

Actors can be humans, animals, technologies, angels and gods. That is, the nature of an actor is not predefined, it is simply linked to the capacity to act, which in turn solely depends on whether the impact of its actions has consequences for other actors. Action is thus not tied to intentionality. In this sense it is radically different from ordinary sociological concepts of behaviour (Parsons 1968).

Applying ANT to media analysis enables us to engage on a more ontological level with the very issue of mediation, in close proximity to other thinkers discussed in previous chapters, such as McLuhan, Benjamin, Baudrillard and Hayles. It can help us understand how mediation is ontologically embedded in the very nature of being. It is on this basis that we can move to more empirical analyses of what media do and how mediation involves various actors in networked practices.

The centrality of the virtual in Latour's work becomes clear when we consider his radical refutation of the assumption that 'reality' and 'representation' are different. Instead, Latour rejects the special status of 'reason' and posits that reasoning is one force among many others. This is, in itself, not an original starting point. For example, Nietzsche (1992) has made very similar claims in the *Will to Power*. The premise or axiom that is shared by Latour and Nietzsche is that history is in effect merely a play of forces and does not have an overarching meaning. It refutes the idea that history can be understood as a 'meta narrative' (Lyotard 1979), for example, Christianity or Marxism. In service of neither salvation not emancipation, history becomes random, pointless and meaningless. It is for this reason that Latour has often been accused of being rather apolitical and nihilistic.

However, a more careful reading of his philosophical position reveals something else. By stressing the centrality of multiplicity and ambivalence, ANT opens a view of history that is open to 'chance' and thus more 'event-like' than random. It is the event which opens up possibilities for ethical and political intervention. No longer predetermined by hypothetical speculations to serve a foregone conclusion, such interventions become truly political and ethical as they entail the ability to be *affected* ('touched' by the encountering of the world).

Networks consist of multiplicities of associations that shift along with the actions that inaugurate them. In this sense, the happening of a network event is a temporal affirmation of social being formed on the basis of the binding nature of 'affect'. The key lesson from ANT is that actions cannot be reduced to intentions or reasons and therefore should not be analysed on the basis of a fixed theoretical conceptual framework.

Instead, theory should be grounded (as theori*zing*) in empirical observations whose descriptions actors can still recognize as a valid reflection of their actions. In this sense, ANT is diametrically opposed to theoretical approaches that engage in forms of conceptual reductionism, such as structuralism (Levi-Strauss), psychoanalysis (Lacan), functionalism (Parsons), historicism (Foucault) and Marxism. All these approaches seek to reduce phenomena to concepts; to reinscribe a narrative logic onto historical events without due regard for the nature of the events themselves.

Media-analyses have, by and large, been plagued by a similar conceptual reductionism. In the stalemate between political economic, semiotic and audience-orientated analyses, the terms of the debates were too often framed in completely introspective 'media studies' discourse. This created impossible questions, such as whether the text or the audience is sovereign in terms of the creation of meaning, or whether media are mere servants of the dominant ideology. These are impossible questions because they have no grounding in any reality of what media do. Empirical analyses then simply become a sideshow to what are in essence lexicogrammatical and semantic issues. That is to say what media, texts, audiences (or dominant ideologies) does not have a phenomenological grounding and thus remain purely speculative constructions in self-referential discursive strategic moves.

Latour (1988b) deploys what he calls 'the principle of irreducibility' as a means to remind us of the fallacy of conflating phenomena to concepts. His proposed 'ethnographic philosophy' (my term not his), is thus an attempt to refocus an analytical logic away from metaphysical assumptions (for example, about human nature) and onto the event of analysis itself. The principle of irreducibility means that what we call 'real' or 'unreal' are only effects of actions by which we put phenomena on trial (that is, phenomena become events). Following the logic that action is what is brought about through force, it follows that 'the reality of a phenomenon is always tried by its strengths and weaknesses'. Indeed, it is on this basis that Latour posits that reality stems from resistance to trials.

Our ability to manipulate phenomena through trials, thus creates a sense of 'non-reality'. That is, if the environment we encounter seems to be completely modifiable at will, our experience of it is that of imagination or fantasy, rather than 'reality'. This is what empowers virtuality. The degree to which the virtual comes across as 'real' depends on the extent to which it is able to impose itself upon its users as an external force. In this sense, 'knowing reality' stems from the experience of resistance to trials. Latour was mainly referring to technoscience, however, it is not difficult to see how media-technologies are not radically different. Media also put reality on trial. Such trials can be understood as forms if mediation that seek to 'pass on' something for something else. That is to represent reality.

Representation and re-presentation

However, at the same time, media-technologies cannot but 're-present' this reality in a mediated form while maintaining that this representation is an unmediated reality, i.e., as if it speaks for itself. The thematic of representation and 're-presentation' is a relatively recent innovation within Latour's (1998, 2005) thinking. His concern with representation has emerged from a reconsideration of the role of religion as a different set of practices from science and art. This can be used effectively to illustrate different dimensions of mediation practices.

Representation is central to the logic of science and empiricism. It is when communication is a form of transmission. This links to what Bolter and Grusin (2000) call the desire for immediacy, i.e., when media attempt to enact mediations as if they reveal themselves without being mediated. This is the underlying force of 'news': to create an immediate presence in which the medium (the intermediary) becomes completely obsolete at the same time it becomes ubiquitous. The logic of news (and of science) is simply to 'present facts' [Allan (1995) called this 'the will to facticity'].

In contrast, representation is the logic of religion; in which communication is a ritual. In religious practices, media are not intermediaries but mediators; the media such as the priest, the liturgy of the word and of the Eucharist, all work together to establish, again and again, the physical ('real') presence of the religious message. The medium never becomes obsolete; the medium becomes the message. In Bolter and Grusin's (2000) thesis on remediation, this is called 'hypermediation'. Hypermediation takes place when the medium explicitly becomes the message. Mediation becomes ritual and re-establishes symbolic exchange. The key force is not the will to facticity, but what Foucault (1979) once referred as 'the will to truth'.

The crucial thesis, however, is that mediation is both representation and re-presentation. Whereas the will to facticity is inscribed in the technological facilitation of representing the world-as-it-happens, the will-to-truth foregrounds the self-reflexive affirmation of the virtual-as-virtuous. We can now perhaps see why Bolter and Grusin (2000) refer to remediation as both transparency and hypermediation. Mediation is neither science nor religion, but borrows from both; it facilitates both transmission and ritual. News work is perhaps closest to science. The news machine produces representations of world events as if they happened without being mediated. Entertainment is closer to a (albeit completely secularized) religion: the ritualistic self-exposure of media for the sake of exposure.

Transduction

Latour's actor networks seem to be motivated only by the need for self-consolidation and enhancing strength, which they can only acquire in association with others. It is because of digitalization that we are able to see that mediation is not actor-specific. The digital expresses a universality of flow; anything can link to anything through digital interfaces: text, image, sound are all exchangeable as digital data; even the protocols that govern them are digital codes (Kittler 1996). The digital testifies to the validity of Latour's view on how networks acquire strength. Consolidation takes place when many actants engage each other through similar or exchangeable protocols (Galloway 2006; also see Mackenzie 2002; Fuller 2005).

In the age of telematics, mediation takes place in an expansive, intensively connected network of flows. Both human and technological actants (but what is the difference?) are meshed together, as in the triple layered virtualities of MUDs. What such networked constellations are able to achieve is overwhelming. They generate a sense of 'reality' that – because it seems capable of resisting most trials – is indistinguishable from the allegedly non-mediated reality of molecular being.

This is what Adrian Mackenzie (2002) has termed '*transduction*'. Echoing C. S. Peirce (1940) for whom *induction* is when a sense of reality is reconstructed on the basis of experiences and *deduction* is when an understanding of reality is derived from abstract ideas, transduction entails a process by which a specific constellation or form (e.g., a medium) emerges out of a range of heterogeneous sources. Transduction is the emergence of metastability (Mackenzie 2002: 16–7). In biology, it is used to describe 'the event in which a virus carries new genetic material in to DNA' (Mackenzie 2002: 17).

Transduction is thus a process by which mediation transforms the nature of the reality it mediates, often very subtly and unnoticeably. A good example of this would be 'protocol' in machine-machine interfaces (convergence). The protocol is something that initially disparate systems share to be able to converse and then converge. The protocol is immutable, but mobile, but never 'pure'; its codes will often be adapted to whatever situational requirements converging systems impose (Galloway 2006). In this sense, the copresence assumed by such a transduction process is, in fact, an illusion. In technical systems transduction takes place when a particular actor network is capable of infusing its own protocol into the established master protocol governing the existing network. As a result, the system becomes something new (often experienced as metastability). When this happens, the virtual becomes both actual and real, and starts to impose itself upon actants as an external reality.

Kittler (1996) suggests that with digitalization, there has been a convergence between alphabetical and numerical forms of communication; this convergence greatly favours transduction as forms of representation (e.g., electronic writing) can now be automatically transformed into tactile processes (electrical currents) through which technical (mechanical as well as informational) systems cannot only operate without external human intervention, but also engage in learning processes that do not need a preset series of fixed principles (axioms), but instead can learn to learn through fuzzy logic:

> The main point is that transduction aids in tracking processes that come into being at the intersection of diverse realities. These diverse realities include corporeal, geographical, economic, conceptual, human and non-human bodies, images and places. They entail new capacities, relations and practices whose advent is not always easy to recognise. (Mackenzie 2002: 18)

However, and this is crucial, because such closures are accomplished by a complex network of interlinked actants – and the particular protocol that prevails is ultimately still arbitrary and only as strong as the alliance that supports it – such closures are rarely permanent. Instead of an 'order', we have orderings. The virtual remains present at every step of the way and offers itself as a portal where one can switch realities, adopt new protocols, forge new links and destroy old ones. Actor networks are not orders, but exist as degrees of orderings, which themselves are nested within wider patterns or orderings. ANT presupposes that there is never an order emerging from total disorder, there are only degrees of ordering, that is degrees of resistance. This opens up a perspective that gives primacy to shifting patterns rather than fixed establishments. Mediation strongly fits in with such a perspective as it focuses our attention on that which establishes and maintains the connections that are being put on trial.

Mackenzie's concept of transduction strongly resonates with Deleuze's *Difference and Repetition* (1994b), in that it urges us to stop thinking in terms of identity as framed by the opposite of same versus difference; instead we should conceptualize ontology on the basis of *repetition*.

Although Latour does not refer to transduction, his usage of 'translation' seems at first to be remarkably similar. Translation enables a shift from one particular set of operations (that are innate to a specific actor network) to another, quite different one. Translation does not require one to engage with the real/representational in terms of identity and equivalence. Instead, identity and equivalence are merely the laboured accomplishments of translations that have established stable forms maintained by force, for example, in the form of patterns generated by repetition (Latour 1988b: 162).

Latour states that 'a force becomes potent only if it speaks for others' (Latour 1988b: 197). The question we must raise is to what extent the force that 'speaks for' remains the same. That is, the question is how what is 'translating' is being identified. The theory of transduction asserts that when a force makes others speak 'as saying it like its allies would have said' (Latour: 1988b: 197), the force itself is already transformed, by repeating itself through its calling upon others.

Only when we accept a concept of translation as going beyond representation can we speak of transduction. We must bear this in mind when invoking ANT to stress that a 'force only becomes an actant if it can enter into translation' (Van Loon 2002). For a force to become potentiality, and thus to engage power (*pouvoir*), it must enter into mediation. This entering into mediation entails a repetition of force *plus* its infusion into networked relationships. This repetition is what Derrida (1974) called a 'supplement' that 'adds to but does not add up' (Bhabha 1990). Hence, translation is only transduction if we mean by it a 'becoming mediated'.

Taking stock, we can see how networked relationships between actors involve transductions. Transductions entail a transformation of matter flows into information flows and *vice versa*. Both are necessary elements in the formation of technical systems; both are dimensions of mediation. There are two specific modalities of analysing such transductions:

- as representations, i.e., as processes by which one particular modality, that of discourse, replaces what it stands in for and the medium vanishes (simulation);

- as re-presentations in which the practice of mediating becomes the message (symbolic exchange).

Mediation, however, is *always both*.

Shannon and Weaver's (1949) model of communication was exactly revolutionary because it stressed that all intelligent entities exist on the basis of patterns of exchanges of information flows. What is passed through networked relationships is information. Kittler (1996) and Fuller (2005) further stress that the electronic revolution entails a capacity to modulate information into action and *vice versa* within the same technical system. Referring to microprocessors, Latour states: 'They are programs of action whose scriptor may delegate their realization to electrons, or signs, or habits, or neurons' (Latour 1996: 223).

Hence, technical systems that involve transduction operate on the basis of connections between disparate actants that are both informational and haptic. The making sense of these connections becomes itself part and parcel of the connecting, which enables the technical system to attain a higher level of complexity, also known as self-referentiality (Luhmann 1990). In ANT, these informational haptic transductions are called 'immutable mobiles'. Immutable, because there is no option to 'mute' them, the force of the network demands each part to accept their significance; mobile because they can be 'passed on' along the lines of networked connections.

Networked technical systems generate immutable mobiles. As they can neither be silenced (muted) nor transformed (mutated), these devices become the primary tools for 'ordering'. In so doing, their job is to silence elements that perform dissonant operations and transform them into consonant ones.

Immutable mobiles govern the *binding-use* of mediation. It is through the binding of actors to the technologically ordered network, that networked being starts to attain a certain (but by no means long-lasting) level of stability. The binding-use also works to integrate (enrol) new, previously unconnected, elements (actants) into the network, as they only need to acquire the definitions of the protocol to be able to converse with the technical system. It is therefore not surprising that most successful media convergences have focused on the attunement and standardization of particular protocols.

Mediation and trust

In the world of digital mediation, it is human-technological interfaciality, also known as the 'network' that provides the anchoring of action. A particularly popular cinematic exploitation of the same ideas is the film *The Matrix*. In this film, the Matrix refers to a omnipresent technological system, which controls all life on earth. In *The Matrix*, 'human' existence is bifurcated into two completely separated aspects. On the one hand, they are the biomolecular resources of machines. Indeed, in their 'real life' physical being, humans are mere embryo-like organisms providing the energy for the Matrix to function. On the other hand, they are virtual beings in a simulated reality, enjoying 'life-as-we-know-it'. However, and here the film betrays its old-fashioned realist assumptions, this virtual world is a fake: a fantasy world created so that the human embryos produce more energy and stay alive longer.

In *The Matrix*, our sense of reality is constantly being questioned by the doubling of 'virtualities'; it is extremely difficult to ascertain what the real reality really is; but a lot easier to accept that there are merely multiple virtualities that can be actualized, even simultaneously. We are constantly reminded of the hypermediated character of any actualized virtuality.

It is against this separation of real life and the virtual that the protagonists form their revolutionary intervention (with Keanu Reeves' Neo as the messianic 'chosen one'). In this sense, *The Matrix* is a reactionary defence of embodiment against processes of disembodiment. Disembodiment generates anxieties. Yet, connecting is inherent to mediation and with expanding mediation so do the number of connections and links (and hence disembodiments) also increase. While some networks, especially those engaged in old-fashioned political strategizing, have centripetal (concentric) tendencies (the proverbial spider's web, Van Loon 2006), the logic of (digital) media networks (especially the Internet) is instead centrifugal and *vortexical*.

Digital media networks operate with a decentralized plurality of nodes, and as a result, the concept of embodiment becomes somewhat problematic unless we are willing to embrace it in relation to 'disembodiment'. Embodiment, after all, still centres attention to a bound, integral, identifiable unit. However, what would natural if association be in a completely disembodied media network?

If transduction is the primary modality of digital/electronic forms of mediation, we need to consider the nature of association in similar terms, as a continuous iteration between matter and information. It is logical to assume that if (following classical sociology perhaps) we accept that associations involve relationships with different degrees and modalities of affect (e.g., trust, solidarity, sacrifice), we need to explore how such modalities of affect are modulated through interfaces. How does trust work in interfaciality?

Take, for example, the Internet. The Internet offers a (deluded?) promise of a totally disembodied, individuated experience. This has placed immense pressure on existing notions of 'trust'. The interface, which allows us to modulate our 'presence' in on-line mediated communities to a far greater extent than any of the preceding media technological forms, has also affected the affective charge of binding-use.

A lot of media attention has been paid to the risks of Internet-based forms of association. At the centre of these concerns are fears that the relative anonymity offered by on-line associations enables paedophiles to assume fake identities to lure children into off-line meetings with potentially devastating consequences. Slightly less extreme, but still cause for concern, is the way in which on-line environments facilitate the domestic consumption of pornographic material. As with the paedophile scares, it is the anonymity which is usually identified as the main reason why so many men dare to consume Internet porn. There are scares over the abuse of credit card details, identity theft and other forms of scamming which are all facilitated by a lack of physiological grounding of on-line interactions and exchanges. Finally, there are concerns about contracting computer viruses, trojans and worms, which lurk beneath deceptive programmes, which lure unsuspected Internet users into rendering their computers completely vulnerable to destruction, spyware or other forms of infiltration.

In all these instances of cybercrime we can detect a similar pattern: the absence of a 'face-to-face', embodied anchoring of persona is deemed to facilitate modes of deception which would ordinarily only be the province of relatively organized criminals. The Internet has turned the illusionary 'man in the street' into an opportunistic fraudster. Hobbesian nightmares about the absence of a Leviathan are easily entertained in such thinking. It is the lack of surveillance, legal muscle and face-to-face moral entrenchment that has loosened the commitment to the common good, and instead awakened the 'wolves within'.

It seems that the lack of affective charge regulating interactions undermines the possibilities to engage in trust. Indeed, all it offers one in its stead is 'blind trust', a form of abandonment to chance with high levels of risk. However, we need to acknowledge, at the same time, that transduction entails a transformation of 'that which has been'. That is, the off-line world has also changed. Of course, there are continuities of engagements and interactions, and friendships totally cultivated via the Internet, for example, are not uncommon (Argyle 1996). In most cases, however, users seek to supplement off-line and on-line modes of interaction (Gauntlett and Horsley 2004). This highlights that the possibilities opened up by digital modes of being affect all modalities of association, being digital is not just something one does in on-line environments.

Cyberenthusiasts have long held the view, so dramatically introduced in William Gibson's (1985) *Neuromancer*, that the meat substance role is no longer of central concern; although most would still stress that the meat still matters, it has become an appendix of the larger, encompassing virtual being of the (in)dividuated (dis)embodied experience. A new articulation has taken place between embodiment and disembodiment and this also affects the relationship between existential being and being-in-the-world, which is the province of mediation (Shields 2003).

As a core issue in this book, we have explored the way in which media technology facilitates the relationship between existential being and our being in the world. In this and the previous chapter, we have focused more closely on issues of embodiment to explore the notion of media as extensions of human faculties. However, are we now at the historically critical threshold beyond which the human ceased to be identifiable as an integral unit within those extended neural networks as Fuller (2005) invoking Kittler (1996) has argued?

Perhaps it is worth while considering this from the point of view of association. That is, whereas perhaps the nodes, the mesh and the links of neural networks are becoming more and more integrated and lose their integrity, there remains a 'social'; that is, there remains a sense of connectedness (association). Following Latour (2005), association implies an ethic of 'being affected'. The boundaries may be vague and ambiguous, the world is not one big homogenous clot of entangled wires in which everything is dissolved in the sameness of ubiquitous connectivity (Mackenzie 2005).

The point to consider here is whether the different modalities of *affect*, which are enabled by the interplay between embodiment and disembodiment, can maintain a sense of differentiation and thereby also maintain a sense of sociation, politics and – underneath both – a continuation of a quest for authentic, i.e., moral, being. This may have been the real challenge laid down by *Neuromancer* (Gibson 1985).

Transduction, which is a transformation of particular established constellations of forces tied to specific bodies (assemblages) does not 'end' with the disembodying and transgressing. That is not the purpose of transduction. Instead, this is followed by a re-embodiment, a rearticulation of an assemblage; new forms are being born. Association continues, it opens up new political spaces and there remains the fundamental ontological question of 'how to be' and thus the possibility for authentic, moral being. Hence, a specific affective modality, such as trust, will not vanish just because the face of it changes. Trust remains a key force in terms of stabilizing associations and enabling authentic being, for it attunes our existential being to a being in the world that is anchored in – for want of a better world – a more sustainable and purposeful way.

The question now becomes not *can* we, but *how* do we develop trust in these new cybernetic virtual worlds? What kinds of attunements between existential being and our being in the world would invoke trust? This can be simplified a bit using a combination of Baudrillard and Mauss. The distinction between symbolic exchange and simulation is that whereas the former engages in a social relationship marked by the giving and receiving of gifts in which a *hau* (moral obligation) is being passed on, the latter are 'dead' non-exchanges because no *hau* is present. This can now be challenged by stating that the *hau* of the gift is not dependent on the matter of the gift itself, but on the matter of the gift relationship, i.e., the process of giving.

The reason why the concept of 'trust' relates to 'the gift' is because if we are to talk about associations, we are invoking relationships that matter to the subjects in it. Trust is nothing but an indicator of the fidelity that such relationships require to qualify as relationships (rather than say connections or links). Trust can feed into solidarity and ultimately into the complete emptying of self in the form of sacrifice as the highest expression of love.

Baudrillard's (1993) model of symbolic exchange requires a notion of a unified subject willing to defend his/her integrity; however, the telematic subject is never unified nor able to defend his/her integrity. Instead, the integrity of the telematic subject is a simulacrum. Nonetheless, it is possible to argue that the *hau* itself does not require a unified, integral subject to be applied to. It can therefore be argued that moral obligations do extend into the virtual.

Runescapism

In order to illustrate the previous point about affective-mediated being, I will use the aforementioned multi-user platform game *Runescape* as an example. *Runescape* is an on-line, multi-user RPG involving over 9 million players worldwide, and in May 2007 it reached the milestone of 1 million paying members. There are servers in the USA, Canada, UK, Australia, Netherlands, Finland and Sweden. The game itself consists of a large map that is duplicated into over 140 parallel universes or 'worlds'. Some worlds are open to subscription fee-paying members only, others are open to all. You can create an account and play for free. The gamers are of all ages, although officially one should be over 13 to play. In my own clumsy attempts to play the game with my own children, we noticed that the vast majority of players claim to be 15 or younger and that male avatars vastly outnumber female ones.

The creators of the game are two brothers, Andrew and Paul Gower, and they set up a company called Jagex, which manages and operates the game. Jagex is extremely concerned about protecting the identity of its clients and has placed a range of measures to ensure that their identities are not disclosed. The only officially sanctioned crossovers between the 'real world' and the 'virtual world' of *Runescape* are the terms of agreement one needs to sign in order to play and, if one wants to become a member, the means by which one sets up the payment (e.g., credit card details).

The game consists of a large number of places and types of activities and engagements one can chose to pursue for leisure or career. There is no real end purpose to the game, one can simply set goals and aim to obtain them. Players choose to be a character and developing a character takes a long time. It is for this reason that for many committed players, runescape is a 'lifestyle'. They can choose which of the 23 skills they want to develop (or all of them) or instead do 'quests' or engage in the various types of minigames. The different skills include various types of combat, but also non-combative skills, such as farming, fishing, cooking and prayer. Scores are listed and ranked and there is a strong competitive element to the game.

Alongside a general 'bulletin board' type of speaking facility, the game also features a 'chatting' (private messenger) facility in which individuals can send others (on their so-called 'friends list') messages privately without anyone else knowing. It is through these messaging systems that players can engage their other 'persona', the self-confessed player behind the screen (i.e., who they claim to be). It is here that we can see the interfaciality of the virtual at work. The players are able to explicate their real life persona in relation to their player identity and they can go even further, as mobile numbers, websites, email addresses, messenger names, etc., do get exchanged frequently, despite the game management's strong warnings against it. In addition to the game, there are also numerous forums and fansites.

Some gamers protect their identity vehemently, others do not. Some gamers use the platform as a means to extend their social networks and friendship groups, however, and they are very quick to sort out who is into this type of association by asking for one's messenger address. Some link their *Runescape* activities to personal websites, such as on MySpace.com, in which they display their own details and offer their email address to anyone wishing to get in touch. Others display video recordings of actual game play on YouTube.com.

It is quite clear then that the gaming platform itself does not foreclose any particular form of virtuality. Its official user protocol favours total anonymity, but the offering of personal details has not been strongly policed. The different strategies of association highlight, however, that gamers do make deliberate choices about how they operate in virtual spaces. This also has profound implications on how they act. Because of this high public visibility, players who make many links with other communication facilities will enable more of a continuity between their *Runescape* persona and other on-line persona. Constructing a gaming persona that is too different from one's real life persona might be costly as one needs to invest a lot of time into creating a corroborating environment. Quite a few players I talked to stressed that being truthful is a key aspect of friendship. It is noticeable that they do not differentiate between the on-line and off-line persona in terms of the imperative of being truthful.

My 10-year-old son is also a gamer on *Runescape*. He once told me of an episode when he felt threatened by another player who approached him in an aggressive manner (of course, displayed only as text on a screen) after my son had rebuked him for making a racist comments about a third player. At another time, he was deeply affected by being cheated by a friend who he knows in real life as they attend the same school. This signals that although there are different layers if virtuality, the game also involves an illusion of transparency, in which all the layers seem to merge into a singular presence. Just like the Evil Clown's violent virtual rape (Dibbel 2001), words uttered in virtual domains can still have a strong physiological and psychological impact.

The call to being truthful is thus not excluded from the virtual interfaciality of the RPG. Neither are the protocols of decency, politeness and friendliness. A visit to *Runescape* offers a wealth of insight into the hypothetical situation of what would happen if 13-year-olds ruled the world. It reveals the intensity of boasting (about levels of achievement), as well as interpersonal nastiness (the swearword 'noob', standing in for 'newbie' or 'beginner', is the most frequently uttered word intended as a 'put down' as other words are censored). There are a lot of complaints about scams (often related to people being misled or tricked while trading) and betrayals. As an indication that central control is difficult, the *Runescape* game management is actively encouraging players to report rule breaking and abusive behaviour.

There is a very low sense of trust throughout the game, and people are very wary of taking risks based on trust. The game management itself heavily invests in promoting caution and prudence. There are a series of rules about desirable and undesirable actions, yet on the generic ethos of the gaming experience (at least in the non-members worlds) is one of the anarchy and chaos of life in a society-without-a-state. Perhaps it is for this reason that the game management have extended the number of player/moderators who function as prefects, ensuring fair play and standards of proper engagement.

The networking enabled by the virtuality of multi-user game platforms, such as *Runescape*, runs across several layers of enpresenting, hovering between the illusion of transparency and hypermediation. Recalling our earlier observations about the triple layering of the virtual sociality of MUDs, we can now make some observations about the way in which the *hau* (which accompanies the gift as a moral obligation) is being mediated. The associations established through *Runescape* have not completely abandoned symbolic exchange; a *hau* remains present. For example, on *Runescape*, it is not uncommon for higher level players to help lower level ones and there is an implicit obligation to reciprocate favours according to both ability and need. In this sense, the world's runescaping teenagers have replicated a moral ordering that is in some (but certainly not all) ways, rather similar to that of the world of their parents. Despite existing in the realm of simulation, something else has remained present.

It is perhaps the need to secure associations that has driven players to create gangs and clans within which reciprocal, *hau*-based symbolic exchanges form the core of the affective charge. This type of association is like a form of tribalism that Mafessoli (1996) identifies as conditioned by taste-based (more random and arbitrary than interest-based) social orientations. It invokes a sense of centripetal solidarity combined with centrifugal hostility and both operating at high levels of intensity. There are thus quite peculiar similarities between runescapism and real-life gang-cultures in terms of their affectively charged relationship between existential being and being in the world.

The triad of virtual being – i.e., avatar, persona and off-line body – exemplifies the process of 'remediation' with exceptional clarity. These three characters do not stand in a simple, representational linear relationship to each other, but are forms of transduction, constantly iterating between immediacy and hypermediation. The 'I' of the acting subject always shifts between these positions, and it is the role of the persona to both fix and transgress the representational relationship between on-line and off-line being.

When considering Latour's approach to representing and re-presenting, an interesting domain on *Runescape* is perhaps the establishment of virtual romance. As this game is played by teenagers and tweenies, one can expect that there will be quite a bit of role-playing in the domains of relationships and sexuality. *Runescape* is clearly a heterosexist ordering and is also steeped in fairly traditional patriarchal sensibilities. Male avatars 'chasing' (and soliciting attention from) female avatars is a fairly common feature and quite a few female avatars make it obvious that they expect presents and other support in exchange for having a *Runescape* relationship. The game itself even allows a marriage in a chapel.

In any case, the multiplication of layers creates tensions and pleasures. Transduction has an affective charge as it travels between avatar, persona and person. It is quite clear that virtuality is not innocent, that trust, fidelity and solidarity have not suddenly vanished in heavily mediated social encounters, and that not all forms of simulation adopted by on-line gamers, for example, are devoid of symbolic exchanges. In this sense, McLuhan's thesis that media are extensions of human faculties still has merits, but we do need to considerably loosen our concept of the embodied human being. The crucial role in transduction is played by the medium of identification: the persona.

The persona is a virtual textualization of the alleged 'real person' behind the keyboard. The persona reveals him or herself through the dialogic modality of the confessional. This textual representation can be purely fictional (and this is why multi-user on-line RPGs, such as *Runescape* are seen as potentially dangerous places where stalkers can easily hide themselves), but regardless of the accuracy of its representation, it will always function as a shuttle between the molecular and digital worlds; it is the medium that transduces and translates affectivities between the different virtualities.

The persona is disembodied as if it is an *intextuation* of a person; yet it embodies the pixel of the avatar and thus enables the *incarnation* of the virtual; by transmitting feelings, emotions and desires. The question becomes to what extent telematics is a process of replacing persons with persona. If we become reduced to keyboard operators, then very little of our life world takes place outside the persona we perform to facilitate our being on-line. This may be the true alienation effect of the simulacrum; we are reduced to shadows on the wall.

Conclusion

Alongside a concern for form, cultural embedding and embodiment, understanding media also needs a strong sense of historical grounding. The point of departure of this chapter has been the specific historic conjuncture which we find ourselves in at the moment, i.e., the digital age. This conjuncture is mainly informed by a radical turning in the relationship between mediation and matter. Whereas until the rise of electronic mediation, the medium always contained a form of matter that entailed rather strict spatiotemporal inhibitions, this became far less central. Beginning with telegraphy, spatiality was being rapidly reconfigured by the emergence of 'wireless' media that used radio waves. Mediation became more independent from the spatial relationship between sender and receiver (Carey 1992; Kittler 1996).

We have seen how we might develop a media analysis that recognizes the radical nature of digitalization or telematics by abandoning the centrality of anthropomorphic embodiment and instead focusing on a concept of human being as itself fragmented, dispersed and networked. Embodiment still matters, but if we are to understand the nature of 'networked being', we have to analyse it in close conjunction with disembodiment as both variations of 'the virtual'. Mediation engenders dense and complex networks that can only be stabilized on a temporal basis, and often not capable of maintaining integrity and consistency of shape and form.

The tetrad of matter, form, use and know-how can be deployed with relative ease to help understand how the emergent digital media-technologies inaugurate a transduction of social relationships and cultural practices. The matter of digital media is electric; it is a form of communication that closely resembles the human body's central nervous system; however, its form, that of touch, is by its very nature extrinsic to the human body. By operating on the basis of 'touch', digital electronic communications can form networks of relationships in which bodies become neurotransmitters of extensive, partly disembodied systemic life forms. This mode of transduction is set-into-work by the binding nature of its use. It does not remain hypothetical, but is set upon the world as the virtualization of reality. This, finally, is reflected in the know-how with which we are attuned to the emergent virtual orderings.

This virtualization, however, does not mean that all that came before it has melted into thin air. The multiplication of interfaces that are enabled by digitalization and expansive networked mediations has not led to a disappearance of an existential moment of 'being there' (*Dasein*). Instead, in all its dispersed existence, *Dasein* is still 'present', albeit in rather fragmented modalities of 'presence', extended over multiple and simultaneous connections and links. The *Dasein* of networked being is by its very nature virtual and partly disembodied. Of course, one would have to say, because regardless of our exact state of embodiment, we still exist. Just because we are no longer existing in purely anthropomorphic forms (one integral and whole body), and just because we are no longer capable of holding together representation, re-presentation and presence *in one interface*, does not mean that we have ceased to be somewhere, somebody or someone.

Latour's approach to theorizing social practices as manifestations of actor networks has proven to provide an excellent tool kit for analysing our mediated being-in-the-world. Moreover, ANT gives empirical credibility to McLuhan's aphorism that media are extensions of human faculties (but also to its opposite, namely that humans are extensions of media) by showing how alliances can be forged between 'humans' and technologies in establishing temporally stable everyday work settings. The relationship between Medium Theory and ANT is, by and large, induced by a sharing of the playful, evasive and provocative philosophical ethos of Nietzsche.

Exploring the Nietzschean connection further would enable us to grasp the philosophical grounding of forms of media analysis that do not reduce human action to human motivations and intentions, but instead is receptive to a more open flow of forces that work with and against each other in attempts to maximize strength. However, there is perhaps also a need to be cautious with an implicit Machiavellian ethos in Nietzsche's writings, which can be pre-empted by insisting that 'strength' is not the same as domination. For example, the refusal to wield one's superior power to gain personal advantage could be seen as an immense act of strength that refutes Machiavellian opportunism, simply because it will so often be interpreted as weakness.

Mediation can only avoid being reduced to pure simulation if it adheres to the basic premise of symbolic exchange as the giving and receiving of *hau*. The *hau* is the binding force of use, or *telos*, that grants mediation its normativity. This is in sharp contrast to the exclusively efficiency driven normativity of know-how (which only values processes on the basis of their outcomes). If mediation is seen as being exclusively concerned with the latter, we will no longer be able to understand how interfaciality can still facilitate trust relations and transduce morality across the various layers of virtuality. This understanding is essential if one is to explain why the game *Runescape* is at all possible as a field of (dis)embodied associations and why it does not necessarily favour the purely cynical, selfish and careless nature if short-term-based opportunistic strategies.

Suggested further reading

Bolter, J.D. and Grusin, R. (2000) *Remediation: Understanding New Media*. Cambridge, MA: MIT Press.
> A landmark piece of work that advances medium theory into coming to terms with the digital age.

Elmer, G. (ed.) (2002) *Critical Perspectives on the Internet*. Lanham, MD: Rowman and Littlefield.
> A collection of critical contributions to understanding the Internet, its social embedding, as well as its implications for social, cultural and political processes.

Gauntlett, D. and Horsley, R. (eds) (2004) *Web. Studies*, 2nd edn. New York, NY: Oxford University Press.
> A collection of accessible chapters covering research and analyses of Internet-related phenomena and processes.

Hemmingway, E. (2007) *Into the Newsroom: Exploring the Digital Production of Regional Television News*. London: Routledge.
> The first full-sized treatment of media analysis from the perspective of Actor Network Theory. It contains a detailed study of how news is actualized in a regional newsroom.

Negroponte, N. (1995) *Being Digital*. New York, NY: Knopf.
> A key text in understanding how the digital revolution is affecting who we are and how we operate.

Shields, R. (2003) *The Virtual*. London: Routledge.
> A detailed, critical and original analysis of the way in which the concept of the virtual affects how we are able to understand the nature of social reality and social relationships.

Trend, D. (ed.) (2001) *Reading Digital Culture*. Oxford: Blackwell.
> A comprehensive anthology of key works associated with a wide range of aspects and issues regarding digital media.

6 CONCLUSION: THEORIZING MEDIA TECHNOLOGY

This book provides a journey across a range of divergent theoretical reflections on mediation that are, nonetheless, united in their critical appreciation of the role of technology in such processes. The central question for this book is: what has been brought about by mediation? This relates to the twofold aim of the book – (1) to explore a range of different approaches to analysing media technology and (2) to show how media-technologies can play a crucial role in the (re-)configuration of social and cultural practices and formations. Both questions have been approached via a range of trajectories. These were divided into three topics: historicity, cultural embedding and (dis)embodiment.

Mediation and 'thirdness'

The nature of media is that they come-in-between. They mediate. Mediation is very similar to what sociologists call 'interaction', but with a crucial exception. Whereas interaction is usually seen as taking place between two actors, *mediation always involves a third*. This becomes clear when we look at mediation as a particular form of conflict management through the intervention of a 'third party'. For example, in marriage counselling or industrial disputes, mediation is a form of settling disagreements. The third party, the mediator, comes 'in-between' the (two) antagonistic parties in conflict to avoid a direct confrontation between them. In this sense, mediation creates the formation of 'poles' of oppositions, and thus for an antagonistic field, or plateau, organized around these poles in which both are placed *vis-à-vis* each other to make sense of the difference in which mediation becomes possible. Indeed, mediation is the creation of a field of interaction in which antagonistic relationships can continue to remain 'in communication'.

Similar 'thirdness' can be seen when considering the 'medium' in, for example, religious practices as well as clairvoyance and communicating with the spirit world ('the dead'). Similarly, during the sacrifice of the mass, the priest literally becomes the medium between God and the congregation of the faithful. Here, mediation also creates a field of communication as ritual that simultaneously functions as an interfacial portal between different 'worlds' (heaven and earth).

All these are instances of mediation, and all highlight the key role of the third element. This is a useful intervention in how we conceptualize communication as in the classical models, communication is generally seen as *immediate*, i.e., taking place between two individuals. What such models of immediate communications overlook is the fact that there is already something coming in between the two communicators: spoken language. Overlooking language as a medium is problematic as it assumes that language is transparent. As the field of sociolinguistics has shown (Bakhtin 1986) alongside philosophy (Derrida 1974; Heidegger 1987), this is far from the case.

Because of an inherent blindness to the medium, classical communication theory treated mediation as that which comes in the way of perfect communication. The medium was at best a 'necessary evil', and always at risk of being corrupted by external interference. Hence, communication theory was forced to invest a lot of additional conceptual work into explaining the role of media in creating 'distortions' or bias as technological shortcomings, rather than inherent in mediation itself (Kittler 1996). Shannon and Weaver's (1949) mathematical model of media communications can be seen as the archetypical model of two-way immediate communication. The medium between sender and receiver is a black box (especially when sender and receiver are identical, as in telegraphy, telephony or two-way radio). The linear model of transmission privileges the intentions of the sender and reduces 'reception' to the art of 'reading well' that is, decoding messages is primarily the art of reading the intentions of the sender. Bias in communication is measured as the discrepancy between the message-as-intended and the message-as-received. The aim of effective communication is to reduce bias; while the aim of effective (strategic) miscommunication is to maximize bias.

The fact that Shannon and Weaver's theory of communication was developed in the context of a military interest in strategic communication does reveal quite a bit about what motivates this interest in bias and effective communication. The radical intervention, however, was not necessarily the idea of appropriating a scientific understanding of communication for strategic military purposes, but the creation of a direct link between communication and action in the form of 'information flows'. It is by virtue of this idea that information engages in action without a subject. It was this breakthrough that enabled Watson and Crick to create a metaphorical analogy of their 'discovery' of the double helix of DNA with a mathematical model of disembodied communications. This inaugurated the possibility of imagining disembodied life within both discourses of communication and genetics. Despite obvious and widely acknowledged (Fiske 1990) flaws in the model, not in the least the rather simplistic emphasis on linearity and intentionality, this model (with its extensive revisions and complexifications) has dominated communication studies to this very day (Carey 1992; Kittler 1996; McQuail 2005).

What we can put in place of models of 'linear communication' is something more radical. It is in a way already contained within Shannon and Weaver's intervention, namely that information does not stand in the place of something else, but is itself what matters. Information-as-content is thus not a representation, but a force (Kittler 1996). This force is bound to the technology by which it comes into being. This technology consists of four key components: form, matter, binding-use and know-how. Hence, media analysis should concern itself with these four aspects that are constitutive of all technologies of mediation.

Mediation as a 'coming-in-between' is thus not a 'passing' of content from 'A' to 'B', but instead the constitution of specific orientations and sensibilities that order (enframe and reveal) how we make sense in terms of perception, thought and communication. That is, we perceive, think and reason by virtue of mediation, and not simply 'through' media. Media are thus part of the fundamental ontology of our own being.

In terms of that ontology, we could distinguish between three specific types of orientation: 'affective', 'intuitive' and 'cognitive' (all three are extended from our central nervous system). The first relates to precognitive dispositions of being that are issued from the mere fact that we exist as sentient beings with senses that perceive (and touch), empirically, the world we inhabit. The second relates to the fact that our sensibilities are anchored in specific associations, which – in the digital age – have become radically exposed in terms of 'networked being'. We constitute our perceptions and thoughts in interpersonal relationships, as well as in relation to specific technological orderings, and these provide the 'ethos' in which we engage with our existence. Finally, the third element relates to reasoning as a deliberate mode of sense-making. This is the realm of discourse; the domain where meanings begin to 'stick' and start to obtain a sense of exteriority (for example, in the form of assertions and arguments).

The model of media analysis that this book advocates is – in essence – based on the straightforward assumption that *mediation is that which attunes our existential being [which Heidegger (1987) calls Dasein] to the ordinary, everyday nature of 'being-in-the-world'*. Existential being is that special feature of consciousness that enables us to reflect on our being 'as if' we engage in a time-out. It is like a shock, a moment of clarity and release from the trance of ordinary, habitual, routine being. Mediation, however, enables us to see that this existential moment which enables us to reflect is never a time-out, but always situated in the world, without being reduced to it (Van Loon 1996a).

What media analysis is, thus, called to be is a way to engage with how this attuning is ordered technologically, in terms of the form, matter, binding-use and know-how that together constitute the medium. In each medium (or media-hybrid), these are articulated in a specific and unique way. Each of these articulations generates a different form of attuning. These different forms of attuning can be analysed in terms of their historical, cultural and biophysiological specificities, and these three different dimensions have been discussed in this book.

Attunement as a historical process

The historical specificity of how media attune our existential being to our being in the world was the starting point of Chapter 2. Analysing media as engaged in historical transformations has been a central aspect of Medium Theory or Media Ecology. Focusing mainly on Innis and McLuhan, Chapter 2 engaged with the issue of media evolution as a dynamic, interactive process between particular media-hybrids ('the medium as the message') and particular environments. Such thinking is strongly orientated towards contextuality, both in terms of environmental factors, as well as particular historical trajectories.

The different, but compatible approaches of Innis and McLuhan to fairly similar questions concerning the role of communication media in processes of social ordering highlight wider tensions between two different versions of 'materialism', namely those of political economy and biophilosophy. The first favours a systemic approach to mediation as an abstracted processing of power, wealth and knowledge, the second favours a more physiological approach to mediation as embodied as well as driven by forces that are irreducible to functions or interests. These forces could be described as 'life affirming' and point towards a vitalist conception of mediation.

However, towards the end of his life, McLuhan attempted to merge his more speculative biophilosophical aphorisms with a more traditional version of historical materialism. The result of this is a fourfold thesis on media evolution [which Levinson (1998) called 'McLuhan's tetrad'], that set the tone for what was later to be called 'new media theory', and structured the work of contemporary media theorists, such as Levinson, and Bolter and Grusin (2000). In more practical analytical terms, the tetrad has given us a means to analyse how media evolve (Levinson 1997: 16).

For each constellation of media, it asks the following questions:

- What does it amplify?
- What does it obsolesce?
- What does it retrieve from the past?
- What does it flip into when it has reached the limits of its potential?

These four elements help us analyse the nature of the bias associated with different technologies of mediation (Innis 1982). That is, it helps us focus in specific terms on the question why people, in a given era and within specific media constellations, attend to the things they attend to? This bias is the specific form of 'attunement', which can take the form of (for example) fear, care, concern, anxiety, but also piety, patience or even ecstasy or exuberance.

McLuhan's orientation towards analysing phenomena associated with technology is non-linear, that is, it does not separate the perceiving (existential) subject (*Dasein*) from the conditions which structure perception (being-in-the-world). Indeed, an analysis of perception has to be part of any analysis of what is being perceived. For medium theory this means that our mapping and analysis of mediation phenomena is itself affected by the mediation of our own being (Curtis 1977). If media are extensions of our faculties, then media are also operating on the modalities of how we feel (affect), understand (intuition) and make sense (cognition).

Sensibility and cultural specificity

This premise of non-linearity, that the position from which we perceive and make sense is not fixed, but itself embedded in the world with which we are trying to come to terms may sound very obvious, its logical implications, however, do not seem to have filtered through to the bulk of media studies. There are exceptions, and we do find quite a few of them in the European traditions of cultural analysis (*Kultur Kritik*). In focusing on the cultural specificity of how media attune us to our being in the world, Chapter 3 aimed to scrutinize how sensibilities are structured in relation to distinctive forms of mediation, and in particular those that have marked the establishment of cultures of modernity, such as cinema, television and photography.

Benjamin's intervention in cultural analysis engages with the radical thesis that the form of mediation, which has shifted towards 'mechanical reproduction', affects not just how meaning is created but, also and equally importantly, how we perceive cultural significance. Although Benjamin's Kantian inclinations (Caygill 1998) may have prevented him from embracing more radically the consequences of his own analysis, the insistence on the cultural embedding of affect, sensibility and sense has enabled a rich pallet of subtle reflections on specific cultural products, i.e., paintings, photographs, films and urban life itself (Shields 1991).

Raymond Williams (1990) also provided a strong historical cultural embedded analysis of television. His work should be seen as taking historical materialism to its logical limits in what it can do in terms of cultural analysis. A concept such as 'structure of feeling', which resembles quite closely Benjamin's concept of aura, enables a more 'sociological' reading of the affective dimension of mediation as attunement, and helps us to see how feelings and intuitions are culturally embedded rather than merely personal idiosyncrasies. Moreover, the strong historical focus provided a means to engage with the historicity of 'binding-use' as the selective principle by which technologies are being stabilized and fine-tuned, and become established.

In theory at least, Williams has provided a possible means to enable us to understand media innovations historically by engaging centrally with the binding nature of use. Use becomes binding over time, as a selective process in which technological applications (such as communications media) are fine-tuned to obtain higher levels of fidelity.

The French tradition that we have drawn upon to develop a framework for media analysis has a somewhat different approach to the binding nature of use. Less emphasis was placed here on use, but more on what we may understand as 'binding'. Binding is the work of the text. The text becomes a medium that assembles affect, intuition and reason not by closing down possibilities through narrative, but by opening up articulations across different domains of affect, sensibility and sense. Indeed, Barthes' notion of textuality was an earlier form of network theory. Textuality is a form of binding (*textere* originally meant weaving, as illustrated by the word 'textile'); in other words, the purposefulness of technology can be analysed in terms of its textuality; that is, how it engages with specific selected registers of sense-making.

It is on this basis that his work on photography can be seen as an attempt to develop a *process semiotics* of mediated cultural production. Barthes triad of denotation, connotation and linguistic message, imposes a separation of different modalities of sense perception that qualify and order the way in which media products assemble (gather) meaning. Here, we can find useful means to stop immersing our concern for media technology into a one-dimensional analysis of 'effects' and 'know-how'. Like form and matter to which it is closely tied, denotation does not engender finality, but is inherently enigmatic; it reveals a particular relationship between our existential being and our common being in the world as one demanding attention (for detail) and care (for possibilities).

In a different pathway within the French trajectory, Baudrillard's (1993) take on media analysis also concentrates on the relationship between mediation and association. That is, the binding nature of use becomes binding in its social anchoring. Social binding is a central theme in Mauss' (1990) work on the gift, which Baudrillard uses to distinguish between symbolic exchange (as involving the giving and receiving of gifts) and simulation (in which no exchange of gifts takes place, but merely an exchange of signs). Mauss argued that gifts are socially binding because of the imposition of the *hau*, the spirit of the gift, which entails maybe not so much an obligation to reciprocate in the same measure, but an obligation to honour the social bond, thus established (for example, by not selling on the gift for profit).

Baudrillard's (1993) thesis is that symbolic exchange is being marginalized as social processes become increasingly mediated. It echoes Virilio's (1997) concerns over escape velocity. Escape velocity is the condition when our ability to re-attune our ability to makes sense to our perceptive capacity is overtaken by the speed at which mediation changes that which we encounter. It is the effect of speed. Changes become so fast that by the time we have been able to make sense of them, the world is already a different place. Binding requires time and time is increasingly becoming scarce. What fills time is an instantaneous circulation of signs. These inaugurate a different type of interaction with the world. Rather than a form of sociation, the circulation of signs inaugurates simulation.

Perhaps Virilio's apocalyptic notion of escape velocity as a threshold and point of no return is somewhat exaggerated. As Mackenzie (2002: 96) has argued, speed is relative and only makes sense in terms of its differentiation. That is, rather than seeing mediated being (following the logic of speed) as that which terminates social being, we should approach mediation and sociation as continuously intersecting. Both are 'binding' our existential being to our being in the world. In this sense, the implosion of culture due to simulation does not mean the end of the world, but instead the transformation of a particular regime of sense-making, one that was dominated by print culture and literacy, to another one, which might be dubbed 'the virtual', although we have to remind ourselves that virtuality also exists in literary media.

Technological being

Technological embodiment has been a theme that, at least since the 1980s, continuously resurfaced in issues over identity and subjectivity. The body is generally understood as the physiological and molecular anchoring of particular subjectivities (Butler 1993b). The latter are culturally and historically specific. The idea that the body itself is subject to cultural and historical modification is perhaps less widely accepted. Indeed, the nature culture distinction is one that has continued to affect how we are to conceptualize the way which technological processes are embodied (Strathern 1992; Frank 1996; Lury 1998; Stacey 1998).

On the most basic level, affect and, to a lesser extent, intuition are difficult to conceptualize without the involvement of bodies. Feeling and sensibility are innately connected to the physiological processes of neurotransmission. Even cognition (in the form of reason), although clearly more susceptible to disembodiment [the 'god trick' as Haraway (1988) once called it], is difficult to conceptualize as completely outside the body (Lyotard 1991). It is for this reason we can only refer to *partial* disembodiment.

However, what exactly do we mean by 'the' body? Indeed, what is 'the' body? The body is itself an abstraction, a myth, when it is asked to perform the incarnation of theoretical speculation. Instead of carnal bodies, we continue to work with *intextuated* ones (de Certeau 1984). Instead, when we are reflecting on the nature of embodiment, we are better off talking about *bodies* in the plural to emphasize that we can only talk about bodies in particular. Moreover, an analysis of mediation that follows a non-linear pathway needs to emphasize not the 'thingness' of media, but mediation as a process.

Feminist analyses of media and culture have exposed the differentiated nature of embodiment. When operating within a feminist perspective, the primordial differentiator is gender. In other words, when we reflect on the matter of mediation which should also reflect on the matter, form, binding-use and know-how of gendered embodiment as technologically enframed and revealed *in mediation*. This is the logical first step in analysing the embodiment of mediation. The bodies that matter (Butler 1993b) are formed along gender specific lines of transduction, and this has an immediate bearing on the binding of use as well as on the performativity of know-how which is retrospectively reconstructed as the primary driving force of technological processes.

For over three decades, feminist media-analyses have exposed the inherent patriarchal bias pervading all aspects of mediation: its political economy, organizational structures, ethos of professionalism, the production process, media products themselves and also the modes of reception and consumption that actualize the mediation. Technology, itself, however, was by and large not a central concern in such analyses.

This relative absence becomes evident in the pornography censorship debate. Both ends of the debate kept the issue in a stalemate exactly because their opposition is in fact an opposition between different versions of modernity: a more liberal individualist one (feminist against censorship) on behalf of the individual, versus an institutional collectivist one (feminist for censorship) on behalf of the 'common good' (of society as a whole and women in particular). The stalemate comes down to an internal tension within modern capitalism as it rests on a balance between two pillars: the market and the (sovereign) nation state.

Moreover, what is striking in this debate is a persistent lack of concern for mediation as a phenomenon, for the technological embedding of pornography as the systemic mediation of sex through commodification and objectification and, last but not least, a concern for the political economy of the porn industry as part of a wider phenomenon of 'cultural industries'. Again, the tetrad of matter, form, binding-use and know-how can be invoked to analyse what exactly is brought about by pornographic mediation.

The matter of pornography varies as it is able to attach itself to a range of media. Each of these particular media inaugurate their own (pornographic) matter. This inauguration highlights technological embodiment. The physiological affects that pornographic mediation is intended to induce, manifest themselves at least partly in forms of embodiment (e.g., sexual arousal). There are of course also non-intended effects (outrage, disgust, etc.), although it is quite likely that some porn is intended to offend. The technological nature of pornography as 'mediated sex' thus reveals that pornography is not just representation, it is also a *practice of re-presentation* and similar to production, consuming pornography is also a *technologically mediated practice*.

The story of pornography provides a powerful testimony to the accuracy of Baudrillard's (and Virilio's) pessimism about mediation becoming pure simulation. Pornography turns human sexuality into a mere resource; desire becomes expropriated from human embodiment and turned into a commodified, thing-like, force: lust. The manufacturing of lust turns mediated sex into a know-how driven technological system, devoid of much care for the process of mediation itself. Binding-use is transformed from a coconstitutive guiding principle into a desired effect. For example, when binding takes the form of addiction.

Feminist work on *media-use*, has been far more receptive towards a careful consideration of media technology. The domestication approach, for example, is strongly influenced by feminist concerns over the ways in which specific practices of *using* technologies have helped shape the matter and form, and (to some extent) can reconfigure the know-how as well. Sadie Plant's example of Ada Byron's influence on the development of computers highlights that (at least in its early stages) in the emergence of a relatively new technological system, the binding nature of use is not by definition marginal. That is, binding-use should not be reduced to the 'consumption phase' when an established technology is introduced to the general public.

In this sense, the feminist critique of technological culture shares its basic premises with those that have influenced non-linear thought. The alienation brought about by an increased reliance on technique (Ellul 1964), stems from a performativity and efficiency-driven orientation to being. For feminism, this orientation is entrenched in the nature of patriarchy as driven by an instrumental rationality following the law of the father, rather than the law of nature (Irigaray 1987).

On a more modest plane, the domestication approach also shows how specific forms of technology-use can alter the nature of technological mediation, and provide an antidote against instrumentalist performativity. It shows that in getting things done practically, intentions may be adapted and modified according to local needs and values. Domestication requires embodiment. Without embodiment, domestication does not become binding; it will remain an empty simulation of the social. The binding nature of use only takes place if it attunes our *Dasein* to our being in the world. That is, the attunement is not optional but necessary.

This can be simplified. Technology-use becomes embodied through routine; routine is a habitualization of technology-use, by means of which it becomes binding. Our bodies are attuned to technology-use when we do things seemingly automatically, for example, when we apply the fine motor skills of holding a pen to write, when we brush our teeth, or use a computer keyboard. This routine attuning, however, also contains a danger. Dwelling technologically, that is inhabiting technology, easily leads to forgetting original purposefulness and its replacement with objectives and goals. This is when technology can become careless, instrumentalized and its use becomes indifferent (Heidegger 1987). We then forget the matter, form and binding-use and only see 'knowhow' [in service of bringing about particular effects, which Lyotard (1979) referred to as 'performativity'] as decontextualized from the world. Our understanding of technology becomes idealist and metaphysical. We then can become ensnared by its hypnotic lure [McLuhan (1964) called this 'the narcissus narcosis'] and turn into automatons. That is, media then cease to be extensions of human faculties, but replacements of them.

It is for this reason that a feminist critique of technology is called to go beyond the immediate politics of male versus female; the identity politics of categorizing and classifying entitlements based on the attribution of sign value. Feminist critique cannot but remind us of the difference within, i.e., gender; the difference within that constitutes us as persons rather than abstractions (Irigaray 2000). It is this differentiated being that can be used to sidestep the dangers of anthropomorphism and anthropocentrism.

When tying feminist critique to a critique of modern technology, we can find interesting connections with, for example, Baudrillard, who insisted on the increasing implosion of meaning in mediated communication. When applied to mediated sex, it is obvious that the objectification of women's bodies and the commodification of sexual pleasure have spiraled into a vortex in which all meaning seems to disappear. All we have are bits, clips, passages, strung together without an apparent logic, meaninglessly simulating sexual pleasure by exchanging signs.

The example of pornography, however, is not exceptional. Instead, it should be seen as an allegory of mediation in modern life. As Kroker and Cook (1988), following Baudrillard (1990) have stated, hypermediation exposes the whole of culture as obscene.

Indeed, the popularity of fly on the wall documentaries, docusoaps, reality soaps and 'reality TV', testifies to this obscenity of ubiquitous exposure. Voyeurism, so well ana-lysed by Laura Mulvey (1975) is not only commonly *accepted*, it is also ubiquitously *expected* as the normativity of mediated engagement. Now everyone is presumed to want Harry Potter's invisibility cloak.

It logically follows that a philosophically coherent feminist media analysis cannot accept instrumentalism, because it would mean a permanent loss of a critical faculty; it would leave the human subject outside of the scope of analysis. It would mean, for example, that one had to posit that the obscenity of hypermediation is reversible and only depends on the political will to see differently. It would call for self-discipline, self-mastery, and a whole range of inherently masculinist associations of neutral, objective points of view from nowhere (Haraway 1988).

Instead, feminist media-analyses, such as those of Haraway and Hayles, have a more ambitious agenda. They aim to reconfigure how we understand life itself. A concept of life as gendered, as differentiated, no longer needs the primacy of a universal subject 'man', but enables one to start with a differentiated, maybe even a networked, set of life affirming processes. Gendered being is open and never really adequately defined. Indeed, Hayles goes as far as to suggest that life itself crosses from the organic, molecu-lar and biological world into forms of textualization and virtualization. Life is infor-mation processing. In such a view of life, the human being is merely a by-product, a facilitator, a vessel that is perhaps only for a short while still necessary for reproduction of information processing media.

Inspiration

Hayles' observations transcend the critical issues of differentiated being but are also a logical conclusion of them. If we accept that one is not one, but two (Irigaray 2000), then we have already set ourselves on the same path as digitalization, which also starts with the premise of the mutual dependency of two oppositional items: the one and the zero. From the initial splitting comes the possibility of exponential multiplication of 2 to the power of n (2^n). This is a founding principle of all non-linear concepts of history: in the beginning there was not one but two [actually three, as the medium (e.g., 'the word') was also there from the beginning].

The pathway, thus constructed, leads us to theorizing mediated being as an iteration between embodiment and disembodiment. Whereas the former has been widely stressed and emphasized within social theory and cultural studies, i.e., is there anyone daring to say these days that the body does not matter? Disembodiment is nowadays vilified as a remnant of Cartesianism. However, we should not be misled by the herd. As Lyotard (1991) has stressed in his seminal work *The Inhuman*, the logic of the modern techno-logical system (he calls it monad) is driven by the quest for developing thought to exist without bodies.

That the age-old quest for eternal life should now have taken on such a technocentric view (in the age of the telematics), testifies to the importance of technology in ordering our relationship, as existential beings, to our (collectively maintained) being-in-the-world. However, disembodiment is as old as human history itself. The attempt to overcome mortality is derived from an archetypical (originary) myth. Indeed, although only a minority of religions have a concept of eternal life, most if not all religions have a concept of life outside the body, be it in the form of angels, spirits, demons or gods.

Instead of invoking a static, dualistic opposition between embodiment and disembodiment, we should perhaps understand it as a binary (thus enabling multiplication) or a relay. This is the core of transduction: processes of embodiment iterate with processes of disembodiment. Networks are a good example of this. Their logic both contains embodiment, in terms of specific nodes, locations, interfaces, and disembodiment, in terms of fragmentation, flow and fluidity.

Technological embodiment takes place alongside technological disembodiment. The former could be seen as a form of *incarnation*. It is when technological applications obtain a form and matter in relation to a binding, use, when, say, human beings start to inhabit (habitualize) technology, i.e., inaugurate a particular technological *habitus* within a technologically mediated habitat. The latter are a form of *intextuation*; a transduction of molecular embodied forms into digital, virtual matters, so as to enable them to 'move' at the speed of light.

What binds together incarnation and intextuation is inspiration (the endowment of a spirit or *hau*). Assembled into a distinctive embodiment, incarnate being dwells technologically, gathers its matter, form, binding-use and know-how; applies these with affect, intuition and/or reason that inform the attuning of *Dasein* to a being in the world. Intextuated being is disassembled as molecules, and reassembled as data flows, that weave new networks and forge new relationships. Inspired being is endowed with the *hau*, the spirit of the gift, which grants him/her a sense of unique personhood, but also brings with it a moral obligation to respect the *hau* and thereby the communal law in which this respect is anchored.

In other words, we do not have to contrast embodied and networked being, not even at the concrete empirical level. The solution, however, is neither simply to see networks as larger order bodies (as in systems theory), nor to see bodies as containers or vessels, but instead to conceptualize bodies as 'open nodes', operating on the basis of a multiplicity of desires. As autonomous forces, bodies have the capacity to enact the assembling, gathering and binding of other forces, through the giving and receiving of gifts. This gathering and binding takes place through media, that is, interfaces. It is through the same interfaces that these bodies can also dissemble, dissipate and disperse, for example, as a multiplicity of desires.

Embodiment and Disembodiment are thus two aspects of the same flow, the flow of networking or transduction. Embodiment is the consolidation, disembodiment the transformation. This flow of transduction is what enables us to counter Baudrillard's

(1993) dualism of symbolic exchange and simulation; it enables us to argue that mediation and association are not necessarily mutually exclusive or antagonistic.

Coevolution

The key figure or trope of conceptualizing 'association' is 'the network' (Latour 2005; Van Loon 2006) In Actor Network Theory, actants forge networked relationships to gather strength and defend their integrity. Latour's inspiration is clearly Nietzschean, but also bears some traces of Darwinism. Darwinism entails an ethos that evolution is inherently meaningless. It does not have a purpose (apart perhaps from 'striving towards greater complexity'). All it is, is a hypothetical explanation of a process of continuous shifting balances between organisms and their environment. The motivation of being is thus reduced to that of survival: we exist in order to be. Apart from being tautological, such a presupposition is also reductionist. The opposite could be equally true – we exist in order to change, i.e., cease to be as we are. This is the essence of symbiosis theory (Margulis 1993; Sapp 1994; Ryan 2003).

Although Darwinism has been generally invoked to argue that evolution entails a movement towards greater complexity, studies have shown this is not necessarily always the case (Wills 1996). That is, it is difficult to see why the principle of survival of the best adapted would *necessarily* lead to greater complexity. Instead, the notion of evolution towards greater complexity entails a theological streak that stems from a cultural orientation of that 'clever beast that invented knowledge' (Nietzsche 2006). It stems from the 'will to know'.

This theological inheritance, which manifests itself in the teleological search for the same meaning (survival of the best adapted in a move towards greater complexity) in every minute manifestation of 'nature', however, has been systematically rejected by Nietzsche and Latour has always been equally suspicious of any teleological reasoning. Instead, the Nietzschean influence on Latour ensured that his understanding of history remains relatively ahistorical; history 'happens' and can only be explained as the outcome of the interplay between forces. It is perhaps for this reason that ANT has a rather underdeveloped conception of sociality. For ANT, sociality is equivalent to association (Latour 2005). Hence, the affective charge of connectivity, which for sociologists, such as Durkheim or Parsons, would still be a morally embedded phenomenon, is within the ANT paradigm merely a collusion/collision of forces; it is a reflection of the investment made (the costs of dissociation are expressed as a loss of value) or power exercised (the costs of dissociation are expressed as a loss of strength).

It is through mediation that our orientation towards the world becomes charged in terms of affect, sensibility and sense. This means that, rather than – or better, primordial to – an instrumental orientation towards gathering strength and enabling survival, our mediated networked being is an existential necessity. As an existential necessity, the affective charge of association is much less tied to the will to power (if this is used in a Machiavellian fashion, which is not necessarily Nietzsche's) as it is to *the will to life* (which is not the same as the will to survive).

This vitalist turn is essential when we are coming to terms with life in an age of digitalization. Digital being, which we have already seen is inscribed in the very fabric of human being as gendered, enables a multiplicity of engagements with our existential disclosedness. These engagements can be called 'desires' in the sense of being '*affirmative*', rather than '*performative*'. Affirmative desires orient us towards our existential being and the will to live. Performative desires are induced by the manipulation of needs that bind us into particular networked relationships, in particular those that we encounter as reified institutional forms, e.g., technoscience, governmentality, commodification, law and warfare. Affirmative desires are a multiplicity and cannot be reduced to anything, not even the will to will. Performative desires are reconfigured around specific formats of object relations, such as need, greed, like, lust, want, aspiration, etc.

Mediation, it could be argued, is also a translation of affirmative desires into performative ones. This is easily exemplified by advertising as a mode of articulating unspecified desires (e.g., a desire to belong) into desires for specific things (the want of a branded product). The problem with ANT is that its own ethnographic orientation enables its analyses to encounter performative desires far more easily than affirmative ones (it suffers from 'a metaphysics of presence'). This, in turn, leads to an all-too-easy acceptance that network behaviour is instrumental and motivated by a desire for strength.

When we consider, however, the dynamic interplay between embodiment and disembodiment, we can regain a bit more vitalism in our media-analyses. And on the basis of this, we can show how mediation can also engender association. From the examples of interactions in on-line multi-user RPGs, it becomes clear that moral considerations are not absent in virtual environments and that mediation does not in itself foreclose the formation of associative bonds. In fact, association is actively pursued by a substantial section of on-line activities because it is an enjoyable part of the gaming experience. The enjoyment is not less real. At the same time, issues of trust and fidelity also apply. As the relationships between avatar, persona and physical body are transductive, it means that they are intertwined and thus affect each other. Trust and fidelity are particular modalities of attuning oneself to being in the world. Digitalization has enabled a greater range of converging modalities of attuning that can be technologically enframed. Violations of trust and fidelity, even if they cross the ontological divides between avatar, persona and physical body, are still violations and morally problematic.

Again invoking affect, intuition and cognition enables us to see how gaming can be understood as a specific form of mediation that attunes our existential being to our being in the world. As we have seen, the triad of avatar, persona and physiological body constitutes a layering of virtualities that enable subjectivities to configure themselves playfully in association with each other. In the first instance, we can understand the role of the persona as primarily shuttling between intextuation and incarnation as it operates as a vehicle between the pixels and the gamers. However, the true realization of the persona is *inspiration*, when it is able to bind into the purposefulness of gaming, a vitalist sense of affirmative desire, when it bestows upon the mediations the spirit of the gift, the *hau*. It is through the *hau* that associations are formed and become binding (for example, in the form of friendships). Binding-use modulates trust and fidelity and provides the moral anchorage of subjectivity.

Inspiration, which binds the persona into the process of mediation, highlights the ontological primacy of the medium for social being. It is here that we may be able to see how in traditional communication theory, the system's model already implied some of this, yet failed to pursue its logical consequences (Fiske 1990; Kittler 1996). It comes with the awareness that media produce bias. Indeed, today's communication models do at least acknowledge that 'bias' is closely related to the technological nature of the mediation process and the idea that language is not a transparent, self-evident medium has become widely accepted beyond the specialisms of philosophy and linguistics.

The concept of mediation, therefore, is not so much a radical innovation, but a useful reminder that all forms of communication evolve three, and not two, nodal points. In other words, if we were to look at the systems model of communication theory through the prism of mediation, it makes perfect sense to echo McLuhan (1964) that indeed, 'the medium is the message'. Quite literally, the space occupied by 'message' between transmitter and receiver is what belongs to the medium. Perhaps those who were quick to dismiss McLuhan's aphorism did so because they believed that speech is an unmediated form of communication and that it is the archetype of all other forms of communication [Derrida (1974) called this 'logocentrism'; also see Bakhtin 1986 and Gardiner 1992].

Although speech is one of the first modalities (media) of communication, its content (language) was already a medium. The content of language might be signs, but these are also media consisting of signifiers and signifieds, as semiotics teaches us. Semiotics also suggests that the signifier is the medium of the signified but that, at least in language, the relationship between the two is arbitrary [this is what C.S. Peirce (1940) calls 'the symbolic']. The signified is the idea or concept, which might thus be then seen as the only immediate origin of communication. Yet, a signified without a signifier is nothing; that is, without a medium giving it some form of expression (a sound, an inscription, an image), the signified is nothing.

Semiotics confirms what Levinson (1997) and others (Ong 1982) have also suggested: from the start of human history, media were part of our human evolution. Biologists would speak of coevolution (for example, symbiosis theory suggests that all animals and zoonotic viruses have coevolved; Margulis 1993; Sapp 1994; Ryan 2003). Modern thought usually subscribes to theoretical propositions based on the singularity of an origin (big bang, selfish gene, etc.), this is central to the linear paradigm (Curtis 1977). However, the concept of coevolution breaks with that tradition to such an extent that when there is no longer a singular origin, it is also difficult to maintain a sense of linear development (or determination).

Coevolution posits that in the beginning there was not one but (at least) two. It is logically linked to a feminist critique of phallocentrism, i.e., that all meaning can be derived from the single signifier – the phallus (Irigaray 2000). Coevolution places the 'difference within' at the heart of its epistemological orientation, and furthermore, cannot but embrace a radical ecological perspective that sidesteps thought organized on the basis of the illusory 'entity-within-environment', but instead stresses the dynamic interplay between all entities as itself constituting an ecological system.

The idea that humans and media have coevolved from the beginning is a premise we should explore in greater detail, both archaeologically but also phenomenologically. It requires that we pay closer attention to the way in which media articulate how we become attuned to our being in the world. This, I would argue, might affirm the theoretical relevance of media studies and provide a clear focal point for its future development.

Medium, space and time

Ontologically speaking, media are an essential part of our human being. More specifically, it is problematic to develop a concept of 'the social' (as some form of 'pure' interaction) that does not consider the role of particular forms of mediation (even if these 'only' involve spoken language in face-to-face situations).

To repeat, according to classical communications theory, the medium is always placed in-between sender and receiver. In more abstract terms, the medium is the 'third term' in communication processes; it comes in-between two interlocutors. This coming-in-between is thus first a mode of *spatial distantiation*. For example, in conflict management, mediation allows the disputing parties to interact, the first premise for settling their dispute, by keeping them apart. However, simultaneously, mediation is also a form of *temporalization* – slowing down; because no longer working through direct face-to-face interactions, the parties in dispute have to take time to evaluate their own and their opponents' positions. Mediation (for example, 'recording') allows the dispute to take (or store) time in which the (promise of a) resolution is deferred to a time-to-come. In short, mediation could be seen as a practice of intervention, a coming-in-between that spatializes a field of possibly conflicting, but at the least non-identical meaning formations, and simultaneously temporizes the formations of meaning by 'giving time' to the rendering of accounts, and opening up possibilities for mitigation, compromise and settlement. Mediation thus closely resembles what Derrida (1982; Van Loon 1996a) refers to as *differance* – the conjuncture of the verbs 'to differ' (distinguish and disagree) and 'to defer' (delay and give in) – to set apart (spatialization) and to delay (temporization).

However, media do not exclusively extend or defer; they also compress and accelerate social processes. Communication satellites are a good example of this space/time compression; through satellites, information travels across the globe in seconds, bypassing nearly all barriers of space and time in the communication process (Virilio 1977, 1997). Mediation changes because media-technologies change. The speeding up of mediation puts pressure on its ability to engender 'differance'. According to Derrida (1992) temporization is essential for the gift to properly inaugurate social bonds. Gifts 'take time'; what they give is time.

What media allow, therefore, is the creation of events; they 'give time' and 'space' to communication processes. That the history of communication media seems to be driven by an oppositional drive – to eradicate space and time – does not negate but actually affirms that media spatialize and temporalize. The desire for immediacy and transparency (Bolter and Grusin 2000) is born out of a realization of *differance*. (Lacanians might call this 'lack'.) This *differance* is what is explored in hypermediation. Hypermediation takes place when media radically actualize McLuhan's aphorism that the medium is the message. It takes place when media become 'self-reflexive' and begin to activate and comment on each other's particularities.

Hypermediation brings to the fore the ubiquitous nature of the virtual. It is perhaps not a coincidence that we have become far more attuned to the mediated character and virtual nature of our own being. This is because our media technological environment has become so steeped in a sense of hypermediation that, whatever desire for immediacy and transparency might drive technological innovation, it will always be accompanied by moments of reflexivity in which we are reminded of our own extended being in media ecologies.

This awareness has become far more prevalent and common-sensical with the advent of digital media. Whereas analogue media, such as photography and radio, always require human intervention in the translation of one type of medium to the next, the digital nature of information facilitates direct communications between media systems. With the increased interconnections (connectivity) between all kinds of different media systems (telecommunications, information servers and data processing, broadcasting media, mobile media), the distinctions between the old-fashioned 'mass-communication' media and other media are no longer hugely relevant. Due to the increased integration and interconnectivity of media, facilitated by digitalization, media have increasingly become mutually adaptable. Anything that can be reduced to a combination of binary codes (one and zero) can be processed in exactly the same way: texts, sounds, images, even tactile sensory stimulations that may simulate 'feelings'. As a consequence of digitalization, almost all media have the potential to become mass media.

In *Remediation*, Bolter and Grusin (2000) argue that media evolutions are always caught up in a double bind. On the one hand, the technological development of media is always geared up towards achieving greater immediacy, i.e., the illusion of transparency (Vattimo 1992); that is, media are optimized as to make themselves less explicitly present. One dimension of this is miniaturization, another is speed (to make communication instantaneous, i.e., more like face-to-face speech). On the other hand, our dependency on a vast and still growing number of media also results in more and more hypermediation, that is, forms of mediation that make explicit reference to the fact that we ourselves are mediated beings.

Bolter and Grusin argue that these two processes always come together because both are, in their extreme states, untenable. Media will never be fully transparent (for they will cease to be media), nor will they exclusively refer to other media (for they will cease to be meaningful). Our relationship with media is always an interplay between 'incorporation' (media becoming part of us, like prostheses) and 'amputation' [media losing their natural habitation as part of our bodies and becoming 'alien objects' (abjects)]. Whatever we think is part of us, or no longer part of us, depends on the specific media ecology in which we live.

Our current age is dominated by digital information processing, which generate a very particular experience of transparency, namely in the form of 'ubiquitous computing' (e.g., wireless technology, including mobile phone/Internet links). We now are accustomed to being able to obtain information 'immediately' about anything, anywhere, anytime we want and we expect to get in touch with most people 'immediately', anywhere, anytime we want. Immediacy is the new form of transparency – time and place do not matter; past and future do not matter; there is only the here-and-now, which – by means of ubiquitous computing – has become anywhere, anytime.

Theorizing media has thus taken us to rather new territory, away from the spheres of media production, organization and consumption. We always need to ask ourselves what media are and what mediation entails. Answers to these questions are never satisfied by simple, methodologically induced observations, but need a 'radical empiricism' to probe deeper, phenomenologically, historically and critically, into the nature of their subject matter. Media theory will have to come to terms with the new challenges posed by ubiquitous computing (indeed, ubiquitous media), these are not simple variations on the same old themes (e.g., representation/performativity, structure/agency, ideology/creativity). Instead, they require new modes of thinking, new frameworks of analysis. I have hoped to show that these frameworks are already out there, perhaps more at the fringes of the subject area, but not beyond it. Analysing media is fundamental if we are to come to terms with the contemporary world, for we have become immersed in forms of mediated being.

GLOSSARY

Actant An entity (human, animal, machine, spirit, god) capable of action. This term has been mainly developed by Latour. In contrast to 'actor' it does not presuppose the acting out of a role. In sociology the most often used term for this would be 'agent'; the problem with that is the thought that an agent always operates on behalf of someone else, represents an institutional function and is therefore too often confused with the concept of 'medium'. A medium can be an actant but not all actants are media.

Actor networks A collection of connected actants; developed by Callon, Latour and Law. Actor networks are forms by which social practices can be consolidated and obtain relative stability.

Affirmative desires Forms of desiring that relate to constituting the presence of existential being. That is, they are authentic forms of human existence. They are expressions of the will to life, in contrast to performative desires (see **performativity** below), which are expressions of a will to power. Affirmation is a key concept within the philosophy of vitalism.

All-at-once-ness A hypothetical condition in which everything is contained in one node at the same time; a term coined by McLuhan (McLuhan and Fiore 1967).

Anthropocentrism An ideology that places 'man' at the centre of the universe.

Anthropomorphism An ideology that models everything on the primacy of 'man' (man as the measure of all things).

Arche From classical Greek word, meaning 'origin' or 'beginning' (as in Archaeology). Nietzsche referred to it with the German word *Ursprung* to argue that it is in fact a myth of beginning (Foucault 1977a); the opposite of **Telos.**

Aura That which gives a work of art its unique features, it reminds us of its singularity in space and time, on our privilege of encountering it, and of the genius of its creator; this concept has been derived from Benjamin (1969).

Autopoiesis A condition in which a system is capable of replicating itself, reproducing itself internally without recourse to its environment; originally developed by Maturana and Varela (1980) in biology, introduced into sociology by Niklas Luhmann (1982; Zolo 1991).

Being-in-the-world   The ordinary, everyday, unreflexive state in which we live and conduct most of our daily affairs; from Heidegger's (1927/1986) *Being and Time*.

Bias   That which we are orientated towards, which makes us attend to the things we attend to; developed by Innis (1982; also see Comor 2003).

Biophilosophy   A philosophical stream that takes as its point of departure the fact that life is itself a non-metaphysical state from which thought emerges; i.e., modalities of thinking that are anchored in the physiological conditions of the thinking-being; mainly associated with Nietzsche, Deleuze and Guatari and 'vitalism'.

Black box   A term coined by Latour to refer to that which is taken for granted in (scientific) practices and cannot be challenged unless at great cost to one's credibility.

Dasein   Literally 'being-there', a term used by Heidegger to refer to existential being, i.e., a mode of being in which one is reflectively aware of oneself as a thinking-being and applies oneself to the question of what it means 'to be'; from Heidegger's (1927/1986) *Being and Time*.

Deduction   A mode of reasoning from abstract principles to logical, empirically observable statements.

Differance   Coined by Jacques Derrida as an amalgamation of the verbs 'to differ' and 'to defer' to help describe how signification is always a doubling of presence (the actual) and absence (the possible), the latter always entails the possibility of becoming present only in so far as it does not happen. In the most simplistic terms, it helps us think about the impossibility of making things fully present in representations (Van Loon 1996a).

Diffraction   A concept used by Donna Haraway (1997) to describe the tension between movement and vision. Diffractions are visual transformations of images by systematically multiplying them, while slightly changing the parameters so that an effect of moving image can be captured in a single visual frame (and thereby connection motion and repetition). Haraway used it to problematize identity thinking and the idea of 'stable' boundaries of being.

Domestication   The process by which technology becomes incorporated into the routine practices of everyday lives (usually placed in 'the home').

Enframing   A term associated with Heidegger's notion of technology as *Gestell* (see below), which is best translated as 'ordering' in the double sense of providing a structure (putting into place) and commanding specific actions.

Entropy   A concept derived from physics referring to a tendency towards disorder within a (closed) system, as energy is being 'lost' to forms that cannot be used. This tendency is also referred to as 'the second law of thermodynamics'.

Ephemeral   That which escapes materialization as 'presence' (a present without a presence); and maintains a 'fleeting' character, impossible to pin down or contain.

Escape velocity   A concept used by Virilio (1997) to describe a critical threshold in modernity in which the speed of mediated communication exceeds our ability to anticipate the changing nature of perception. At this critical threshold, cognition can no longer validate or invalidate speculation and past, present and future collapse into one 'point of view'. That is, they become intensities of exposure.

Existential being   The momentary and by no means ordinary revelation of one's unique, irreducible 'presence' as existent in the world. It is a form of consciousness that reflects back upon its own existence as here/now in the world.

Functionalism   A particular mode of thinking based on the premise that the existence of norms, values and institutions is derived from a selective evolution in which those elements that were most in tune with the needs of the wider social system were more likely to be reinforced. As a result, norms, values and institutions exist because they function to support the needs of the wider social system of which they are a part. The main proponent of this type of thinking was the American sociologist, Talcott Parsons.

Habitus   'A system of shared social dispositions and cognitive structures which generates perceptions, appreciations and actions' (Bourdieu 1988: 279). The habitus mediates between individual and collective experiences and expressions. It provides the ingrained logic of how we orient ourselves towards the world and is informed by our past experiences as well as by forms of socialization (family, school media, etc.). Also see Bourdieu (1977).

Hau   A word from Maori, meaning 'spirit of the gift'. It was used by Marcell Mauss to describe how the giving and receiving of gifts, among the Maori, entailed an entering into a social relationship that was itself an expression of a moral obligation to not exploit the social relationship for personal gains. In Heideggerian terms, the *Hau* reflects the binding use of the gift.

Hermeneutics   Hermeneutics is concerned with understanding the world through interpretation. It is derived from the Greek mythological character Hermes, who was a traveller. Hermeneutics consist of understanding the world not from the outside, but from the inside; by being 'under way' as a member of the very world one seeks to understand. In Heidegger's sense, it is a form of understanding Being in terms of one's being in the world.

Humanism   An ideology that seeks to develop modes of reasoning derived from human values based on the primacy of human being. Premodern forms of humanism (e.g., that of Erasmus) were primarily directed against the formalistic traditions of scholasticism (which derived knowledge from logical principles). It meant a return to interpretative origins in their original context. In the modern age, humanism became a secular philosophy that embraced the central premise of modern thought as 'man as the measure of all things'. Whereas the first form of humanism was merely an intervention; the second is best understood as an extension of modern technoscience as it feeds into a range of institutional practices, as well as legitimations of forms of disciplinary power.

Hybrid media   A term coined by McLuhan to describe what happens if media meet; i.e., when the medium-as-the-message affects mediation. This is easiest understood as the moment when a new medium is being introduced and it affects the consistency of the existing media-*Gestell*, for example, the introduction of the camcorder and the rise of 'reality television'.

Hypermediation   A term coined by Bolter and Grusin (2000) to describe the process of media-becoming-message in an endless movement of reflexive mediation. Here, media foreground the mediated nature of our existence by exposing how our very understanding of the world is always already mediated.

Hyperreality   A term used by Baudrillard to describe the sense of intensified reality due to the expansion of simulation. Media simulate reality into hyperreality and create worlds that are 'more real than the real thing'. It is a reality in which every detail can be scrutinized; as all our senses are being amplified by media-technologies.

Ideological State Apparatus (ISA)   A term coined by Louis Althusser to describe aspects of the state in capitalist systems that are primarily concerned with reproducing the existing order (mode of production) through sustaining an integration of the majority of people into modes of thinking that provide 'an imaginary relationship . . . to their real conditions of existence' (Althusser 1971: 162) that does not challenge the system, but helps people to 'fit in'; schools, media, trade unions, even hospitals are ISAs.

Immutable mobile   A concept developed by Latour (1987) to conceptualize a process by which networking relationships are established through media that themselves remain constant and are not effected by the relationship. They are in that sense like protocol in computer interfaces, without which systems would not be able to communicate.

Indexicality   It means two different things in two different disciplines. In sociolinguistics it refers to the situation specific nature of speech. For example, when people use 'this' or 'here' the meaning of such words depends entirely on the setting in which the language exchange takes place. In social semiotics (particularly the work of Charles Sanders Peirce), it refers to a specific mode of signification that is distinct from both icon (e.g., an image) and symbol (text). The index refers to a relationship between sign and referent that is one of causation and has physical properties, thereby working as a tracing device. In this sense, smoke is an index of fire, just a photosynthesis (using chemical properties) enables light to form an image on photographic paper in analogue photography. When these two things are combined (context specificity and physical, causal relationships), indexicality becomes a concept to describe how 'pointing towards' (e.g., the index finger) establishes a virtual material doubling of meaning that is by its very nature, spatially anchored.

Induction   The process of bringing about an event or change. In social settings it is used to describe a usually intensive (immersion) process of introducing 'new members' to the life world of institutional settings. In the philosophy of science it means the process by which theses are being derived from repetitive observations. It is also used in electromagnetic physics to describe how electric currents can be generated from magnetic fields and *vice versa*. In all cases, it refers to a transformation of matter that brings about a specific effect.

Instrumentalism   An ideology that reduces some actants to mere passive objects, which are completely at the disposal of other actants. In this sense, it reflects a disavowal of some forms of agency and an exaggeration of others. It usually applies to perceptions that reduce technology to being mere 'tools', thereby imposing on their being a selective logic derived from the intentionality of those who deploy them. It reduces the fullness of meaning as multiple possibilities to what was intended as 'meant to be'.

Interfaciality   The process of linking different types of systems. It is usually referred to as that which connects human systems and technological systems. For example, in computing, they can be both 'hardware', such as the screen, the keyboard and the mouse, but also software (e.g., specific graphical applications that serve as control panels). These devices all mediate between human beings and computers and make it possible for humans to engage with computers, but is becoming more evident with the spread of neural networks and fuzzy logic. Interfaces also enable computers to interpret human thought and actions.

Intersubjectivity   That which exists between subjects. It designates the social and discursive space that is created by interactions between subjects. It also highlights that this 'in-between-ness' is meaningful in its own terms and cannot be reduced to the sum of subject-ivities involved. An exchange of some kind between the subjective forms constituting intersubjectivity is essential, although such an exchange does not have to be limited to verbal forms.

Isomorphism   The ideology that insists on the unity and integrity between form and content. That is, it insists that things are part of a single group if they have the same form. Just as isotherm refers to a consistency of the value of temperature, isomorphism refers to the consistency of the value of form. It is in effect a prerequisite for essentialism; the ideology that there are essential characteristics to specific modes of being (e.g., gender, ethnicity, race).

Jouissance   A concept developed by Jacques Lacan (1977). It literally means 'enjoyment', but Lacan used it in contrast to Freud's 'pleasure principle' to refer to what lies beyond the limitations of pleasure (i.e., pain). It has a sexual connotation that is related to the orgasm.

Linear paradigm   The idea that cause and effect exist in a single serial relationship that can be chronologically traced in time. Although essential in ancient Greek geometry (Euclid), it finds its most famous application in the laws of physics, as developed by Isaac Newton. Newtonian physics have found many applications in other fields, such as economics and biology. In the latter it became associated with views of evolutionism that were simplified applications of Darwin's crucial insights into random variation and natural selection. Whereas random variations do not really sit comfortably with linear paradigms, the latter's effect on understanding natural selection resulted in extremely deterministic views on evolution that were often reduced to the slogan 'survival of the fittest'. The same problems emerge when applying this to media-evolution, as it assumes that there has been a linear sucession of media forms, whereas in reality changes in media have been far more divergent and complex, resembling more the shape of fractals than of lines.

Longe durée   This means 'in the long term' and refers to the fact that history entails a slow, gradual dual process of solidification and modification. Long duree is a time perspective that favours slowness and continuity.

Mediascape   A variation on the world 'landscape' to represent – in terms of a spatial metaphor – the concept of a media ecology. Just as landscape combines the visual and spatial representation of a natural environment with connotations of 'orderliness' and 'patterns'.

Mediatization   The process by which social, political, economic and cultural processes, interactions and transactions increasingly involve media.

Metaphysics of presence   A particular predisposition in thought that assumes an equivalence between being and presence. The term was used by Derrida as a critique of ontologies that imply that the relationship between the 'sign' and the 'referent' is timeless.

Modality   In grammar, modality refers to the commitment between the subject and the action (expressed in the verb). In philosophical terms, modality is often synonymous with 'form' or 'mode of engagement' (as in 'modalities of power').

Myth   A concept made famous by Levi-Strauss and, above all, Roland Barthes (1993). Whereas for Levi-Strauss myths were part of the basic structures of meaning and thus, fundamental to all cultural forms. Barthes took a more critical line by arguing that myths were distortions of history. They turned historical, socially constructed and, therefore, politically motivated significations into a timeless, naturalized sense of 'always already' there.

Non-linear paradigm   In contrast to the linear paradigm, a non-linear paradigm is formed on the basis of the assumption that causes and effects are not necessarily chronologically related. That is to say, it is based on the principle of multiple determinants that do not add up. The non-linear paradigm is central to chaos theory.

Performativity   A term associated with the work of Judith Butler. She uses it to refer to the way in which subjectivity is not given, but enacted. However, in the work of Lyotard, performativity refers to an ethos of modernity, more specifically the technological drive to maximize efficiency.

Phenomenology   A philosophical approach that seeks to develop an ontology of thought on the basis of perception and experience. It is associated with the work of Edmund Husserl and has been one of the most influential streams in modern continental philosophy.

Post-human   A term that refers to that into which the human being is thought to evolve through its increased reliance on digital technology (also referred to as 'cyborg').

Post-structuralism   A philosophical approach closely associated with literary theory, which developed as a critique of structuralism, undermining the latters insistence on the primacy of forms and relations of determination and creating a view of more fluid, historically specific, ambivalent and non-determinate accounts of social and cultural processes.

Pure war   A term developed by Virilio (1993) to describe the condition in which war permeates every aspect of life; war is no longer declared, but continuous and ongoing; everything that exists functions in the mobilization of war capacity, and there is no distinction between preparation for war and actual combat.

Remediation   A concept developed by Bolter and Grusin (2000) to describe how media-evolutions have always entailed two processes: (1) a drive towards immediacy and (2) a drive to hyper-mediation. It is, in essence, a further development of McLuhan's (1964) aphorism that 'the medium is the message'. Remediation thus suggests that human evolution entails an increased reliance on mediated being, but that this has two rather different manifestations: on the one hand, our world seems to become ever more immediate and transparent; and on the other hand, we become completely dependent on media which also mobilize other media as content to further enhance the extent of our mediated being.

Semiotics   This is usually defined as the 'science of science' (in which case it would be more properly called 'semiology'). However, a more accurate definition of semiotics would be the 'creation of meaning', which is not exclusively limited to the work of academic interpreters, but includes everyone involved in the process of signification.

Signification   The attribution of significance; which is an essential part of the creation of meaning. Significance has to be understood both in terms of an imposition (attachment) of possible interpretations, as well as the imposition (evaluation) of what matters.

Simulacrum   A copy of which no original exists.

Simulation   Simulations are a device by which 'reality is played out' under controlled conditions (e.g., such as in flight simulators or role-play simulations). It has been used as a concept by Baudrillard (1993) in contrast to symbolic exchange to refer to a process by which signs become exchanged for signs without any transfer of social significance. It is dominant in a world in which media can create completely self-enclosed environments in which the reality engaged is only one created by other media.

Slave morality   A term used by Nietzsche to criticize the underlying motives of modernist politics of emancipation. It is derived from a critique if Hegel's Master-Slave dichotomy, which forms the basis of the latter's approach to dialectics. The basic tenet of slave morality is that domination is bad therefore the master is bad and the slave is good and, *therefore*, occupies a morally superior position. Slave morality informs most emancipatory movements of the modern age including socialism, feminism and anti-racism. It is also linked to the idea that by fighting evil one automatically becomes sanctified (George W. Bush's justification for the war on Iraq).

Social/cultural determinism   The idea that societal changes are solely caused by human intentions, actions or motives. The social variant stresses relationships in terms of interests and struggles over power; the cultural variant stresses (collective) attributions of meaning.

Sociation The process by which 'the social' is formed. It is based on relationships and interactions between 'members'. These relationships differ according to the 'affective charge', which determines the strength of the 'bond' (which Durkheim refers to in terms of 'social solidarity').

Society of the spectacle A phrased used by Guy Debord (1969/1994) to describe how capitalism evolves through a massive expansion of symbolic goods, produced and disseminated by media. The phrase covers both political-economic and cultural aspects of understanding social reproduction in capitalist societies.

Structuralism An ideology associated with a specific theoretical stream of twentieth century cultural theory in which meaning was believed to be based on deep-seated 'hidden' structures. The basic model most often used to explain this is one developed by the Swiss linguist Ferdinand de Saussure who distinguished between langue, the deep-seated structures of language (e.g., grammar) and parole, which is the way in which language is used and manifests itself practically.

Structure of feeling A concept developed by Raymond Williams in an attempt to analyse how material conditions of existence can frame subjectivities, not simply in terms of their needs, or in terms of ideas (ideology), but also in terms of their psychological being. Key to this concept is the emphasis on the collective, shared nature of such feelings, which are thus far from idiosyncratic or subjective, but instead objective and socially produced.

Symbiosis The biological process by which two different organisms constitute a relationship that becomes so intertwined that they start functioning as a single organism. In essence it relates to the interaction between two different types of genome, for example, animal DNA and viral RNA (see Margulis 1993; Sapp 1994; Ryan 2003).

Symbolic exchange A concept that has been central to the work of Jean Baudrillard (1993) to describe the transference of significance between subjects again in forms of communication that resemble an exchange of gifts. Key to this is that the symbolic nature of the gifts is closely connected to and embedded in the social processes that grant it significance. This is not the case in the opposite of symbolic exchange, simulation, where no such transference takes place.

Technique A concept associated with the work of Jacques Ellul (1964) to describe the particular way in which technology orders the world (in modern society) by putting everything else (including human beings) at its disposal as a resource to be used.

Technological determinism The ideology that presupposes that all societal change (including economic change) is generated by technological forces and innovations.

Telematics Derived from *tele* (=distance) and *matica* (operation). It literally means 'operations at a distance' and is refers to the linking of telecommunications and information processing. This is the basis of what is known as connectivity, the convergence between different types of media (communications, information platforms and entertainment).

Telos From classical Greek, meaning (final) destiny; in contrast to **arche**. The prefix *tele* (as in television) refers to distance; *telos* is therefore what is being projected to in terms of final aim toward which we are destined.

Tetrad This literally means 'four-fold'. It is used by McLuhan to identify four core questions as the basis of any medium analysis: (1) What does the new medium amplify? (2) What does it obsolesce? (3) What does it retrieve from the past? (4) What does it flip into?

Transduction A concept coined by Simondon and developed by Adrian McKenzie (2002) a process by which a new medium emerges out of a diverse range of existing media. By engendering a new medium, transduction is thus a process by which mediation evolves into ever-changing assemblages.

Virtual   That which is suspended in time in terms of a 'not yet'. In space, it is what shuttles between presence and absence, in metaphysics it links the actual and the possible, it is what unites subjects and objects.

Vitality   Life force that is innate to all being regardless of its 'organic' status.

Vortex   A spiralling movement, that can be either centripetal (in which things get sucked in) or centrifugal, in which things spin out of control. Vortex is associated with non-linear paradigms and is the opposite of index. Whereas index points towards a specific causal relationships and this singles out a 'line', vortex multiplies links and lines (like a fractal) and creates complexity, either in terms of an implosion (centripetal vortex) or explosion (centrifugal vortex).

REFERENCES

Adam, B. (1990) *Time and Social Theory*. Cambridge: Polity Press.

Adams, P. (1993) In TV: On 'Nearness', on Heidegger and on Television, in T. Fry (ed.) *R U A TV? Heidegger and the Televisual*. Sydney: Power Publications, 45–66.

Adorno, T.W. and Horkheimer, M. (1979) *Dialectic of Enlightenment*. London: Verso.

Allan, S. (1995) News, truth and postmodernity: unravelling the will to facticity, in B. Adam and S. Allan (eds) *Theorizing Culture. An Interdisciplinary Critique after Postmodernism*. London: UCL Press, 129–44.

Allen, G. (2003) *Roland Barthes*. London: Routledge.

Althusser, L. (1971) *Lenin and Philosophy and Other Essays*. New York, NY: New Left Books.

Anderson, B. (1983) *Imagined Communities Reflection on the Origin and Spread of Nationalism*. London: Verso.

Ang, I. (1985) *Watching 'Dallas': Soap Opera and the Melodramatic Imagination*. London: Methuen.

Ang, I. (1992) Living-room wars: new technologies, audience measurement and the tactics of television consumption, in R. Silverstone and E. Hirsch (eds) *Consuming Technologies: Media and Information in Domestic Spaces*. London: Routledge, 131–45.

Ansell-Pearson, K. (1997) *Viroid Life. Perspectives on Nietzsche and the Transhuman Condition*. London: Routledge.

Argyle, K. (1996) Life after death, in R. Shields (ed.) *Cultures of Internet: Virtual Spaces, Real Histories, Living Bodies*. London: Sage, 133–42.

Augé, M. (1995) *Non-places: An Introduction to an Anthropology of Supermodernity*. London: Verso.

Babe, R.E. (2000) *Canadian Communication Thought: Ten Foundational Writers*. Toronto: University of Toronto Press.

Bakardjieva, M. (2005) *Internet Society. The Internet in Everyday Life*. London: Sage.

Bakhtin, M.M. (1986) *Speech Genres and Other Late Essays* (V.W. McGee transl., C. Emerson and M. Holquist eds.). Austin, TX: University of Texas Press.

Barthes, R. (1977) *Image Music Text*. London: Fontana.

Barthes, R. (1993a) *Camera Lucida. Reflections on Photography*. London: Vintage.

Barthes, R. (1993b) *Mythologies*. London: Vintage.

Baudrillard, J. (1990) *Fatal Strategies. Crystal Revenge*. New York, NY: Semiotext(e).

Baudrillard, J. (1993) *Symbolic Exchange and Death*. London: Sage.

Bauman, Z. (2001) *The Individualized Society*. Cambridge: Polity Press.

Beck, U. (1997) *The Reinvention of Politics. Rethinking Modernity in the Global Social Order*. Cambridge: Polity Press.

Beck, U. (1998) *Was ist Globalisierung?* Frankfurt am Main: Suhrkamp Verlag.

Beck, U. and Beck-Gernsheim, E. (2002) *Individualization*. London: Sage.

Benjamin, W. (1969) *Illuminations. Essays and Reflections*. New York, NY: Shocken.

Benjamin, W. (2006) *Berlin Childhood Around 1900*. Cambridge, MA: Belknap Press.

Berker, T., Hartman, M., Punie, Y. and Ward, K.J. (eds) (2006) *Domestication of Media and Technology*. Maidenhead: Open University Press.

Berman, M. (1982) *All that is Solid Melts into Air, the Exploration of Modernity*. New York, NY: Penguin Books.

Bhabha, H. (1990) DissemiNation: time, narrative, and the margins of the modern nation, in H. Bhabha (ed.) *Nation and Narration*. London: Routledge, 291–322.

Blumler, J. G. and Katz, E. (1974): *The Uses of Mass Communication*. Newbury Park, CA: Sage.

Bolter, J.D. and Grusin, R. (2000) *Remediation: Understanding New Media*. Cambridge, MA: MIT Press.

Bourdieu, P. (1977) *Outline of a Theory of Practice*. Cambridge: Cambridge University Press.

Bourdieu, P. (1984) *Distinction: a Social Critique of the Judgement of Taste*. Cambridge, MA: Harvard University Press.

Bourdieu, P. (1988) *Homo Academicus*. Stanford, CA: Stanford University Press.

Boyle, K. (2005) *Media and Violence. Gendering the Debates*. London: Sage.

Briggs, A. and Burke, P. (2002) *A Social History of the Media. From Gutenberg to the Internet*. Cambridge: Polity Press.

Bristow, J. (1997) *Sexuality*. London: Routledge.

Bromberg, H. (1996) 'Are MUDs Communities?' in R. Shields (ed.) *Cultures of Internet: Virtual Spaces, Real Histories, Living Bodies*. London: Sage, 143–52.

Butler, J. (1993a) Endangered/endangering: schematic racism and White paranoia, in R. Gooding-Williams (ed.) *Reading Rodney King. Reading Urban Uprising*. London: Routledge, 15–22.

Butler, J. (1993b) *Bodies that Matter. On the Discursive Limits of Sex*. London: Routledge.

Canetti, E. (1962) *Crowds and Power*. New York, NY: Farrar, Strauss and Giroux.

Carey, J.W. (1992) *Communication as Culture. Essays on Media and Society*. London: Routledge.

Castells, M. (1996) *The Rise of the Network Society*. Oxford: Blackwell Publishers.

Caygill, H. (1998) *Walter Benjamin: the Colour of Experience*. London: Routledge.

Chambers, D., Steimer, L. and Fleming, C. (2004) *Women and Journalism*. London: Routledge.

Charlesworth, S. (2000) *Phenomenology of the English Working Class*. Cambridge: Cambridge University Press.

Church Gibson, P. (ed.) (2004) *More Dirty Looks: Gender, Pornography and Power*. London: BFI.

Clark, N. (1997) 'Infowar/Ecodefense: target-rich environmentalism from Desert Storm to Independence Day. *Space and Culture* 2: 50–74.

Cockburn, C. (1992) The circuit of technology: gender, identity and power, in R. Silverstone and

E. Hirsch (eds) *Consuming Technologies: Media and Information in Domestic Spaces*. London: Routledge, 32–47.

Cockburn, C. and Fürst-Dilic, R. (eds) (1994) *Bringing Technology Home. Gender and Technology in a Changing Europe*. Buckingham: Open University Press.

Comor, E. (2003) Harold Innis, in C. May (ed.) *Key Thinkers for the Information Society*. London: Routledge, 87–108.

Connell, M. (1998) Body, mimesis and childhood in Adorno, Kafka and Freud. *Body and Society* 4(4): 67–90.

Connolly, W. (2002) *Neuropolitics. Thinking, Culture, Speed*. Minneapolis, MN: University of Minnesota Press.

Copjec, J. (1989) The orthopsychic subject. Film theory and the reception of Lacan. *October* 49 (Summer): 53–71.

Cottle, S. (1993) *TV News, Urban Conflict and the Inner City*. Leicester: Leicester University Press.

Couldry, N. (forthcoming) Actor Network Theory and Media: do they connect and on what terms? in A. Hepp (ed.) *Cultures of Connectivity*. Mahwah, NJ: Hampton Press.

Crossley, N. (1996) *Intersubjectivity: the Fabric of Social Becoming*. London: Sage.

Curtis, J.W. (1977) *Culture as Polyphony*. London: Routledge and Kegan Paul.

Curtis, N. (2006) *War and Social Theory. World, Value and Identity*. Basingstoke: Palgrave Macmillan.

Dahlgren, P. (1995) *Television and the Public Sphere*. London: Sage.

de Certeau, M. (1984) *The Practice of Everyday Life*. Berkeley, CA: University of California Press.

de Kerckhove, D. (1996) *Gekoppelde Intelligentie. De opkomst van de WEB-maatschappij*. Den Haag: SMO.

de Regt, A. (1984) *Arbeidersgezinnen en Beschavingsarbeid. Ontwikkelingen in Nederland 1870–1940*. Meppel: Boom.

de Tocqueville, A. (2000) *Democracy in America*. (H. Mansfield and D. Winthrop, transl.). Chicago, IL: University of Chicago Press.

Debord, G. ([1969]1994a)*The Society of the Spectacle*. New York, NY: Zone Books.

Deleuze, G. ([1969]1994b) *Difference and Repetition*. London: Athlone.

Deleuze, G. (1986) *Cinema 1: the Movement-Image*. London: Athlone.

Deleuze, G. (1989) *Cinema 2: the Time-Image*. London: Athlone.

Deleuze, G. and Guattari, F. (1983) *Anti-Oedipus: Capitalism and Schizophrenia I*. London: Athlone.

Derrida, J. (1974) *Of Grammatology*. Baltimore: Johns Hopkins University Press.

Derrida, J. (1982) *Margins of Philosophy*. Hemel Hamsptead: Harvester Wheatsheaf.

Derrida, J. (1992) *Give Time I; Counterfeit Money* (P. Kamuf, transl.). Chicago, IL: University of Chicago Press.

Descartes, R. (1960) *Meditations on First Philosophy*. London: Macmillan.

Descombes, V. (1980) *Modern French Philosophy*. Cambridge: Cambridge University Press.

Dibbel, J. (2001) A rape in cyberspace; or how an evil clown, a Haitian trickster spirit, two wizards and a cast of dozens turned a database into a society, in D. Trend (ed.) *Reading Digital Culture*. Oxford: Blackwell, 199–213.

Dovey, J. (1996) The revelation of unguessed worlds, in J. Dovey (ed.) *Fractal Dreams. New Media in Social Context*. London: Lawence and Wishart, 109–35.

Doyle, R. (2003) *Wetwares: Experiments in Postvital Living*. Minneapolis, MN: University of Minnesota Press.

Durkheim, E. (1984) *The Division of Labour in Society*. London: Macmillan.

Durkheim, E. (2001) *The Elementary Forms of Religious Life*. Oxford: Oxford University Press.

Dyer-Witheford, N. (2002) E-capital and the many-headed hydra, in G. Elmer (ed.) *Critical Perspectives on the Internet*. Lanham, MD: Rowman and Littlefield, 129–63.

Eisenstein, E. (1983) *The Printing Revolution in Early Modern Europe*. Cambridge: Cambridge University Press.

Ellis, J. (1992) *Visible Fictions, Cinema, Television, Video*. London: Routledge.

Ellul, J. (1964) *The Technological Society*. New York, NY: Vintage.

Ellul. J. (1965) *Propaganda. The Formation of Men's Attitudes*. New York, NY: Alfred A. Knopf.

Elmer, G. (ed.) (2002) *Critical Perspectives on the Internet*. Lanham, MD: Rowman and Littlefield.

Featherstone, M. and Burrows, R. (eds) (1996) *Cyberspace Cyberbodies Cyberpunk. Cultures of Technological Embodiment*. London: Sage.

Fiske, J. (1990) *Introduction to Communication Studies*, 2nd edn. London: Routledge.

Fiske, J. (1994) *Media Matters, Everyday Culture and Political Change*. Minneapolis, MN: University of Minnesota Press.

Florida, R. (2002) *The Rise of the Creative Class. And How It's Transforming Work, Leisure and Everyday Life*. New York, NY: Basic Books.

Foucault, M. (1969) *L'Archéologie du Savoir*. Paris: Éditions Gallimard.

Foucault, M. (1970) *The Order of Things, an Archeology of the Human Sciences*. New York, NY: Vintage Books.

Foucault, M. (1977a) *Language, Counter-Memory, Practice, Selected Essays and Interviews*. Oxford: Basil Blackwell.

Foucault, M. (1977b) *Discipline and Punish, the Birth of the Prison*. New York, NY: Vintage Books.

Foucault, M. (1979) *The History of Sexuality, an Introduction; Volume 1: the Will to Know*. New York, NY: Random House.

Frank, A. (1996) Reconciliatory alchemy: bodies, narrratives and power. *Body and Society* 2(3): 53–72.

Franklin, M. (2003) Walter Benjamin, in C. May (ed.) *Key Thinkers of the Information Society*. London: Routledge, 12–42.

Franklin, S. (1997) *Embodied Progress. A Cultural Account of Assisted Conception*. London: Routledge.

Freedman, D. (2003) Raymond Williams, in C. May (ed.) *Key Thinkers of the Information Society*. London: Routledge, 173–90.

Freud, S. (1989) *Civilization and Its Discontents*. New York, NY: W.W. Norton and Company.

Fry, T. (1993) 'Switchings' in T. Fry (ed.) *R U A TV? Heidegger and the Televisual*. Sydney: Power Publications, 24–44.

Fuller, M. (2005) *Media Ecologies. Materialist Energies in Art and Technoculture*. Cambridge, MA: MIT Press.

Gallen, G. (2006) A woman's world. *XBIZ World Magazine*. Available at: http//xbiz.com

Galloway, A.R. (2006) Protocol. *Theory Culture & Society* 23(2–3): 317–20.

Gardiner, M. (1992) *The Dialogics of Critique. M. M. Bakhtin and the Theory of Ideology.* London: Routledge.

Gauntlett, D. and Horsley, R. (eds) (2004) *Web.Studies*, 2nd edn. New York, NY: Oxford University Press.

Gellner, E. (1983) *Nations and Nationalism.* Oxford: Basil Blackwell.

Genosko, G. (1998) *Undisciplined Theory.* London: Sage.

Gerbner, G. and Gross, L. (1976) Living with television: the violence profile. *Journal of Communication*, 26, 172–99.

Gibson, W. (1985) *Neuromancer.* London: Victor Gollancz.

Giddens, A. (1985) *The Nation State and Violence. Volume Two of A Contemporary Critique of Historical Materialism.* Cambridge: Polity Press.

Giddens, A. (1990) *The Consequences of Modernity.* Cambridge: Polity Press.

Giddens, A. (1991) *Modernity and Self-Identity.* Cambridge: Polity Press.

Gillis, S. (2004) Cybersex, in P. Church Gibson (ed.) *More Dirty Looks: Gender, Pornography and Power.* London: BFI, 92–101.

Gottdiener, M. (1995) *Postmodern Semiotics: Material Culture and the Forms of Postmodern Life.* Oxford: Blackwell.

Gramsci, A. (1971) *Selections from the Prison Notebooks* (Q. Hoare and G. N. Smith, transl.). New York, NY: International Publishers.

Gray, A. (1992) *Video Playtime. The Gendering of a Leisure Technology.* London: Routledge.

Haddon, L. (2003) Domestication and mobile telephony, in J. Katz (ed.) *Machines that Become Us: the Social Context of Personal Communication Technology.* New Jersey, NJ: Transaction Publishers, 43–56.

Hall, S. (1980) Encoding/decoding, in S. Hall, D. Hobson, A. Lowe and P. Willis (eds) *Culture, Media, Language. Working Papers in Cultural Studies 1972–1979* London: Unwyn Hyman, 128–38.

Hall, S., Critcher, C., Jefferson, T., Clark J. and Roberts, B. (1978) *Policing the Crisis, Mugging, the State and Law and Order.* London: Macmillan Press.

Haraway, D. (1988) Situated knowledges: the sciences question in feminism and the privilege of partial perspective. *Feminist Studies* 14(3): 575–99.

Haraway, D. (1989) *Primate Visions Gender, Race and Nature in the World of Modern Science.* New York, NY: Routledge.

Haraway, D. (1990) A manifesto for cyborgs: science, technology and socialist feminism in the 1980s, in L. J. Nicholson (ed.) *Feminism/Postmodernism.* New York, NY: Routledge, Chapman and Hall, 199–233.

Haraway, D. (1991) *Simians, Cyborgs and Women.* London: Free Association Books.

Haraway, D. (1997) *Modest Witness @ Second Millenium. FemaleMan© Meets Oncomouse™.* London: Routledge.

Hardt, M. and Negri, A. (2000) *Empire.* Cambridge, MA: Harvard University Press.

Harrison, J. (2000) *Terrestrial Television News in Britain: the Culture of Production.* Manchester: Manchester University Press.

Hartley, J. (ed.) (2005) *Creative Industries.* Oxford: Blackwell.

Harvey, D. (1989) *The Conditions of Postmodernity.* Oxford: Basil Blackwell.

Hayles, N.K. (1999) *How We Became Posthuman.* Chicago, IL: University of Chicago Press.

Hayles, N.K. (2002) *Writing Machines.* Cambridge, MA: MIT Press.

Heidegger, M. ([1927]1986) *Sein und Zeit*, 16th edn. Tübingen: Max Niemeyer Verlag.

Heidegger, M. (1977) *The Question Concerning Technology and Other Essays*. New York, NY: Harper & Row.

Heidegger, M. (1987) *Over Bouwen, Wonen en Denken*. Nijmegen: Sun.

Hemmingway, E. (2007) *Into the Newsroom: Exploring the Digital Production of Regional Television News*. London: Routledge.

Herlihy, D. (1997) *The Black Death and the Transformation of the West*. Cambridge, MA: Harvard University Press.

Heyd, T. and Clegg, J. (eds) (2005) *Aesthetics and Rock Art*. Aldershot: Ahsgate.

Heyer, P. (2003) *Harold Innis*. Lanham, MD: Rowman and Littlefield.

Hoggart, R. ([1957] 1990) *The Uses of Literacy: Aspects of Working Class Life*. Hammondsworth: Penguin.

Holland, P. (1983) The Page Three girl speaks to women, too. A sun-sational survey. *Screen* 24(3): 85–102.

Inglis, F. (1990) *Media Theory. An Introduction*. Oxford: Blackwell.

Innis, H. (1972) *Empire and Communication*. Toronto: University of Toronto Press.

Innis, H. (1982) *The Bias of Communication*. Toronto: University of Toronto Press.

Irigaray, L. (1987) *This Sex which is not One*. Ithaca: Cornell University Press.

Irigaray, L. (2000) *To Be Two*. London: Athlone.

Jacobs, D. and Yudken, J.S. (2003) *The Internet, Organizational Change, and Labor*. London: Routledge.

Jameson, F. (1994) *Postmodernism or the Cultural Logic of Late Capitalism*. London: Verso.

Jordanova, L. (1989) *Sexual Visions: Images of Gender in Science and Medicine Between the Eighteenth and Twentieth Centuries*. Hemel Hempstead: Harvester Wheatsheaf.

Juffer, J. (2004) There's no place like home: further developments on the domestic front, in P. Church Gibson (ed.) *More Dirty Looks: Gender, Pornography and Power*. London: BFI, 45–58.

Karim, K.H. (2003) *Jacques Ellul*, in C. May (ed.) *Key Thinkers of the Information Society*. London: Routledge, 65–86.

Kelly, K. (1998) *New Rules for the New Economy: 10 Radical Strategies for a Connected World*. London: Penguin.

Kittler, F. (1996) The history of communciations media. Available at: http://ww.ctheory.net/articles.aspx?id=45

Kittler, F. (1997) *Literature Media Information Systems*. Amsterdam: OPA.

Kroker, A. and Cook, D. (1988) *The Postmodern Scene. Excremental Culture and Hyperaesthetics*. London: Macmillan.

Lacan, J. (1977) *Écrits. A Selection*. London: Routledge.

Lash, S. (2002) *Critique of Information*. London: Sage.

Lash, S. and Friedman, J. (eds)(1992) *Modernity and Identity*. Oxford: Basil Blackwell.

Latour, B. (1987) *Science in Action. How to Follow Scientists and Engineers Through Society*. Buckingham: Open University Press.

Latour, B. (1988a) Mixing humans and non-humans together: the sociology of a door-closer. *Social Problems* 35 (3): 298–310.

Latour, B. (1988b) *The Pasteurization of France*. Cambridge, MA: Harvard University Press.

Latour, B. (1996) *Aramis or the Love of Technology*. Cambridge, MA: Harvard University Press.

Latour, B. (1998) How to be iconophilic in Art, Science and Religion? in C.A. Jones and P. Galison, with A. Slaton (eds) *Picturing Science Producing Art*. New York, NY: Routledge.

Latour, B. (2005) *Re-Assembling the Social An Introduction to Actor-Network-Theory*. Oxford: Oxford University Press.

Latour, B. and Woolgar, S. (1979) *Laboratory Life. The Social Construction of Scientific Facts*. London: Sage.

Law, J. and Hassard, J. (1999) *Actor Network Theory and Beyond*. Oxford: Blackwell.

Le Bon, G. (1896) *The Crowd: A Study of the Popular Mind*. Kitchener: Batoche Books.

Leslie, E. (2001) *Walter Benjamin, Overpowering Conformism*. London: Pluto.

Levinson, P. (1997) *The Soft Edge. A Natural History and Future of the Information Revolution*. London: Routledge.

Levinson, P. (1998) *Digital McLuhan. A Guide to the Information Millennium*. London: Routledge.

Loader, B. (1997) *The Governance of Cyberspace. Politics, Technology and Global Restructuring*. London: Routledge.

Lodziak, C. (1995) *Manipulating Needs. Capitalism and Culture*. London: Pluto.

Lodziak, C. (2001) *The Myth of Consumerism*. London: Pluto.

Luhmann, N. (1982) *The Differentiation of Society*. New York, NY: Columbia University Press.

Luhmann, N. (1990) *Essays on Self-Reference*. New York, NY: Columbia University Press.

Lundell, A. (1989) *Virus*. Chicago, IL: Contemporary Books.

Lury, C. (1998) *Prosthetic Culture. Photography, Memory and Identity*. London: Routledge.

Lyon, D. (2001) *The Surveillance Society: Monitoring Everyday Life*. Buckingham: Open University Press.

Lyotard, J.F. (1979) *La Condition Postmoderne, rapport sur le savoir*. Paris: Les Éditions de Minuit.

Lyotard, J.F. (1991) *The Inhuman: Reflections on Time*. Cambridge: Polity Press.

Mackenzie, A. (2002) *Transductions: Bodies and Machines at Speed*. New York, NY: Continuum.

Mackenzie, A. (2005) Untangling the unwired: Wi-Fi and the cultural inversion of infrastructure. *Space and Culture* 8(3): 269–85.

Mackenzie, D. and Wajcman, J. (eds) (1985) *The Social Shaping of Technology*. Buckingham: Open University Press.

Mafessoli, M. (1996) *The Time of the Tribes*. London: Sage.

Manovitch, L. (2001) *The Language of New Media*. Cambridge, MA: MIT Press.

Marcuse, H. (1964) *One Dimensional Man. Studies in the Ideology of Advanced Industrial Society*. Boston, MA: Beacon Press.

Marcuse, H. (1974) *Eros and Civilization: A Philosophical Inquiry into Freud*. Boston, MA: Beacon Press.

Margulis, L. (1993) *Symbiosis in Cell Evolution. Microbial Communities in the Archean and Proterozoic Eons*, 2nd edn. New York, NY: Freeman and Company.

Martin, E. (1987) *The Woman in the Body. A Cultiral Analysis of Reproduction*. Buckingham: Open University Press.

Martin-Murphy, B. (2002) A critical history of the Internet, in G. Elmer (ed.) *Critical Perspectives on the Internet*. Lanham, MD: Rowman and Littlefield, 27–45.

Marx, K. ([1867] 1990) *Capital, Volume I* (Ben Fowkes, transl.). London: Penguin.

Mattelart, A. and Mattelart, M. (1992) *Rethinking Media Theory*. Minneapolis, MN: University of Minnesota Press.

Maturana, H. and Varela, F. (1980) *Autopoiesis and Cognition: The Realization of the Living*. London: Reidl.

Mauss, M. ([1924] 1990) *The Gift: The Form and Reason for Exchange in Archaic Societies*. London: Routledge.

May, C. (2003) Lewis Mumford, in C. May, (ed.) *Key Thinkers of the Information Society*. London: Routledge, 109–34.

McLuhan, M. (1962) *The Gutenberg Galaxy. The Making of Typographic Man*. Toronto: University of Toronto Press.

McLuhan, M. (1964) *Understanding Media. The Extensions of Man*, 2nd edn. Hammondsworth: Penguin.

McLuhan, M. (1982) *Introduction to the Bias of Communication*. Toronto: University of Toronto Press.

McLuhan, M. and Fiore, Q. (1967) *The Medium is the Message: an Inventory of Effects*. New York, NY: Bentam.

McNeill, W.H. (1976) *Plagues and Peoples*. Harmondsworth: Penguin.

McQuail, D. (2005) *Mass Communication Theory*, 5th edn. London: Sage.

Mead, G.H. (1934) *Mind Self and Society: From the Standpoint of a Social Behaviourist*. Chicago, IL: University of Chicago Press.

Merrin, W. (2005) *Baudrillard and the Media*. Cambridge: Polity Press.

Meyrowitz, J. (1985) *No Sense of Place. The Impact of Electronic Media on Social Behavior*. New York, NY: Oxford University Press.

Miller, D. (1987) *Material Culture and Mass Consumption*. Oxford: Blackwell.

Miller, J. (1971) *McLuhan*. London: Collins.

Millet, K. (1970) *Sexual Politics: the Classic Analysis of the Interplay Between Men, Women, and Culture*. New York, NY: Doubleday.

Moores, S. (1993) *Interpreting Audiences. The Ethnography of Media Consumption*. London: Sage.

Moores, S. (2005) *Media/Theory. Thinking about Media and Communications*. London: Routledge.

Morgan, R. (1978) *Going Too Far: the Personal Chronicle of a Feminist*. New York, NY: Random House.

Morley, D. (1986) *Family Television: Cultural Power and Domestic Leisure*. London: Comedia.

Morley, D. (2007) *Media, Modernity and Technology. The Geography of the New*. London: Routledge.

Mulvey, L. (1975) Visual pleasure and narrative cinema. *Screen* 16(3): 6–18.

Mumford, L. (1961) *The City in History: its Transformations and its Prospects* New York, NY: Harcourt, Brace and World.

Murdock, G. and Golding, P. (1977) Capitalism, communication and class relations, in J. Curran, M. Gurevitch and J. Woollacott (eds) *Mass Communication and Society*. London: Arnold.

Negroponte, N. (1995) *Being Digital*. New York, NY: Knopf.

Nietzsche, F. (1966) *Beyond Good and Evil. Prelude to a Philosophy of the Future*. New York, NY: Random House.

Nietzsche, F. (1992) *Der Wille zur Macht. Versuch einer Umwertung aller Werte*. Farnkfurt am Main: Insel Verlag.

Nietzsche, F. (2006) On truth and lies in a non moral sense, in *The Nietzsche Reader*. Oxford: Blackwell, 114–23.

Nowotny, H. (1994) *Time: The Modern and Postmodern Experience*. Cambridge: Polity Press.

O'Connor, A. (1989) *Raymond Williams on Television*. London: Routledge.

Ong, W.J. (1982) *Orality and Literacy. The Technologizing of the World*. London: Routledge.

Parsons, T. (1968) *The Structure of Social Action. A Study in Social Theory with Special Reference to a Group of Recent European Writers Volume I*. New York, NY: Free Press.

Parsons, T. (1973) *The Evolution of Societies*. Englewood Cliffs: Prentice Hall.

Peirce, C.S. (1940) *The Philosophy of Peirce. Selected Writings*, J. Buchler (ed.). London: Kegan Paul, French, Trubner and Company.

Plant, S. (1995) The future looms: weaving women and cybernetics. *Body and Society* 3/4 (November): 45–64.

Porquet, J.L. (2003) *Jacques Ellul: l'homme qui avait (presque) tout prévu*. Paris: Le Cherche Midi.

Poster, M. (1984) *Foucault, Marxism and History; Mode of Production versus Mode of Information*. Cambridge: Polity Press.

Poster, M. (2001) *What's the Matter with the Internet?* Minneapolis, MN: University of Minnesota Press.

Postman, N. (1987) *Amusing Ourselves to Death. Public Discourse in the Age of Show Business*. London: Methuen.

Postman, N. (1992) *Technopoly. The Surrender of Culture to Technology*. New York, NY: Knopf.

Rheingold, H. (2000) *The Virtual Community*. Cambridge, MA: MIT Press.

Rifkin, J. (2000) *The Age of Access. How the Shift from Ownership to Access is Transforming Modern Life*. London: Penguin.

Robins, K. (1996) Cyberspace and the world we live in, in J. Dovey (ed.) *Fractal Dreams. New Media in Social Context*. London: Lawrence and Wishart, 1–30.

Ryan, F. (2003) *Darwin's Blindspot. Evolution Beyond Natural Selection*. New York, NY: Thomson Texere.

Saetnan, A. R., Oudshoorn, N. and Kirejczyk, M. (eds) (2000) *Bodies of Technology. Women's Involvement with Reproductive Medicine*. Columbus, OH: Ohio State University Press.

Sahlins, M. (1997) The Spirit of the Gift, in A.D. Schrift (ed.) *The Logic of the Gift*. London: Routledge, 70–99.

Sapp, J. (1994) *Evolution by Association*. Oxford: Oxford University Press.

Schlesinger, P. (1987) *Putting Reality Together. BBC News*. London: Methuen.

Segal, L. (2004) Only the literal: the contradictions of anti-pornography feminism, in P. Church Gibson (ed.) *More Dirty Looks: Gender, Pornography and Power*. London: BFI, 59–70.

Seiter, E., Borchers, H., Kreutzner, G. and Warth, E.M. (eds) (1989) *Remote Control: Television, Audiences and Cultural Power*. London: Routledge.

Shannon, C. and Weaver, W. (1949) *A Mathematical Model of Communication*. Urbana, IL: University of Illinois Press.

Shields, R. (1991) *Places on the Margin. Alternative Geographies of Modernity*. London: Routledge.

Shields, R. (ed.) (1996) *Cultures of the Internet: Virtual Spaces, Real Histories, Living Bodies*. London: Sage.

Shields, R. (2003) *The Virtual*. London: Routledge.

Silverstone, R. and Haddon, L. (1996) Design and the domestication of information and communication technologies: technical change and everyday life, in R. Mansell and R. Silverstone (eds) *OUP Communications by Design*. Oxford: Oxford University Press, 44–74.

Silverstone, R. and Hirsch, E. (eds) (1992) *Consuming Technologies: Media and Information in Domestic Spaces*. London: Routledge.

Smith, A. (1990) Towards a Global Culture? in M. Featherstone (ed.) *Global Culture: Nationalism, Globalization and Modernity*. London: Sage, 171–91.

Spigel, L. (2001) Media homes: then and now. *International Journal of Cultural Studies*, 4(4): 385–411.

Stacey, J. (1998) *Terratologies. A Cultural Study of Cancer*. London: Routledge.

Storey, J. (1993) *An Introductory Guide to Cultural Theory and Popular Culture*. Hemel Hempstead: Harvester Wheatsheaf.

Strathern, M. (1992) *After Nature. English Kinship in the Late Twentieth Century*. Cambridge: Cambridge University Press.

Sunday Times (2007) *Police Investigate Sex Abuse in Virtual World* (13 May), p. 10. Available at: http://www.timesonline.co.uk/tol/news/uk/crime/article1782086.ece

Thompson, J.B. (1995) *Modernity and the Media*. Cambridge: Polity Press.

Trend, D. (ed.) (2001) *Reading Digital Culture*. Oxford: Blackwell.

Tuchman, G. (1978) *Making News: A Study in the Construction of Reality*. New York, NY: Free Press.

Van Loon, J. (1996a) A cultural exploration of time: some implications of temporality and mediation. *Time and Society* 5: 61–84.

Van Loon, J. (1996b) Technological sensibilities and the cyberpolitics of gender: Donna Haraway's postmodern feminism. *Innovation* 9(2): 231–43.

Van Loon, J. (1999) Whiter shades of pale: media-hybridities of Rodney King, in A. Brah, M. Hickman and Mairtin Mac an Ghaill (eds) *Thinking Identities: Ethnicity, Racism and Culture*. London: Macmillan.

Van Loon, J. (2000) Enframing/revealing: on the question of ethics and difference in technologies of mediation, in D. Berry (ed.) *Ethics and Media Culture Practices and Representations*. Oxford: Focal Press, 54–72.

Van Loon, J. (2002) *Risk and Technological Culture. Towards a Sociology of Virulence*. London: Routledge.

Van Loon, J. (2006) Network. *Theory Culture & Society* 23(2/3): 307–14.

van Zoonen, L. (1994) *Feminist Media Studies*. London: Sage.

Vattimo, G. (1988) *The End of Modernity*. Cambridge: Polity Press.

Vattimo, G. (1992) *The Transparent Society*. Cambridge: Polity Press.

Vattimo, G. (1997) *Beyond Interpretation. The Meaning of Hermeneutics for Philosophy*. Cambridge: Polity Press.

Virilio, P. (1977) *Speed and Politics*. New York, NY: Semiotext(e).

Virilio, P. (1993) *Pure War* (with S. Lothringer). New York, NY: Semiotext(e).

Virilio, P. (1997) *Open Sky*. London: Verso.

Wajcman, J. (1991) *Feminism Confronts Technology*. University Park, PA: Pennsylvania State University Press.

Wajcman, J. (2004) *Technofeminism*. Cambridge: Polity Press.

White, L.T. (1962) *Medieval Technology and Social Change*. Oxford: Clarendon.

Williams, K. (2003) *Understanding Media Theory*. London: Hodder Arnold.

Williams, R. (1965) *The Long Revolution*. Hammondsworth: Penguin.

Williams, R. (1983) *Keywords*. London: Fontana.

Williams, R. (1990) *Television and Cultural Form*, 2nd edn. London: Routledge.

Wills, C. (1996) *Yellow Fever. Black Goddess. The Coevolution of Peoples and Plagues*. New York, NY: Addison Wesley.

Winter, C. (1996) *Predigen unter freien Himmel. Medienkuliurelle Funktionen von Bettelmönchen*. Bardowick: Wissenschaftler Verlag.

Wittel, A. (2000) Ethnography on the move: from field to net to Internet. *Forum: Qualitative Social Research* Vol 1(1). Available at: http://www.qualitative-research.net/fqs-texte/1–00/1–00wittel-e.htm

Wolf, E. (1982) *Europe and the People Without History*. Berkeley, CA: University of California Press.

Yaklef, A. (2004) Global brands as embodied 'Generic Spaces'. The example of branded chain hotels. *Space and Culture* 7(2): 237–48.

Zhang, X. (2007) *The Origins of the Modern Chinese Press: The Influence of the Protestant Missionary Press in Late Qing China*. London: Routledge.

Zolo, D. (1991) Autopoiesis: critique of a postmodern paradigm. *Telos* 86: 61–80.

INDEX

References in **bold** are included in the glossary.